To Father Christian —
May Father Bui's
story have meaning
and inspiration for
your priesthood.
The mercy of Jesus
and Mary is awesome!
With love & admiration,
Dee Harkins
June 9, 2009

ACCLAIM FOR *A MOTHER'S PLEA*

This is the vividly personal story of a priest in a Chicago parish coming to terms with what the priesthood demands of a man in a great modern city. Profoundly conscious of the sin and unbelief that distort human lives and that touch him too, Father Buś, CR, is sometimes desperate in face of the hostile disregard for the Church so prevalent today. Yet his encounter with The Divine Mercy and his closeness to the Blessed Virgin Mary enable him to consecrate his life as a priest totally to them. This book will rejoice the hearts of faithful Catholics and will touch especially the hearts of priests and those preparing for the priesthood.

Francis Cardinal George, OMI
Archbishop of Chicago

This compelling story of the Mercy of God acting through one of His priests breaks through our shrouds of complacency and indifference to move hearts and minds to seek greater union with Christ through his Church. Generations from now, people will be reading *A Mother's Plea* to find inspiration and understand how God's Divine Mercy was manifested in our days in hidden but extraordinary ways. Like the story of St. Maria Faustina herself, *A Mother's Plea* is a story of grace building on nature, trust overcoming fear, and mercy vanquishing sin and death. It is the convincing clarion call for the construction of the Sanctuary of The Divine Mercy, a building for the indwelling of The Divine Mercy in our earthly existence and a beacon reminding the world that God's merciful call to return to Him continues even in the noise and distractions of today's secularized civilization.

Dr. Denis McNamara, Assistant Director
The Liturgical Institute, University of Saint Mary of the Lake,
Mundelein Seminary
Author, Heavenly City

Long before the genocide in Rwanda, the Blessed Mother said that sincere prayer of the Rosary in each village would stop the terrible situation that was going to happen (the genocide). She requested a chapel as well, and obviously we didn't listen until it was too late! I challenge you to listen to her, those who still have time. I don't have any doubt that her sanctuary will be a great gift not only to the people of Chicago but also to the whole world. The world needs prayer more than anything especially in these apocalyptic, troubled time!

We are all called to be instruments of the Mother of God. Thank you, Fr. Anthony, for listening and responding to her call again and again. You are not alone and you are a blessing to many!

Immaculee Ilibagiza
Author
Left to Tell: Discovering God Amidst the Rwandan Holocaust

A Mother's Plea is an absolute must for one's "spiritual library!"At a time when humanity faces grave spiritual dangers and the priesthood has been besmirched by scandal and attacked by the secular media, Father Anthony Buś, in this inspiring work, shows the beauty and power of God's love in his priesthood. His own journey, met with trials and triumphs, is a story that is extremely moving and will forever touch your heart.

This powerful work reflects the beauty of abandonment to God, the intercession of the Blessed Virgin Mary, and the power of trust in The Divine Mercy.

It has inspired me and will stir in you the desire to seek greater holiness. This is a "must read" for fellow priests and for anyone searching for greater meaning in their lives and a more intimate relationship with God.

Drew Mariani
Award-Winning Journalist and Nationally Syndicated Radio Host

Take it from a non-Catholic, this book is a blessing and should be in every hotel/motel, just like the Gideon Bible.

Connie Melvin-Culver
Culver Methodist Ministries, The Villages, Florida

An unusually rare and compelling look into the soul of a Roman Catholic priest, this timely and timeless diary will rekindle hope in the ancient, but ever so new quest for union with God.

Against the backdrop of the high tech world of the Third Millennium, the looming threat of international and domestic terrorism, and a Church floundering to regain credibility in the wake of countless scandals, Fr. Anthony Buś weaves a bold thread, through the intensely personal sharing of his own journey, to reconnect with the deeper meaning and purpose of life.

This provocative story of an inner-city Chicago priest will profoundly move the hearts of Christians and non-Christians alike to recognize the abiding mystery of a hidden presence that sustains and transforms the human person confronted with forces that undermine the dignity and nobility of life.

Fr. S. Seraphim Michalenko, MIC
Rector Emeritus of the National Shrine of The Divine Mercy and
Vice Postulator Emeritus for St. Faustina's Cause of Canonization

This intensely personal journey toward holiness and obedience to a call is inspiring in its enduring faithfulness to God's mercy. The witness this story gives, of confronting spiritual trials and elusive triumphs with greater prayer, is a lesson in hope. It details how faith and trustful surrender sustain the hope that waits for what is unseen. That is why this book has no ending ... yet. The sequel should be earth-shattering.

Sheila Gribben Liaugminas
Former Time Magazine Reporter
Emmy Award Winning NBC-TV show Co-Host

A Mother's Plea calls forth heroism in the face of evil, integrity in the face of deceit, and trust in the face of vulnerability. If you have the courage to lift the sword of mercy, step into the battle larger than humanity, and on your knees plead salvation for the world — this book is for you.

Margaret B. Poole
Chicago Public High School Teacher

A Mother's Plea constitutes an inspiring diary of the life of a contemporary parish priest amidst the agonies and ecstasies of today's parish realities. Founded upon the pillars of Eucharistic Adoration, Our Lady's role as Mediatrix of All Graces, and a priestly humility in pursuit of holiness, this little work encourages an openness of the heart to Heaven's design for every Catholic parish: to be a sanctuary of Divine Mercy through the intercession of Our Lady, Mediatrix of Mercy.

Dr. Mark I. Miravalle, S.T.D.
International President
Vox Populi Mariae Mediatrici
Professor of Theology and Mariology
Franciscan University of Steubenville, Steubenville, Ohio

A MOTHER'S PLEA

Lifting the Veil in Sanctuary

A MOTHER'S PLEA

Lifting the Veil in Sanctuary

Father Anthony Buś, CR

MARIAN PRESS
STOCKBRIDGE, MA 01263

2008

*Cover Design, Book Design and
Photo Illustrations for Chapters 1, 8, 27 by*
Chris Deschaine
www.braintrustdesign.com

Cover Photograph and page 324 by
Richard Hein
As published in the Chicago Sun-Times.
Copyright 2007 by Chicago Sun-Times, Inc.
Reprinted with permission.

Portrait of Mary Stachowicz in Chapter 16 by
Laura Stone
art_indigo@yahoo.com

Back Cover Photograph and Photograph for Chapter 4 and 24 by
Dimitre
www.dimitre.com

The Iconic Monstrance of Our Lady of the Sign
Image in Chapter 24
Stefan Niedorezo, Sculptor
Malgorzata Sawczuk, Conservator/Gold Gilding

Sanctuary Schematic Designs
McCrery Architects
www.mccreryarchitects.com

Nihil Obstat
Most Reverend J. Basil Meeking, S.T.D.
Censor Deputatus
July 7, 2004

Imprimatur
Most Reverend Edwin M. Conway, D.D.
Vicar General
Archdiocese of Chicago
July 8, 2004

Library of Congress Catalog Number: 2007937814.v
ISBN: 978-1-59614-184-1

Available from the Association of Marian Helpers,
Stockbridge, MA 01263
Tel. 1-800-462-7426 or www.marian.org

Third Printing
January 2008

A Mother's Plea is dedicated to those who,
through reflection on this diary, have the courage
to enter into the drama of God's unfolding plan for
His people. I would also like to acknowledge and thank the
countless people who have patiently stood by me in this
journey and continue to walk with me in faith.

To my family, whose home and land I left so many years ago
to follow the call, I assure you of my love
and daily prayers.

Finally, to the Blessed Virgin Mary who, indeed,
is not frozen in the pages of Sacred Scripture,
but ever active in the world today, I say thank you for
your *yes* to God that we be saved and that
Jesus be known, loved, and served.

CONTENTS

FOREWORD 21

PREFACE 25

PRELUDE 31

1   OUR LADY'S PARISH 37
     Friendship with God 39
     The Message of The Divine Mercy 40
     Jubilee Pilgrimage 43
     The Icon of The Divine Mercy 44
     The Death of Carl Demma 46
     Return of the Icons 47
     Adoration Begins 49
     The Outdoor Sanctuary 50
     The Mother of Our Lord Leads Us 53

2   INVITATION TO DRINK AT THE
     FOUNTAIN OF MERCY 55
     Mary Teaches Us to Pray 55
     Our Lady's Plan 58

3   NEVER ALONE IN GETHSEMANE 65
     Intimacy with the Christ 66
     Hollywood and St. Maria Faustina 69
     Our Lady Prepares the Ground 71
     The Television: Our Lady's Tool? 74

4   ALLURED BY THE CHRIST 79
     Descent into Nothingness 81
     Grace Abounds in God's Hiddenness 84
     From the Desert to the Dark of Night 87

5   THE CARNIVAL THAT DROPPED
     OUT OF HEAVEN 91

6 IN THE SHADOW OF TERROR 95
   Unceasing Prayer 96
   To Live in True Freedom 99

7 CALLED TO BE A PRIEST 103
   The Seed of My Vocation 104
   Come into My Heart 106

8 BREAD FROM HEAVEN THAT
   WE NOT COLLAPSE 113
   Pledge of His Presence Among Us 114
   An Intimate Encounter 117
   Becoming What We Consume 120

9 SATAN'S TRAP 123
   To Awaken Satan 124

10 OUR LADY'S INTERVENTION 129
   Seek Refuge in God 130

11 THE FOUR O'CLOCK APPARITION 133
   Disciples of Mercy 135

12 THE PROSTITUTION AND RAPE
   OF THE HOLY FAITH 139
   Holiness of Life 140
   The Sacred Character of the Christ 142

13 UPON THIS ROCK 145
   She Will Not Abandon 147
   Steered towards Safe Harbor 148
   The Rock is the Christ 150

14 AND HE WEPT 155
   Through the Prism of History 156
   The Time of Our Visitation 158
   Reform to the Standard of the Christ 161

15   AT THE LAST HOUR 163
        Spiritual Maturity. 167
        A Sheer Miracle 169

16   MURDERED OR MARTYRED?
        THE DEATH OF MARY STACHOWICZ. . . . 173
        On the Front Lines 175
        The Flame in Her Heart. 177
        The Kingdom of Heaven Suffers Violence 179

17   BRING BACK THE ANGELUS 185
        Her Summons to Pray 186
        The Ultimate Act of Humility 187

18   THE SEARCH FOR SANCTUARY 189
        Disposed to the Holy Encounter. 189
        Revival of Catholic Mysticism 191
        From the Cenacle to Gethsemane 194
        Sowing the Seeds of Sanctuary 196
        Custodian of the Sanctuary 198

19   AWAKENING THE SLEEPING GIANT 201
        His Light Exposes the Darkness 202
        The Virtue of Discipleship 203

20   JESUS IS KNOCKING. 205
        Awakened to the Sound of God's Voice 206
        In His Image 208
        To Speak to Our Hearts 210

21   MEETING WITH THE CARDINAL. 211
        The First Sign 214
        The Second Sign 217
        The Third Sign 219
        To Serve and Nurture Catholic Spirituality 221

22   THE DEMISE OF
        THREE MILLION DOLLARS. 223

23   THE STATUE OF THE DIVINE MERCY
        GOES TO THE CONTINENT OF AFRICA 231
        Shrine of Our Lady of Kibeho 235

24   DEFENSE OF THE
        ICONIC MONSTRANCE 241
        Courage in Battle 242
        Woman of the Apocalypse 247
        The New Evangelization. 250

25   FROM THE EYE OF THE STORM,
        SHE GUIDES US 255
        Reorientation of the Sanctuary 257
        Gifts through Prayer and Devotion. 259

26   THE CALL TO ARMS: DEFINING
        THE PRIESTHOOD. 265
        Symbols of Consecration 266
        Formed in Our Lady's Spirituality. 268
        Satan Befriends the Priest. 269
        The Sacrificial and Sacred Character
        of the Priesthood. 271
        The Life-Giving Gift of Celibacy. 273
        The Mission 277

27   LET THE CHILDREN COME UNTO ME . . 281
        Priestly Formation. 284
        The Devil's Illusory Love. 287
        The Heroism of Holiness. 290
        The Chorus of Fiats 294
        The Power of Humility. 296

28   AN APOCALYPTIC AWAKENING 303
        Pilgrimage Prayers. 304
        On the Island of Patmos. 306
        A Perpetual Imprint 312
        The Wounds of Her Son. 316
        Preparation for Victory. 319

EPILOGUE 322

A FATHER'S PLEA. 324

THE PROPOSED SANCTUARY
OF THE DIVINE MERCY. 326
Sanctuary Mission and Vision 326
Sanctuary Schematic Designs 328
The Theology of the Sanctuary of
The Divine Mercy 330
The Spirit of Our Efforts 335
Special Perpetual Novena Prayer to
Our Lady of Good Remedy 348
Afterword. 350

PRAYERS REFERENCED IN
A MOTHER'S PLEA. 359
Message of The Divine Mercy 359
The Chaplet of Divine Mercy 364
The Angelus. 365
The Act of Consecration. 366
Prayer to St. Michael. 366

BROTHER BOGDAN JANSKI
FOUNDER OF THE RESURRECTIONISTS . . 367
From Addiction to Conversion:
The Story of Brother Bogdan Janski,
Founder of the Resurrectionists. 369
St. Stanislaus Kostka Catholic
Church Parish History 380

TRIBUTE TO MARY STACHOWICZ. 387

SOURCES 389

AUTHOR'S BIOGRAPHY. 391

THE SUICIDE OF AGUSTIN: A CLARION CALL TO SANCTUARY

Foreword to the Revised Edition of
A Mother's Plea: Lifting the Veil in Sanctuary

T his updated edition of *A Mother's Plea* is a further testimony to the drama of this story, which continues to unfold – or perhaps better said, the curtain continues to rise as the readers are invited no longer to be mere spectators, but rather to take their place in the drama. They may not be characters in this specific story, but the plea of the Mother resounds throughout the world, calling for an active participation in the life of a loving God.

Each of us is a character in the story of God's self-revelation in history. The Gospel is perpetually written through the lives of those who have courage to respond to the call. I say courage, because no one who answers the call will go forward unscathed. But the sweet taste of victory brings a joy enveloped in the mystery of God who is ever present in the sanctuary that remains, too often hidden, in the deep recesses of the soul. The inner peace found there is the knowledge that we are never actually alone and that the road to journey's end has meaning and purpose.

An additional chapter has been added to this book that brings to a dramatic finale the story that forms *A Mother's Plea*. The change in the subtitle from *Journey into the Light* to *Lifting the Veil in Sanctuary* is indicative of the Blessed Virgin Mary's yearning to give us the means to make the journey, equipped with the grace of the Holy Spirit and armed for the fight that brings victory. In sanctuary, the veil is lifted and we are prepared for the journey of life with a renewed understanding. Our eyes and ears are opened to the *ancients of old*, so we can give attention to God ever active in the here and now, but always with a view to the future.

The suicide of a young man I counseled compels me to more aggressively lift the veil to the hidden presence of God in sanctuary. Agustin Garcia had come to me wrapped in his own darkness of disconnect. He was 21 years old and at the age of 13 had left home to begin a futile search for himself and some semblance of love. His quest took him to the wrong places and to the wrong people.

Just five weeks ago, at this juncture in his journey, he came to me with a burning desire to be free from the darkness enveloping his young life. He felt trapped. I know with certitude that my encounter with him opened a door that could set him free. I became instantly a *father* to a *son*. I felt the infusion of God's grace opening to him the fount of mercy and love. Agustin had begun the walk and wanted to make it in communion with others. He was reaching out and just beginning to touch with the tips of his fingers the freedom he sought. But he lived deep on the south side of Chicago, far from this parish where he was beginning to discover a refuge from the demons that haunted him.

Sometimes it takes great courage and strength to live in a world whose spirit militates seductively and powerfully against the truth that we are worthy of God's love and created for a noble purpose. I think Agustin had the courage, but he didn't have the strength. He took his own life — hanging himself from the light fixture of his room in an apartment he shared with several other young men.

His body dangled there for three days before someone opened the door in search of him. Near his body was a handwritten note. In his last words before he died, he asked pardon for his offense and that I celebrate Mass for him in the sanctuary where he felt loved and where he had found peace. As I now write, I am only a few hours from receiving his body into the church for the Rite of Christian Burial. After Mass, we will send his body to his parents and siblings in Mexico.

Agustin's death has left me with a heavy heart and in deep sadness. It rekindles in me an urgency to lift the veil in sanctuary in all places and for all people. We should never have come to these times when God seems so inaccessible — so hard to find. The disconnect felt so painfully today is our doing.

This revised edition of *A Mother's Plea* is an attempt to bring the story afresh into the lives of others. It brings the promise of hope to a world still so new to the third millennium. Since its initial publication in 2005, *A Mother's Plea* has become a religious bestseller. The book has crossed over the Atlantic to Ireland and to several countries in Africa. Recently it has jumped the Indian Ocean into India and Sri Lanka. It is my hope that the voice ringing through the pages of *A Mother's Plea* might fortify men and women with the courage and sacrificial strength needed to reconnect a weary, wayward, and wondering people with the God of life.

PREFACE

May 30, 2004

When I began to write *A Mother's Plea*, it was neither my intention to write a book, nor did I anticipate the sharing of my personal quest for union with God. The writing began as a mere response to a request by Archdiocesan personnel, that I should write a justification for wanting to build a sanctuary on parish property.

Having been pastor of this poor parish for just over four years, I realized how absurd my vision of the sanctuary must have seemed, since the parish barely had the funds to make ends meet from one month to the next. In addition to this, the church and school needed millions of dollars for repair. Even so, I trusted a voice within that beckoned me to open the doors to sanctuary while, at the same time, calling me to give myself unreservedly to Jesus Christ.

Not quite sure how to articulate the call, the moment I sat down to write, it was as if I had been suddenly infused with the grace of a single-hearted purpose to be unabashedly true to the Spirit moving through my soul. I had a keen sense that no matter how suspect my discernment may be perceived, the message was not only for my personal transformation, but also that others would be assisted in their own journey towards the light of the often imperceptible, but ever abiding presence of God.

Now, as I look back, I am utterly amazed at the ease with which I conveyed the words that Our Lady spoke to me nearly five years ago when she asked that I give her the parish and make her its Mother and Queen. I am amazed because normally I would have kept such an experience to myself for fear of ridicule and rejection. Such a claim is viewed with an almost scrupulous skepticism in the climate of the modern world and like most human beings I, too, want to be accepted.

I am also amazed at the ease with which I speak of Satan and the spiritual warfare that permeates my life and, indeed, all sectors of society where loyalty to God is a serious concern. The devil and his adversaries, with the ensuing battle waged against God and his disciples, were lightly treated in the formative years of my preparation for the priesthood. If the topic would surface from time to time, it seemed a cause for embarrassment as some sort of barnacle of an outdated theology or demonology still clinging to the hull of the Church.

After all is said and done, though, popular theological speculation and inquiry yields to the sacred magisterium, that is, the teaching authority of the Church whose mission is the preservation of Christian dogma and doctrine. The sacred magisterium enjoys the charism of divine protection from teachers who *tickle the ears*, leading the faithful to the fantasy of fable no matter how sophisticated the whim may be. That the Blessed Virgin Mary shares in the redemptive work of her Son and that the devil wages war on her children are dogmatic and doctrinal truths of the Catholic faith.

Our Lady's solicitous concern for the salvation and sanctification of humanity is woven throughout this diary of personal reflections. While the unfolding story contains intriguing twists and turns interlaced with the repetition of complementary themes, it remains a diary whose chapters were not premeditated nor written in view of preceding chapters. The stirrings of the Spirit compelled me to write, giving me no rest until the thoughts milling through my mind were put to paper. Any barriers to the free flow of words were lifted only when I turned my eyes away from myself and looked to the Holy Mother of God. Through her heart, her thoughts were heard and, indeed, constitute the story of *A Mother's Plea*.

If the Blessed Virgin Mary shows a particular concern for an *Anawim*, that is, the little flock of simple believers, there is no reason to believe that the remnant cannot encompass the whole world. Reflectively and prayerfully read, I hope this book will inspire the reader to recognize a similar stirring of God's Spirit already active in his or her own soul, or perhaps open the soul to the invitation to embark on the adventure of a gracious God, ever active in the lives of His people. This is certainly the longing and the yearning of the grieving Mother.

Our Lady's example 2,000 years ago when she walked the earth has shown that we should never underestimate the sacred power that emanates from a people whose lives are entrusted to the mysterious design of God's action in the world. The ramifications of their lived faith ripple through history. We are the fruit of their lived faith and the same seed of faith germinates in our souls to ensure the possibility for the interior peace of our children. Without God there can be no genuine peace — the two are synonymous.

The Resurrection Prayer

by Fr. Frank Grzechowiak, CR

O Risen Lord, the way,
the truth, and the life!

Make us faithful followers
of the spirit of Your Resurrection.

Grant that we may be inwardly renewed,
dying to ourselves in order that You may live in us.

May our lives serve as signs of the
transforming power of Your love.

Use us as Your instruments
for the renewal of society,
bringing Your life and love to all,
and leading them to Your Church.

This we ask of You, Lord Jesus,
living and reigning with the Father,
in the unity of the Holy Spirit, God forever.

Amen.

PSALM 107

"Give thanks to the LORD who is good,
whose love endures forever!"

Let that be the prayer of the LORD'S redeemed,
those redeemed from the hand of the foe,
those gathered from foreign lands,
from east and west, from north and south.

Some had lost their way in a barren desert;
found no path toward a city to live in.
They were hungry and thirsty;
their life was ebbing away.

In their distress they cried to the LORD,
who rescued them in their peril,
guided them by a direct path
so they reached a city to live in.

Let them thank the LORD for such kindness,
such wondrous deeds for mere mortals.
For He satisfied the thirsty,
filled the hungry with good things.

Some lived in darkness and gloom,
in prison, bound with chains,
because they rebelled against God's word,
scorned the counsel of the Most High,

who humbled their hearts through hardship;
they stumbled with no one to help.
In their distress they cried to the LORD,
who saved them in their peril,
led them forth from darkness and gloom,
and broke their chains asunder.

Let them thank the LORD for such kindness,
such wondrous deeds for mere mortals.
For He broke down the gates of bronze
and snapped the bars of iron.

II
Some fell sick from their wicked ways,
afflicted because of their sins.
They loathed all manner of food;
they were at the gates of death.

In their distress they cried to the LORD,
who saved them in their peril,
Sent forth the word to heal them,
snatched them from the grave.

Let them thank the LORD for such kindness,
such wondrous deeds for mere mortals.
Let them offer a sacrifice in thanks,
declare His works with shouts of joy.

Some went off to sea in ships,
plied their trade on the deep waters.
They saw the works of the LORD,

the wonders of God in the deep.
He spoke and roused a storm wind;
it tossed the waves on high.
They rose up to the heavens,
sank to the depths;
their hearts trembled at the danger.

They reeled, staggered like drunkards;
their skill was of no avail.
In their distress they cried to the LORD,
who brought them out of their peril,
hushed the storm to a murmur;
the waves of the sea were stilled.
They rejoiced that the sea grew calm,
that God brought them to the harbor they longed for.

Let them thank the LORD for such kindness,
such wondrous deeds for mere mortals.
Let them praise Him in the assembly of the people,
give thanks in the council of the elders.

III

God changed rivers into desert,
springs of water into thirsty ground,
fruitful land into a salty waste,
because of the wickedness of its people.

He changed the desert into pools of water,
arid land into springs of water,
and settled the hungry there;
they built a city to live in.

They sowed fields and planted vineyards,
brought in an abundant harvest.
God blessed them, they became very many,
and their livestock did not decrease.
But He poured out contempt on princes,
made them wander the trackless wastes,
where they were diminished and brought low
through misery and cruel oppression,
while the poor were released from their affliction;
their families increased like their flocks.

The upright saw this and rejoiced;
all wickedness shut its mouth.
Whoever is wise will take note of these things,
will ponder the merciful deeds of the LORD.

Christ Jesus,
though He was in the form of God,
did not regard equality with
God something to be grasped.
Rather, He emptied Himself,
taking the form of a slave,
coming in human likeness;
and found human in appearance,
He humbled Himself,
becoming obedient to death,
even death on a cross.
Because of this, God greatly exalted Him
and bestowed on Him the name
that is above every name, that at the name of Jesus
every knee should bend,
of those in heaven and on earth and under the earth,
and every tongue confess that
Jesus Christ is Lord,
to the glory of God the Father.

Phil 2:6-11

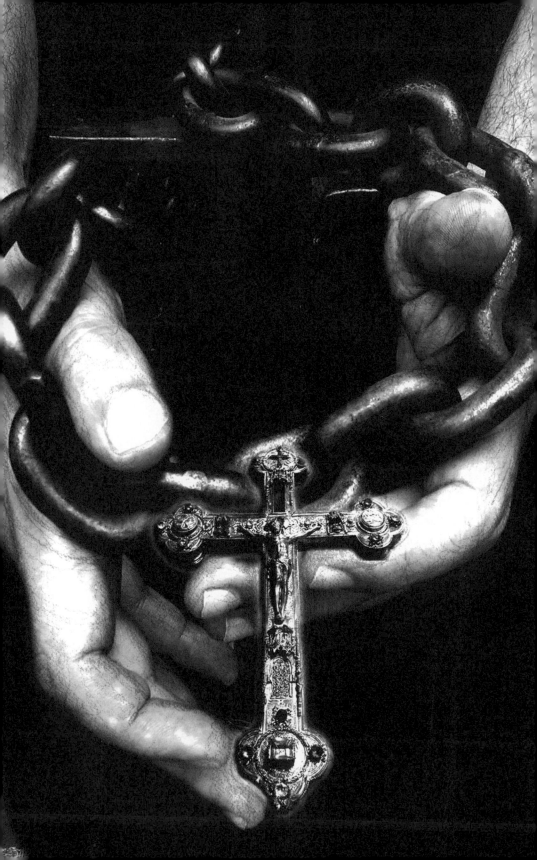

1

OUR LADY'S PARISH

June 3, 2001

On the occasion of the 15th anniversary of my ordination to the priesthood, May 25, 1999, a darkness was lifted that enabled me to pray with greater ease, especially to pray the Rosary. For years I had prayed the Rosary with great difficulty. Just lifting the rosary into my hands was a burden. It had the weight of a rock. This troubled me since I had always been devoted to the Blessed Virgin Mary.

My vocation to the priesthood and religious life was born from and deeply woven in a spirituality that was Eucharistic and Marian, but in the past several years my perception of those spiritual realities had become obscured, if not totally hidden. It was an anniversary card that I received from Sister Maria Guadalupe — a Missionary of Charity — that lifted me from the spiritual aridity that I had endured for about ten years. The card read, quoting Mother Teresa of Calcutta, "Holiness is nothing special for a priest. It is a duty for a priest to be holy because he comes in such close contact with Jesus. Be a true lover of the cross of Jesus in which lies the mystery of your priesthood." Sister Guadalupe also added these words of Mother Teresa. "Mary has a very tender love, a special protection also, for every priest, if he would only turn to her." Deeply touched by these words, I laid the card aside and took the rosary from my pocket. It suddenly had the feel of a feather. I began to pray. From that day the Rosary became anew, the chain that bound me to God. And I began praying the Mysteries daily.

Not surprisingly, by August I found myself preparing for the total consecration of my life to Jesus through Mary following the direction of St. Louis Marie de Montfort, the 17th century devotee to the mystery of the Incarnation and the role of the Blessed Virgin Mary in God's plan of salvation. It was a gnawing desire and need to deepen my priestly and religious consecration that led me to St. Louis Marie de Montfort.

Two weeks into the 33-day preparation for consecration, I had entered into a formal hour of prayer feeling oppressed by the weight of my responsibility as pastor of the very diverse parish of St. Stanislaus Kostka. The parish was financially insecure. We needed $400,000 for a roof. The facade on the exterior wall of the church was falling, and the pillars in the interior of the church were crumbling. During the previous four years, I had tried unsuccessfully to secure money for the parish, and I was tired and overwhelmed. It was during prayer that I interiorly heard Our Lady say in a distinct and direct way, "Give me the parish. Make me Mother and Queen of the parish." In that moment, I consecrated the parish to the Blessed Virgin Mary with total confidence, and the burden was lifted. Three days later I received word from the Archdiocese that St. Stanislaus Kostka Parish was to receive an $850,000 Archdiocesan grant and that work on the church should begin immediately. It had been months since I had talked with anyone about the financial problems of the parish.

FRIENDSHIP WITH GOD

Having consecrated the parish to the Virgin Mary, I continued preparation for my own personal consecration. As I approached the final week of preparation, I struggled with the concept of slavery to Mary. This is at the heart of St. Louis Marie de Montfort's consecration. The disciple makes himself a slave. The word slave was oppressive to me, and every fiber of my being rejected this idea of enslavement.

When I had begun the 33-day preparation for consecration I chose to wear a rosary around my neck. On the last day, the morning of September 13th, I was preparing to go to the gym for exercise. I saw myself in the reflection of the mirror with the rosary hanging from my neck. I remember thinking how odd I looked — as if in bondage, and I asked myself why I thought it necessary to continue wearing the rosary.

While exercising, the rosary seemed to press against my chest in a way that irritated me. I was doing nothing to force its weight against my chest. Finally, the rosary broke and fell to the floor. When I stooped to pick it up, I noticed immediately that the chains had visibly turned gold, a definite change from their previous bright silver. I knew then that in the evening, as the vigil for the Feast of the Triumph of the Cross began, I would have no problem completing the preparation and would entrust my life to Our Lady as a slave.

It was God's providence that I should make the consecration on the Feast of the Triumph of the Cross. I didn't plan it this way. When I celebrated Mass the following morning, I was struck by what was written in the second reading. St. Paul says in his letter written to the Philippians, "Christ Jesus, though He was in the form of God, did not deem equality with God something to grasp at. Rather, He emptied Himself and took the form of a slave, being born in the likeness of man" (Phil 2:6-7). And so I understood that I was inspired to do a good thing; to act in imitation of Christ is the sure means to friendship with God.

THE MESSAGE OF THE DIVINE MERCY

During the final weeks of my preparation, it seemed a little flock was forming. We shared a few things in common. Devoted to the Blessed Virgin Mary, grounded in the Holy Sacrifice of the Mass and devoted to Christ in the Blessed Sacrament, we were drawn to The Divine Mercy. The image of The Divine Mercy and entire message and devotion to The Divine Mercy led us to begin the Hour of Great Mercy on Sundays at 3:00 p.m.

The urgent call to proclaim The Divine Mercy comes as a plea to the Church through the mystic and prophet, St. Maria Faustina Kowalska, who died in Poland in 1938 at the age of 33. She was canonized a saint on April 30, 2000. At the age of 20, Maria Faustina Kowalska was at a dance. In her own words she describes what happened:

> Once I was at a dance (probably in Lodz) with one of my sisters. While everybody was having a good time, my soul was experiencing deep torments. As I began to dance, I suddenly saw Jesus at my side, Jesus racked with pain, stripped of His clothing, all covered with wounds, who spoke these words to me: "How long shall I put up with you and how long will you keep putting Me off?" At the moment the charming music stopped, and the company I was with vanished from my sight; there remained Jesus and I. I took a seat by my dear sister, pretending to have a headache in order to cover up what took place in my soul. After a while I slipped out unnoticed, leaving my sister and all my companions behind and

made my way to the Cathedral of St. Stanislaus Kostka. It was almost twilight; there were only a few people in the Cathedral. Paying no attention to what was happening around me, I fell prostrate before the Blessed Sacrament and begged the Lord to be good enough to give me to understand what I should do next. Then I heard these words: "Go at once to Warsaw; you will enter a convent there." *(Diary of St. Faustina, 9-10).*

And so, it began. Maria Faustina went to Warsaw, entered a convent and Jesus commissioned her to begin recording His plea for humanity's return to God.

Through St. Maria Faustina, Jesus shows us how to prepare for the day of justice. He reminds us that we are living in a time of grace and that all people have the chance during this time to turn from darkness to light, to turn from evil to good, to rise from death to life. He awaits the return of fallen humanity. He desires to bathe humanity in the water and blood that flows from His pierced side — from His wounded Heart. It is a message of mercy — a message of forgiveness — a call to conversion and transformation — a call to be free in the love and peace of the suffering, crucified and risen Jesus.

The image and the entire devotion to The Divine Mercy are especially understood in the celebration of the Holy Sacrifice of the Mass and in adoration of the Blessed Sacrament. The soul is transformed by the grace and mercy which flows from the Sacred Species, enabling us to be true disciples of mercy through our prayer, our words, and our actions.

There has been a strong call from the Holy Father to establish chapels for adoration of the Blessed Sacrament throughout the world. I, too, felt the need for such a chapel here at St. Stanislaus Kostka from the beginning of my pastorate. Life in the parish is all consuming with little time available even to think about such an endeavor, but the desire for a sanctuary continued to burn. While Our Lady's work on the exterior of the church was under way, I began to labor over the possibility of establishing a Divine Mercy Chapel of perpetual adoration of the Blessed Sacrament. We had the space but no money, so I resigned myself to the belief that if Our Lady wanted the sanctuary, she would provide the means.

One morning after celebrating a Mass for the Missionaries of Charity, I asked the Sisters to add to their prayers our discernment for the chapel. Sister Guadalupe said, "Father, you will have the chapel." She told me to call Oscar I. Delgado, who had been a war correspondent for NBC and had come into some money. Not knowing what to do with the money, he prayed and soon after felt the call to spread the message of The Divine Mercy. He had helped to establish perpetual adoration chapels throughout the world in addition to using other means for the spread of the message.

I wasted no time calling Oscar, who already had done much to make the mercy of Jesus known. We met at the parish in February 2000. I showed him the space for the chapel and explained what we wanted to do. I had also mentioned that it would be consoling to have the 33-foot Icon of Our Lady of the Millennium at the parish overlooking the Kennedy Expressway. This pilgrim statue of the Blessed Virgin Mary draws innumerable people to prayer as it is taken throughout the Chicagoland area, mostly hosted by parishes for a week at a time. The icon's eventual and permanent home has yet to be decided. As I raised the question of St. Stanislaus Kostka as a possible home for the icon, the former NBC journalist proposed the idea of having a similar statue sculpted of The Divine Mercy.

THE JUBILEE PILGRIMAGE

Towards the end of March, I led 42 pilgrims through the Holy Land and Rome to celebrate the Great Jubilee Year 2000 of the Incarnation. En route to Israel, we had a short layover in Milan where we celebrated the first Mass of the pilgrimage. We prepared the altar in the airport's concourse near the gate where we would board our flight to Tel Aviv. People from all over gathered for the Mass. I asked the pilgrims to include in their daily intentions a request for the Lord's guidance — a vivid sign that it is, in fact, Our Lady's desire for the sanctuary. Throughout the pilgrimage we celebrated Mass daily, and prayed the Rosary each morning and the Chaplet of The Divine Mercy in the afternoon.

On March 31st, after ten days in the Holy Land, we left Israel and arrived in Rome late that Friday afternoon. Once settled in our hotel, I asked the Roman guide to secure a chapel in St. Peter's Basilica for the last Mass of the pilgrimage. She returned to our hotel later Friday night to inform me that all the chapels in the Vatican were taken, but that the Church of the Holy Spirit was available and was reasonably close to our hotel. So, we were scheduled to celebrate our last Mass in the Church of the Holy Spirit on Sunday evening at 5:00.

Saturday morning I woke up early, and by 5:00 a.m. had walked to St. Peter's Square to pray the Rosary. The plaza was closed, so I continued my prayer, walking through the nearby streets. I came upon a small church. Alongside the doors of the church were banners announcing the upcoming canonization of Blessed Maria Faustina Kowalska on April 30. I entered the church and saw Sisters of the Blessed's congregation praying before the Blessed Sacrament. Enthroned behind the Blessed Sacrament was an impressive image of The Divine Mercy. To the side of the nave there was another chapel to The Divine Mercy and a statue of Blessed Maria Faustina.

My heart jumped a few beats as I felt this was the sign I had sought, that, in fact, it was Our Lady's intention to establish a sanctuary to The Divine Mercy at St. Stanislaus Kostka Parish. At breakfast I shared my discovery with the pilgrims and our Roman guide said, "Oh, the church you speak of is the Church of the Holy Spirit." And so, in thanksgiving for all the graces received in our Jubilee pilgrimage, we gathered on Sunday evening in the Church of the Holy Spirit, located only a few blocks from the Vatican. There we celebrated our last Mass in Rome's official Sanctuary to The Divine Mercy.

THE ICON OF THE DIVINE MERCY

We returned to Chicago, and a few days passed before I received the first photos of a bronze statue of The Divine Mercy, which was being sculpted in Mexico. This was further confirmation that the Holy Spirit was guiding us towards the establishment of a sanctuary to The Divine Mercy in accordance with Our Lady's plan.

It seemed providential to me that the icon was being sculpted in Mexico. While the donor knew nothing of the history of this parish, Our Lady did. St. Stanislaus Kostka Parish was founded in 1867 and was the first parish in the Archdiocese of Chicago with an apostolic mission to the immigrants from Poland. At the turn of the century, it was one of the largest parishes in the world. During the last several decades, the parish has also become the home to immigrants from the Latin American countries, with the majority of these immigrants coming from Mexico.

Indeed, God shows no partiality since the devotion of The Divine Mercy comes to us through a Polish nun, St. Maria Faustina, while the statue comes to us through a Mexican sculptress, Gogy Farias. The parish's membership today is Anglo, Hispanic, Polish, Asian, and African. This diversity reflects the challenge to true catholicity — that God is the God of all people. All who profess and live the faith of the Church are welcome to take their place at the altar of sacrifice — the table of the banquet.

Meanwhile, from September until June, the artist Ray Garza began designs for the chapel. I had known Ray for four years. He was going through an inner conversion and had been fully reconciled with Christ and the Church. He stayed close to the parish and made himself available to assist in a variety of odd jobs. The death of his grandmother, who was deeply devoted to the Blessed Virgin Mary, had a strong impact on Ray and inspired his daily devotion to the Rosary. He also became more and more interested in the message of Divine Mercy and felt very much a part of Our Lady's plan for the parish of St. Stanislaus Kostka.

In the first days of June, we began preparing for the arrival of the newly sculpted Icon of The Divine Mercy. With the help of Carl Demma, we would send the icon to parishes throughout the Archdiocese of Chicago. Carl was the inspiration behind the 33-foot statue of Our Lady of the Millennium. Considering his expertise in matters pertaining to touring the statue of Our Lady, he agreed to oversee the travels of the 18-foot Icon of The Divine Mercy. In the meantime, as the Icon of The Divine Mercy would visit parishes, a pedestal would be prepared so that the icon could be erected upon its return to the parish the following October. At that time, the parish also expected to host the statue of Our Lady of the Millennium for a week of prayer and devotion.

THE DEATH OF CARL DEMMA

The Icon of The Divine Mercy finally made its way from Mexico into Chicago on June 23rd and was blessed at the parish in an outdoor Mass on the Feast of Corpus Christi, June 25th. Carl had prepared the icon to tour through the Archdiocese the following Tuesday. That Sunday evening, the Feast of Corpus Christi, he came to the church. At around 9:00, he and I began to talk about the significance of both statues. He told me he believed the Icon of Our Lady would also find a permanent home here at St. Stanislaus Kostka. His last words to me that night were, "Her Son has arrived." He sat in his car, prayed the Rosary and seemed to be in deep contemplation, his eyes fixed on the icon.

Around midnight, Carl's wife, Francine, called and asked what time Carl had left the church because he had not yet arrived home. There was nothing we could do but wait. At 6:00 the following morning, as I prepared to leave to celebrate Mass for the Missionaries of Charity, I called Francine. She informed me that Carl had, indeed, come home. She found him outside their home in his parked car. He had apparently died of a heart attack. By 6:30, in the convent chapel of the Missionaries of Charity, I began the Mass for the repose of Carl's soul.

The death of Carl Demma caught the attention of the media. It inspired a front page article in the *Chicago Tribune* on the mystique of iconography — "the pull of tactile and visual symbols on the religious imagination." When I was interviewed by Steve Kloehn, the newspaper's reporter, he asked me to explain the attraction. Pointing to a weeping woman on her knees before the icon, I told him to ask her. Drying her eyes, she simply said she felt cleansed and had her faith in Christ restored. In his report, Kloehn quoted Fr. Richard Fragomeni, a scholar of worship at Catholic Theological Union. Father Fragomeni explained:

> Deep within the icon, deep within the material world, something profoundly other is making itself known to us. They become the ways in which the attention is focused so that all our senses can know God *(Chicago Tribune, June 27, 2000).*

RETURN OF THE ICONS

Within a few weeks, we began to tour the Icon of The Divine Mercy with Ray Garza now designated as its caretaker. Ray took great pride in this mission, and his eyes danced as he talked about the excitement and the manifestation of faith shown by the people everywhere the icon went. Also, he spoke about their sadness when the icon left.

By October, we were preparing for the return of the Icon of The Divine Mercy and the visitation of Carl Demma's Icon of Our Lady of the Millennium. A temporary outdoor adoration chapel was being erected as well as an outdoor sanctuary for the celebration of the Mass. Parishioners were decorating the grounds and people were asked to remove their cars from adjacent streets to make room for the arrival of the icons.

The bells of the church had not been working for a couple of years, so I called the service personnel to schedule their repair. Unable to speak directly with anyone, I left a message on the service center voice mail, but never received a return call. Since I had many other pressing concerns, I did not pursue the issue.

Ray had done some touch up work on the Icon of The Divine Mercy, which was being kept in a warehouse the week before its return to St. Stanislaus Kostka. On Thursday, October 5th, he retrieved a 16-foot photo image of St. Maria Faustina from the rectory basement. In celebration of her being raised to sainthood, the photo image of St. Maria Faustina had hung from the rectory until the wind finally blew the image loose. Ray repaired the slightly damaged image and hung it in the church until he could return on Monday to enthrone it behind the outdoor sanctuary overlooking the icons. To our amazement, it occurred to us that October 5th was the saint's first feast day. Ray also commented how providential it was that he was born April 30th, the day of her canonization. He had developed a strong relationship to The Divine Mercy, acknowledging that Christ had been good to him. Ray recognized a wonderful manifestation of Our Lord's mercy in the love he shared with his wife, Leona.

Saturday morning I got a call from Ray's brother-in-law, who informed me that shortly after midnight on October 7th, the Feast of the Holy Rosary, Ray had suffered an aneurysm to the brain. The prognosis was not good. I was back and forth, to and from the hospital in those few days. Leona was holding on to every ounce of hope that he would pull through.

Tuesday morning, October 10th, the icons arrived at the church. When the statue of Our Lady was raised in an upright position, birds came from everywhere and seemed to dance in flight around the icon to the exuberant joy of the students of the parish school who stood by watching.

When the Icon of The Divine Mercy was hoisted from a flatbed truck and lowered to the ground, the bells began to ring, which caught everyone's attention. I ran to the sacristy of the church and found a gentleman repairing the bell system. He must have noticed the astonished look on my face because he just looked at me and said, "We got the message to repair the bell system days ago, but we've been busy." The next moment I walked into the rectory office to receive an incoming call. It was Leona informing me that they were taking Ray off life-support. He was pronounced dead soon thereafter. After his funeral Mass, Ray's body was carried to the Icon of The Divine Mercy where we prayed the Chaplet. The cortege then peacefully and quietly made its way to the cemetery where Ray's body was laid to rest.

ADORATION BEGINS

After the weeklong prayer, the Icon of Our Lady left the parish to continue its pilgrimage through the Archdiocese while the Icon of The Divine Mercy remained at St. Stanislaus Kostka, to our delight. We still needed money for the pedestal and were not sure exactly where to erect it.

In the meantime, life and ministry in the parish intensified as we entered November. We also bid farewell to Juan Ibarra, one of our deacons who, following the footsteps of his saintly father, had been a true adorer of the Blessed Sacrament and a humble devotee to the Blessed Virgin Mary. Juan had made all the necessary preparations to lead the parish in the Novena to Our Lady of Guadalupe. Two days before the nine-day prayer began, he, too, died suddenly. His body was escorted into the church moments before we began the first evening of prayer to Our Lady.

The manifestation of faith in those days of prayer took the sting out of Juan Ibarra's death. The idea of the chapel lingered in the back of my mind. Our Lady of Guadalupe's words to Juan Diego seemed to re-echo with new urgency in this "our" time. Nearly 500 years ago in her apparitions on the Hill of Tepeyac, Our Lady said to Juan Diego:

> Know and understand, you, my littlest child, that I am the ever Virgin Mary, Mother of the true God through whom you live: the creator of all that is; the Lord of heaven and earth. I deeply wish that a temple be erected here so that in it I may show and give all my love, compassion, help, and defense, for I am your merciful mother. To you, and all the inhabitants of this land and to all those who love me and put their trust in me know that I hear the cry of my children and I come to relieve their miseries and pain.

The idea of the chapel lingered on. Advent and Christmas passed. Winter had set in and before we knew it Lent was almost upon us.

Still no chapel, still no pedestal, but my heart continued to burn. Our Lady had the plan. What next? Finally, about two weeks before Ash Wednesday, I felt every barrier to the building of a chapel had lifted. Rather than wait for money to do major reconstruction in the space allotted for the chapel, we opened a small adoration chapel to The Divine Mercy in the rectory parlor. While not a permanent chapel, nor a perpetual adoration chapel, for at least 12 hours a day from 8:00 in the morning to 8:00 in the evening, people could come to pray.

The Outdoor Sanctuary

Lent came and as we entered into the celebration of Holy Week and prepared for the first official observance of

The Divine Mercy Sunday, we began to move forward with plans to construct the base of the icon.

After a number of bids were taken, a contractor was selected, and we scheduled a meeting for a morning in May to study his proposed drawings of the pedestal. The day before the meeting, I had received a telephone call from Maureen Murphy of the Archdiocesan Office of Legal Services. She said that someone had left some money in a will. The money was designated specifically for a chapel. Maureen said that the executor of the will had been given my name and would contact me. Within hours the executor's call came, but I was out of the office. I tried to return the message, but my efforts were in vain.

During the meeting the following day, the contractor showed us the drawings of the pedestal and then surprised us with a beautiful sketch of an outdoor sanctuary to enclose the icon. The cost of the sanctuary would exceed $100,000. It could easily cost as much as $130,000 — perhaps $150,000 — or even as much as $200,000. I was excited at the thought of such a beautiful sanctuary. The problem was, of course, that we had no money.

I quietly left the meeting to make a phone call. The gentleman who answered thanked me for calling. He proceeded to tell me that his mother was the executor of a will, and there was some money left over for a chapel. He estimated that about $120,000 to $135,000 remained in the will. The man and his mother met me in the rectory two days later. I shared with them the story of my walk in faith from the moment Our Lady requested the parish to the present day. They listened with caution, but with rapt attention.

Before leaving, the mother shared with me a dream she had had some years ago. She saw an image of Our Lord in vivid detail unlike any she had ever seen. Weeks later, the same image was enthroned in her parish church. It was the image of The Divine Mercy. Then, when I shared with her my hope that we would dedicate the sanctuary on September 8th, the Feast of Our Lady's Birth, the woman's eyes sparkled. She told me that she and her husband were married on September 8th. Although he had died five years ago, I could see that her pain was still deep and her love very much alive.

Confident that the money would be designated for the sanctuary, I waited patiently for a response from the donors. Nearly two weeks had passed, and I had heard nothing. I felt deeply humbled by my premature enthusiasm and thought perhaps I had said something wrong to the donors, or perhaps my discernment had been somehow misguided. I sincerely asked the Lord to forgive my presumption and lift me from the darkness that enveloped me.

In desolation, I went to the next meeting that was scheduled with the contractor. Since I had no money, I had no good news to give him. We decided that we would dispense with the idea of a sanctuary for now and build a patio around the icon. After the meeting, I reluctantly called the donor and left a voice mail message, asking if the parish was still being considered for the money.

An hour later I received a call with an apology. Apparently, the donor's son had left a message on our parish voice mail two weeks ago on the day after we met. He regretted that I didn't get the message, but said, "Yes, my mother wasted no time in her decision to give the money to St. Stanislaus Kostka Parish for the outdoor sanctuary."

As we seemingly move closer to having a permanent chapel for adoration of the Blessed Sacrament and a sanctuary of The Divine Mercy, we are humbled. Our Lady, in the meantime, continues to manifest herself.

THE MOTHER OF OUR LORD LEADS US

Nearly two years ago on the Feast of the Triumph of the Holy Cross, I entrusted my life to Jesus through Mary. Not long after, I took the crucifix and the zucchetto (or skull cap) as symbols of my submission and began wearing them daily.

I took the crucifix for obvious reasons. The crucifix is the most vivid symbol of Jesus' submission to the will of the Father in atonement for the sins of the world through His suffering, death, and resurrection. The idea of also wearing a skull cap as a sign of submission came to me as I walked the corridors of the Vatican Museum while on a pilgrimage in Rome. Some of the artwork in the Museum portrayed priests and religious of an era long gone donned in the skull cap and the simple religious garb of their day. Something in those images spoke to me of the total and undivided attention they gave to God. As I reflected on these paintings, the symbol of the skull cap was slowly redefined and took on new meaning in relation to my personal consecration. I felt that the distinction and uniqueness of wearing the skull cap in this world of the Third Millennium could be a bold symbol, provoking inquiry as to its meaning and providing me with opportunities to speak to the mysteries of religious faith in Christ Jesus.

Whatever message these symbols might have for the outside world, for me they seal the enslavement of my life to God. If for no other reason, the daily wearing of the crucifix and skull cap reminds me of the sacrificial and sacred character of my consecration.

As I celebrated Mass that morning, I felt confirmed in the decision to establish a Divine Mercy adoration chapel. The words of the preface to the Eucharistic Prayer set me free from any lingering doubt as I prayed, "Everywhere we proclaim Your mighty works for You have called us out of darkness and into Your own wonderful light."

Yet, there is still darkness. We are in exile. We are strangers in a foreign land, and there's a storm on the horizon. The battle is waged; the warfare is intense. It is true what we read in the Book of Revelation, "The huge dragon, and ancient serpent known as the devil or Satan, the seducer of the whole world...wages war on her offspring, on those who keep God's commandments and give witness to Jesus" (Rev 12:9, 17). It is a lonely walk, it is the way of the cross, but God is with us. And so, we let the Mother of Our Lord lead us, for we belong to her. The Blessed Virgin Mary has a very tender love, a special protection, for all her children, if we only turn to her.

2

INVITATION TO DRINK AT THE FOUNTAIN OF MERCY

June 29, 2001

Alongside Chicago's Kennedy Expressway, at the crossroads where north meets south, I envision an oasis of Catholic spirituality. Here, at the parish church of St. Stanislaus Kostka, heaven reaches out in a gesture of mercy to satisfy the thirst of the spiritually poor through the symbols of Catholic mysticism. This mysticism — expressed in the Icons of Our Lady of the Millennium and The Divine Mercy — weaves itself into our collective religious imagination. Both Marian and Eucharistic, this spirituality is grounded in the ancient tradition of the Church.

MARY TEACHES US TO PRAY

At the entrance to our outdoor Sanctuary of The Divine Mercy, the Icon of Our Lady of the Millennium, in a posture of prayer, points to Jesus whose gesture of blessing is directed away from her and towards a pilgrim people. The pilgrims are symbolized in the flow of traffic moving north and south on the Kennedy Expressway. For the pilgrims drawn to the sanctuary, the praying Mary leads them through the Via Dolorosa to the Font of Mercy, the Icon of Jesus.

The water that cascades down the Icon of The Divine Mercy's pedestal represents the Blood and Water flowing from the Heart of Jesus. The fountain itself symbolizes the birth of the Church. This birth was realized and continues to be sustained through the Sacraments, principally the Holy Eucharist and the Sacrament of Reconciliation. The Eucharist, instituted at the Last Supper, perpetuates the sacrifice Jesus made of Himself on Golgotha. Through this sacrifice humanity was set free from its slavery to sin and death. The redeeming grace of the Eucharist continues to transform the lives of a pilgrim people who sin unceasingly and have yet to die. Through the Holy Sacrifice of the Mass, a perpetual outpouring of mercy brings humanity out of slavery and into freedom, from darkness into light, from death to life. This process will continue — without ceasing — until the end of time, when Jesus comes in glory. To enter into this sacred mystery, the pilgrim must pass by way of the Blessed Virgin Mary.

Mary of Nazareth, a creature like us, was by a singular grace of God, exalted far above the angels and all the other saints. The mere size of the Icon of Our Lady of the Millennium gives testimony to this singular grace. Conceived without original sin, she, who remained sinless, was chosen by God to be mother of the Messiah and mother of the messianic people. The messianic people are a pilgrim people in exile, but in journey towards their homeland. The Blessed Virgin Mary is the necessary means to the pilgrim's true knowledge and true experience of Jesus. She gives a wandering people direction. The Holy Mother of the Incarnate Word guides us to a proper spirituality where we discover that we are known and loved by God.

The Icon of Our Lady of the Millennium shows the Virgin in the posture of prayer. This is reminiscent of those moments when in her home in Nazareth the Angel Gabriel greets her as the one chosen by God to be the Mother of the Christ. In the Annunciation, Mary teaches us to pray.

In her prayer, she is first and foremost attentive. Her eyes are fixed on God. Second, Our Lady surrenders her life — she submits her mind, her body, her soul, and her spirit to God. She abandons to God her memory, her understanding, and her entire will. Third, she is acting in obedience to the divine will of God. And finally, Mary, in all humility, shows herself to be a woman of faith and trust. Her faith and trust are expressed in her *fiat*, "let it be done to me as you have said." In her *yes* to the will of God, the Incarnation happens — the Word is made Flesh — Jesus is conceived and formed in the Virgin Mary.

Mary of Nazareth says *yes* on behalf of all humanity, but before the world sets its eyes on Jesus, He remains hidden in her womb. She is the Ark of the Covenant. She is the tabernacle, concealing the Holy of Holies until the appointed time. Then, in the little town of Bethlehem, the dark of night gives way to the light of day. In unceasing prayer, the Virgin Mary will nurture the Incarnate Word for thirty years until the wedding feast at Cana of Galilee. There, at her request, the drama begins to unfold toward the long awaited hour.

Outside the walls of Ancient Jerusalem on the Hill of Calvary, the hour arrives. It is His hour. It is her hour. It is the Hour of Great Mercy. It is the great hour of reconciliation resounding in the cry of Jesus, "Father, forgive them."

It is the hour of marriage. It is the hour of birth. On Golgotha, Jesus, the Incarnate God, is wedded to His people in the person of Mary — she is the virgin bride without the stain of sin. There at the foot of the cross, the Virgin Mary becomes mother of the messianic people, recalling the words of the prophet Isaiah, "In one moment's time the Daughter Zion suffers the pain of labor and gives birth to a children she never conceived." In the Blood and Water flowing from the sacred wounds of Jesus, Mary is in the pain of labor — she is birthing her children.

So, appropriately, it is by way of the Icon of Our Lady that the pilgrim must enter into the Sanctuary of The Divine Mercy. As it was, so it is and so it will be. This is Catholic spirituality.

Through Our Lady's posture of prayer, her response to God's call and her pondering the mysterious action of God in her life and in the lives of her children, she prods the pilgrim people to go forward. She inspires them to walk the Via Dolorosa to the fountain of The Divine Mercy.

Mary is a creature like us in the order of nature, but by the order of grace she is far above the angels and all the other saints. She is by God's grace exalted and forever contemplates her Son who is her God. It is through this perpetual contemplation of The Divine Mercy and in the strength so powerfully conveyed through the Icon of Our Lady that pilgrims find the courage to go where she has already trod.

OUR LADY'S PLAN

It is towards Jesus that she leads the pilgrim people. She will walk with them and show them the way. In her invitation to drink from the fountain of mercy, she does not deceive. She crushes the head of the ancient serpent, bringing to light the darkness of his deceptions, his seductions, and all the illusions that keep her children from the truth of who they are and who God is. The way to The Divine Mercy is the difficult way of the cross, but Our Lady will guide the pilgrim people. She will accompany those who veer off the Kennedy Expressway as they venture into the Sanctuary of The Divine Mercy. There, the spiritual thirst of a pilgrim people will be satisfied even as Jesus' own thirst for souls will be quenched. This is Our Lady's plan.

It is her plan that the pilgrim people drink at the true fount of The Divine Mercy, which is the Holy Eucharist. The Sanctuary of The Divine Mercy has the ultimate purpose of leading the pilgrims to the chapel to adore and to contemplate the Blessed Sacrament of the Holy Eucharist — where the Body and Blood, together with the Soul and Divinity of the Lord Jesus Christ is truly, really, and substantially contained in the Blessed Sacrament.

And so, in the heart of Chicago, heaven reaches out to humanity in a gesture of mercy to enkindle within the soul a desire for God. Our Lady, the tabernacle that so long ago concealed the Holy of Holies, continues in her apostolic mission to make Jesus known, loved, and served and to gently and tenderly, gracefully and mercifully remind a wayward, wandering, and wondering people that they, too, are known, loved, and served by a living God.

Two thousand years ago when the Virgin of Nazareth spoke her *yes* on behalf of all humanity, she was not alone. There were others, too, who awaited the fulfillment of the promise made to Abraham. Attentive to the voice of the prophets, they were a people keeping vigil. Holy Scripture calls these faithful people the *Anawim* — the Poor of Yahweh, the Holy Remnant, the Daughter Zion. There were Elizabeth and Zachariah, Anna and Simeon, and Joseph, the husband of Mary, to name a few. It was through their vigilant faith that

Jesus came the first time and as it was then, so it will be when He comes again in glory. The Blessed Virgin Mary in a singular and most perfect way represents all the believing people of God.

In the Gospel, in a rather chilling way, Jesus asks, "When the Son of Man comes in glory, will He even find faith in the world?" Our response is, *yes*. We say *yes* because we recall the words Jesus spoke the night before He was crucified. In His farewell discourse, He directed His words to His little flock and prayed to His Father on their behalf and on behalf of those who would believe in their testimony. He promised that He would not leave them orphaned.

And so, at Our Lady's invitation, the Sanctuary of The Divine Mercy leading to the chapel of adoration of the Blessed Sacrament testifies to the truth of Our Lord's words that He would be with us always.

The sanctuary and the adoration chapel constitute holy ground — a place of refuge for a vigilant people — an oasis in the desert journey through the trials and tribulations of life in this world.

Increasingly the world shows hostility to the way of Christ, and increasingly the Catholic is perceived as a stranger in a foreign land. Nonetheless, walking humbly in solidarity with sinful humanity, there remains in a sincere Catholic a deep-felt need to keep vigil and to intercede on behalf of all for the atonement of sin.

Whether or not the multitude responds to heaven's reaching out in a gesture of mercy to satisfy the thirst of the spiritually poor, it is to the vigilant flock that Our Lady shows particular concern. They are disciples in mission. They know themselves to be in exile — strangers in a foreign land. They know there's a storm on the horizon. The war is waged: The battle is intense. Our Lady knows too well the truth of what is written in the Book of Revelation, "the huge dragon, and ancient serpent known as the devil or Satan, the seducer of the whole world, wages war on her offspring, on those who keep God's commandments and give witness to Jesus."

It is in her plan to transform the little flock and keep them strong, because they are sharers in her apostolic mission and it is to them that the world unknowingly will be indebted. They atone for sins and keep the faith alive. In the name of humanity, they will receive the Messiah when He comes in His glory. Theirs is a lonely walk, it is the way of the cross, but God is with them and Mary will lead them — they belong to her.

She, then, knowingly and consciously, draws them to the fountain of The Divine Mercy. She insures for them a resting place in the crossroad of Chicago's Loop on the grounds of the parish church of St. Stanislaus Kostka. It is here that they will drink from the fountain of mercy. It is here that the mysticism of the Church weaves itself into the religious imagination so that Jesus be known and loved and served.

The Icon of Our Lady of the Millennium and the Icon of The Divine Mercy are heaven's plea for humanity's return to God. They symbolize the marriage between God and His bride, the Church. It is the mission of the Church to proclaim the message of The Divine Mercy before Jesus the Christ returns in glory as the just Judge. This is Our Lady's time — this is a time of grace. This is the only time we have. Our indifference to her call would be chilling. Our silence would be condemning.

So now, O children,
listen to me;
instruction and wisdom do not reject!
Happy the man who obeys me,
and happy those who keep my ways.
Happy the man watching daily at my gates,
waiting at my doorposts;
for he who finds me finds life,
and wins favor from the Lord.

Proverbs 8:31-35

3

NEVER ALONE IN GETHSEMANE

August 18, 2001

In Luke's Gospel Jesus says:

> Gird your loins and light your lamps and be like servants who await their master's return from a wedding, ready to open immediately when he comes and knocks. Blessed are those servants whom the master finds vigilant on his arrival.

Vigilance is synonymous with waiting. Since I consecrated my life to the Blessed Virgin Mary two years ago, she has taught me the necessity of keeping vigil in patient expectation and to do so in complete trust and total surrender to the will of God.

That my life changed on the day of the consecration is perhaps an understatement. I not only began pondering the request of the Blessed Virgin that a Sanctuary to The Divine Mercy be established on the grounds of the parish, but the eyes of my soul were also opened to reflect on the extent to which I had not previously opened myself to the transforming power of God's grace. While I had always been perceived as a good and faithful priest, the consecration has graced me with the painful realization that I had not been single-minded in my devotion to God: Instead, I have too often lived under the control of my own ego. The seriousness with which I consecrated my life to the Holy Mother of God has made me aware of the seriousness with which my life has been received by God for His sole purpose and plan.

There is a price to be paid in the surrender of one's life to God's specific will. The cost of discipleship is the purgation of the senses from inordinate attachment to the things of the world so that the impediments to friendship with God be lifted. Even when not possessed by creatures, things, or ideologies, the death to the self is an annihilation that is deeply personal, deeply spiritual and, indeed, the cause of intense pain. That Jesus freely and fully accepted His own death gives me courage not to resist the sacrifices God may be asking of me in the conformity of my will to His. The knowledge that I am known by God and called into His divine will brings the joy that sustains me in the garden of sorrows.

Nearly two years ago, when I made the first of three pilgrimages to the Holy Land, I heard Jesus call me into Gethsemane. This was only two months after I had entrusted my life to the Blessed Virgin Mary. This was also before the events surrounding the devotion to The Divine Mercy began to unfold. An interior darkness began to envelop me in November of 1999 as I was en route to the Holy Land.

Intimacy with the Christ

After arriving in Tel Aviv, I took a cab to Tiberias to meet the pilgrims assigned to my spiritual direction. After I introduced myself to the driver, he told me to sit back and relax. It was rush hour, so he estimated that the trip to Tiberias would take about two hours. I sat in the back seat. With my eyes closed, I began to wallow in darkness, feeling very much alone and terribly lonely. Perhaps a half an hour later, I silently begged Jesus to take away the enduring loneliness and lift me from the darkness. I had no sooner made this request when the cab driver broke the silence saying, "Anthony, don't worry. Your first time in the Holy Land — the good God will grant your wish." Naturally I perked up as it seemed he had taken the thoughts from my mind.

He told me that tradition has it that for first-time arrivals to the Holy Land, the good God will grant any request so long as the petition is placed at the Wailing Wall. Then the driver shared his own experience of this tradition. He is Jewish and came from France. Twelve years ago, he had made his first trip to the Holy Land. At the Wailing Wall, he asked the good God to send him a wife. He had asked that she be Israeli and a virgin, and he shyly added the request that her name be Denise. His reply came two years later when, back in France, he actually met an Israeli woman. She was a virgin and her name was Denise. Not long after their meeting, they were married. They now make their home in Tel Aviv.

The driver and I bonded spiritually and shared many things, even stopping for dinner to prolong the trip to Tiberias. When we reached the hotel, I thanked him and told him how grateful I was to God for putting me in his cab. He said the gratitude was mutually shared. He had had little work, even calling his wife to tell her that the day had been unproductive. She said, "Not to worry — the good God will provide." He no sooner hung up the phone when he met with my request to go to Tiberias. So, the good God provided him with a day's wage, and I found consolation through the wise counsel of this fine man of God.

Following the driver's advice, I left my petition at the Wailing Wall. It seems to me that if in the last couple of years I have been intrigued by the concept of spiritual warfare, it is because I experience it at a deep level — both interiorly and exteriorly. The consecration of my life to the Blessed Virgin Mary put me on the frontline in the heat of battle. Naturally, I don't want to fight this battle alone. So, in one of my petitions at the Wailing Wall, I asked God to bring somebody into this battle with me.

As I reflect back, I think that in the Holy Land Jesus was preparing me. Of all the religious sites, I was most deeply moved in Gethsemane. There, at the site of His agony, His betrayal, and His arrest, my soul begged Jesus to allow me to accompany Him in the garden. I longed for intimacy with the Christ and wanted to accompany Him in His darkest hours. He assured me that I would.

Jesus was preparing me for the "sweat of blood" and for the lonely walk of interior purgation. I realize now that it was not I who would accompany Him, but rather He would accompany me. He had answered my petition, but not exactly as I had expected. He and He alone would be with me in the trenches to fight this battle, and I would have to learn to walk in faith and put all my trust in Him.

If I am being purified, it is because my will and the will of the parish are not yet conformed to the will of God. For my part I must continue to decrease, to lose myself, and to die to myself. In short, Our Lady's plan for the parish requires this. Jesus must increase; He must be found; He must live. As St. John so clearly says, "The world with its lust is passing away, but he who does the will of God abides forever."

I fail Jesus and Mary far too often. This is cause for personal grief and it robs me of interior peace, but they remain lovingly faithful and this is the cause of my joy. Heaven, knowing how frail, how weak, how pitiful we really are, treats us with mercy and patient expectation, believing more in us than we believe in ourselves.

Sanctification is a holy work. It is God's work in us. I have come to understand that I cannot make myself holy, but

I must cooperate with God's grace as it mysteriously transforms my life. What is needed is proper disposition in vigilant prayer — the prayer of waiting — a waiting with patient expectation that God will do what He intends to do.

I pray for the grace to be that blessed servant whom the master finds vigilant on His arrival. As pastor, I recognize my duty to open the door without delay when He comes and knocks. Something wholly unique is happening here at St. Stanislaus Kostka, and Our Lady continues to prepare the way in perfect conformity to the will of God. For my part, I walk in faith.

HOLLYWOOD AND ST. MARIA FAUSTINA

While the garden of sorrows is a deep-felt reality and Jesus, the redeemer lifting me up, the journey of faith is shared by others who hear the call in the deep recesses of the soul and respond with generosity of heart. The Blessed Virgin Mary's request for Sanctuary has drawn others into her story.

Thankfully, I enjoy the support of others whose eyes and ears are open to the same vision and the same call. As the story unfolds, we recognize the need for patient and persevering prayer for the personal sanctification of our lives, coupled with unceasing intercession that God's mercy may envelop the whole world. As the overall plan for the sanctuary grows, I realize we will not have the Sanctuary of The Divine Mercy by September 8th, as I had hoped. The $135,000 that was promised to us remains in the care of the Archdiocese and may not be released until there is certainty that the whole project is financially secured.

In my previous reflections, I mentioned Oscar I. Delgado, a former NBC war correspondent who covered conflicts in Latin American, the Persian Gulf, and Bosnia-Herzegovina. While he was in Latin America, Oscar won the

Mexican Lottery. Being a man of faith, he waited for God to direct him as to how to use this money.

While Oscar was in the Persian Gulf, his assignments included a Christmas Eve interview with Sadaam Hussein, only a few weeks before the Persian Gulf War began. Later he was assigned to cover the war in Bosnia-Herzegovina. While there, Oscar visited the little village of Medjugorje, the site where it is alleged that the Blessed Virgin Mary has appeared to young people beginning on the Feast of St. John the Baptist, June 24, 1981. It is said that these apparitions continue to this day.

In Medjugorje, Oscar had a personal religious experience. It was there that he felt called by God to use the money he won in the lottery to spread the prophetic message given to St. Maria Faustina, the message of Divine Mercy. Since that time, Oscar has assisted in the building of adoration chapels throughout the world, using various means to make this message known. In an effort to promote this message of Divine Mercy, Oscar donated the 18-foot bronze Icon of The Divine Mercy to the sanctuary here at St. Stanislaus Kostka Parish.

Some years ago, Oscar left NBC and became executive producer of the two radio shows, "Night Flight" and "The Road Less Traveled," which air on Catholic Family Radio. He is also a Hollywood movie producer, preparing now for the premiere of his first major motion picture. While secular in nature, the movie has a moral message. Oscar intends to use this MGM-OCE movie, "The Learning Curve" as a springboard into religious films.

Just two weeks ago, the theater exhibitors, Marcus, AMC, Loews and Regal announced the world premiere of Oscar's movie for October 5th. Although it was unknown to them, the Feast of St. Maria Faustina is on the same day. Since the message of The Divine Mercy is at the heart of what Oscar does, the date of the movie's premiere is not viewed as a mere coincidence. Those who walk in faith recognize God's providence in the small details of daily life.

In my previous reflections, I mentioned the possibility of having the Icon of Our Lady of the Millennium at the entrance to the Sanctuary of The Divine Mercy. There has been some debate as to where the eventual home of the traveling Icon of Our Lady will be. Understandably, many parishes are vying for possession of the icon.

What is certain is that an image of Our Lady must be near the entrance to the Sanctuary of The Divine Mercy. I began ruminating over the possibility of having an icon sculpted of Our Lady of Guadalupe in the event that St. Stanislaus Kostka is not chosen as the permanent home of Our Lady of the Millennium. The Virgin of Guadalupe is Patroness of the Americas.

OUR LADY PREPARES THE GROUND

Another person who has stepped providentially into Our Lady's story is Gloria Hernandez. I met Gloria for the first time when, unknown to her, she came to the parish as an instrument of God's providence. At that time, I was being pressured to publicize and communicate the upcoming arrival of the Icon of The Divine Mercy, which was en route from Mexico. It was May, a typically busy time in the parish. Inundated with countless other things to do, I could not yield to the pressure to publicize the upcoming event. It was the farthest thing from my mind, yet I was still bothered by the burden of the pressure.

Still weakened by the weight of responsibility to publicize the arrival of the Icon of The Divine Mercy, one Friday evening after celebrating Mass, I was sharing with parishioners the story of The Divine Mercy and presented them with the first photos of the icon, which I had received only a few days earlier. I noticed a woman I had never seen before listening with attention. Afterwards, she came to me and introduced herself as Gloria Hernandez. She handed me her business card. Amazed by divine providence, I breathed a sigh of relief as I read her card identifying her as the Hispanic Director of Communications for the Archdiocese of Chicago. When she left work that evening, she had planned to go to Mass and, since she was so close to downtown, Gloria decided to come to St. Stanislaus Kostka.

Gloria generously covered the arrival of the Icon of The Divine Mercy and reported the story in the Catholic press. It was through her effort that the events surrounding the icon received front page coverage in *Chicago Catolico*. At the same time, it was Carl Demma's death that inspired a front page article in the *Chicago Tribune* on the mystique of iconography and the story of The Divine Mercy. The story caught the attention of the secular and religious media. I did not view this as mere coincidence, but rather, the humbling manifestation of God's grace aware of human limitations.

Now, over a year since the statue's arrival from Mexico, Gloria reappeared. I hadn't spoken to her since the day the Icon of The Divine Mercy was blessed a year and a half ago. I was happy to see her when she recently came to join us in prayer at the Holy Hour of The Divine Mercy. Eager to give her an update on the status of the sanctuary, I shared bits and pieces of the story with her. As I talked, she began to smile and something in her eyes told me that the Blessed Virgin Mary may have arranged our meeting.

Gloria enthusiastically gave me an update of her endeavors during the course of the past year. She had coordinated and directed Cardinal Francis George's pilgrimage to Mexico for the Feast of Our Lady of Guadalupe. As a result of the pilgrimage, she and other volunteers organized a group called the Juan Diego Solidarity Committee to assist the children of the indigenous peoples of Mexico. Juan Diego was the Indian to whom Our Lady appeared on the Hill of Tepeyac in 1531. It is there beside the Hill of Apparitions that the Basilica of Our Lady of Guadalupe stands. That shrine draws more pilgrims yearly than any other Catholic shrine throughout the world.

The Mexican Church donated huge rocks cut from the Hill of Tepeyac as a gift to the Church in the United States of America. Some were destined for a sanctuary to Our Lady of Guadalupe that was to be erected in Los Angeles, California. Just recently, the Church had appointed the Juan Diego Solidarity Committee as the caretakers of the rocks in Los Angeles. Intrigued by the story that continues to unfold here at St. Stanislaus Kostka, Gloria suggested the possibility of bringing the rocks to the Sanctuary of The Divine Mercy to be used as a foundation for the statue of Our Lady of Guadalupe.

The words that Our Lady spoke to Juan Diego on the Hill of Tepeyac nearly 500 years ago re-echo with new urgency in this our time, *"I deeply wish that a temple be erected here so that in it I may show and give all my love, compassion, help, and defense, for I am your merciful mother. To you, and all the inhabitants of this land, and to all those who love me and put their trust in me know that I hear the cry of my children and I come to relieve their miseries and pain."* Indeed, there is much misery and pain. As a priest, I see it daily in the lives of our people. Often their eyes betray a deep sadness and an inner turmoil, which is void of any hope or joy.

Certainly I am not exempt from the experience of sadness and inner turmoil, but I have the sure hope that the battle within me is a necessary purgation that precedes a deep and genuine holiness of life. I live daily with the burning desire that Jesus reproduce His life in mine. I choose to be as bold as St. Therese of Lisieux in saying with conviction that I want to be a saint.

It was Mother Teresa of Calcutta who reminded us that sanctity is not the privilege of the few, but rather, the ordinary responsibility of all God's people. It is when we admit our desire to be saints that we begin to walk in humility. Today, though, more than ever we need heaven's help, and, indeed, heaven is reaching out. To be holy is God's greatest work in us. Knowing that we are destined to share fully in the holiness of God already brings relief from the pain and miseries of our lives lived in exile.

The Television: Our Lady's Tool?

Today is Monday, August 20th, the Feast of St. Bernard. I completed the previous reflections early Saturday afternoon. As always, I remain focused on my pastoral responsibilities to the parish and the parishioners as the story of the sanctuary continues to evolve. With so little time to spare in the course of a day's work, I cannot neglect my prayer life, and I will continue to write as long as the inspiration burns in my soul. I believe that the events unfolding here at the parish are not meant for my private reflection alone. This is Our Lady's story, and we are all instruments in this, her plan. Because I firmly accept this in faith, I am compelled to continue telling the story.

While I wonder how to secure potential donors to finance the sanctuary, I trust that the Blessed Virgin Mary will provide the means and the people necessary to bring her call to fruition.

While some have suggested media exposure to promote the story, I readily admit that I have a personal phobia for cameras. As an introvert and loner, I shy away from such attention. I am perfectly content being the medium through my prayer and my writing, as well as in my discussions with our people through homilies and in personal sharing. From this standpoint, I welcome others to reach out if they feel called, but I'd rather remain hidden and consumed by the apostolic mission of the parish. If the truth were known, I would prefer to follow my heart's desire to be enveloped in prayer and solitude on the top of a mountain in France, and wrapped in the silence of the hermitage I once visited there.

A few days ago, I experienced what for some may be mere coincidence, but for me is another manifestation of God's providence. Saturday evening I was celebrating the Mass. There were few people in the church, so I immediately noticed a couple who entered the church shortly after the Mass began. They sat perhaps a dozen rows from the ambo and may have been the only people seated on that side of the church. I don't recall that there were others. I had never seen this couple before.

During the homily, the couple sat almost directly in front of me as I expounded on the evils of television and how we seem to be unaffected by the media's propagation of ideas, behaviors, and language that run counter to our Judeo-Christian values and principles. I noted that in most homes, sofas and recliners now encircle the television, giving the impression that the television has become the supreme authority governing our lives. I think our grandparents would "roll over in their graves" at the sights and sounds that fill the minds and hearts, the bodies, and souls of the people of this generation.

I went on to explain that I have not watched television since I consecrated my life to Our Lady two years ago. The only time that I might catch a glimpse of the television anymore is when I go to the gym and am subjected to six different stations being broadcast simultaneously on six different sets. The only sound that drowns out the noise of those televisions is the blare of the radio — an experience, at times, nauseating. I am sure I likened the television to the Antichrist as I delivered the homily.

After the Mass, the visiting couple came to me and thanked me for the Mass and told me how beautiful the church was. They said they felt something special about being in this church. I thanked them for coming and asked for their prayers. I didn't say much about our walk in faith except that Our Lady is leading us and we want to be faithful and strong in the ensuing spiritual battle that has the potential for disturbing our peace. I gave them some earlier reflections on the unfolding story, but the gentleman had already picked them up from the back of the church.

They introduced themselves as John and Mary Ambull, directors of the Catholic Views Television Network. The network runs six hours of Catholic Television on EWTN, the Eternal Word Television Network. On their way to Mokena, Illinois, they just happened to be passing our church along the Kennedy Expressway and decided to exit. Mr. Ambull said in parting, "We'll be in touch."

While the television has a dark side that is governed by the flesh lusting against the spirit, it also has the potential for great good. Acting in conformity to the will of God, the Blessed Virgin uses every means at her disposal to bring Jesus to us and us to Him.

You are the light of the world.
A city set on a hill cannot be hidden.
Men do not light a lamp
and then put it under a bushel basket.
They set it on a stand,
where it gives light to all in the house.
In the same way,
your light must shine before men
so that they may see goodness in your acts
and give praise to your heavenly Father.

Matthew 5:14-16

4

ALLURED BY THE CHRIST

August 23, 2001

Having just completed three days of conferences for the Missionaries of Charity, I find myself again reflecting on the words of Mother Teresa. In writing to a priest, Mother Teresa said:

> You have said 'yes' to Jesus and He has taken you at your word. The Word of God became Jesus, the poor one. And so this terrible emptiness you experience. God cannot fill what is full. He can only fill emptiness — deep poverty — and your yes is the beginning of being or becoming empty. It is not how much we really 'have' to give — but how empty we are. Let Jesus be the victim and priest in you.

After sixteen years in the priesthood, I am almost ashamed to admit that I am only beginning to be empty. God has, indeed, waited with patient expectation even while inflicting wounds to seemingly force me into submission. As I look back over the years, since childhood, I can clearly see how God's hand has unceasingly guided me. I can also see how from the deepest recesses of my soul, I have always desired the Christ. At the same time, I have resisted the descent into my nothingness to claim that hidden treasure. I knew it was there. I knew it was mine and I knew it would always be there.

Upon entering the seminary at the age of 21, I was extremely naïve and idealistic. For this reason, I felt torn when all around me I was faced with the challenge of dealing with blatant contradictions to the ideals that consumed me. The ideals I held concerning the holiness of life, self-renunciation, and zeal for the propagation of the faith were hampered by the prevailing psychology of the day, which emphasized an exaggerated preoccupation with the self and the false promise of resurrection without the sorrows of Calvary.

It was the image of sunshine, blue skies, green grass, and flowers that captivated the attention of the post-Vatican II Church. It was an era of great so-called "liberation" for priests and religious, many of whom threw aside what was viewed as the yoke of an "oppressive regime." In doing this, they expected to savor the freshness of a newfound identity.

For my part, all I could identify with was the crucified Jesus. He was my consolation. As I entered the seminary, it seemed that Jesus, who had previously *allured* me to Himself, had thrown me high into the sky and let me drop into a million pieces. That first year I was sustained by a photograph that I had seen in a book. It became an icon for me. I meditated daily on the image which showed a man, infested with sores, lying almost dead in the streets of Calcutta. He was being lifted out of the gutter by Mother Teresa. In my mind, I was that man, and she was the Christ.

Throughout my nine years of seminary, I sought refuge in the Blessed Sacrament. There in the silence of my heart Jesus not only sustained me, He assured me that He was with me, that He wanted me and that He would instruct me. This He did. Had Jesus not fulfilled His promise to me, I would never have permitted myself to be ordained a priest, nor would I have made a public profession of vows as a religious in the Church.

Feeling totally out of sync with the prevailing norms of a secularized religious life and priesthood, I painfully tried to let go of my idealism and rise above my naiveté. I tried, but I could not. For the most part, the naiveté has long since past, but the idealism continues to consume me.

The language, attitudes, and lifestyles on the contemporary religious scene left me feeling rather odd and out of touch. Intimidated by the intelligence and eloquence of countless priests and religious, I felt myself being coerced into dying to my ideals. However, no matter how close I came to letting go, the idealism would always reemerge with a fascination that would overwhelm me. The ideal I speak of is that of a total and undivided consecration of one's life to Christ. It is being able to say with St. Paul, "It is no longer I who live, but Christ Jesus who lives in me."

Descent into Nothingness

Although as a seminarian I felt disillusioned by the prevailing attitudes of a secularized religious life and priesthood, I was nonetheless illuminated by Jesus in the Blessed Sacrament. He gently invited me to go where I feared to go — into complete nothingness.

I believe it was really into nothingness that Jesus invited the young man who asked the Lord what he should do to inherit everlasting life. Jesus asked him if he had kept the commandments, and the young man said he had done so since his youth. So Jesus told him to sell all his possessions, give to the poor, and follow Him. Hearing this, the young man became sad and walked away. Even so, the Gospel says Jesus looked on him with love. Jesus knew that the young man would return.

The invitation to descend into nothingness, and there to claim the hidden treasure, is an invitation that eventually comes to all of us. Jesus knows when the time is opportune for each of us. In the interim, even as we wrestle with the thought of letting go, He never takes His loving gaze from us.

The time for me to descend into my own nothingness had not yet come, but I did, indeed, wrestle with the inevitable. In stark contrast to the nine difficult years spent in seminary formation, my first six years in the priesthood were like an extended honeymoon. For the most part, I have been graced with much consolation in prayer during both the difficulties of the seminary and the joys of my first years in the priesthood. It was only when I was assigned to the parish of St. Stanislaus Kostka that I experienced a sudden change in my prayer life, as I began what would be a rather long sojourn through the desert.

The parishioners received me with a great deal of warmth, and I have always been humbled by their acceptance of me in spite of my shortcomings. Most of the time I feel undeserving of the attention they give me, but it brings me great joy, and this joy helps to sustain me. It is for them as well as for me that I want to descend into nothingness, so that Christ can be everything. I want to love them with His love. I want to look on my parishioners with the same eyes that Jesus fixed on the young man who walked away sad because he had too many possessions.

With this change in assignment, I became like an infant having to learn to communicate in a language that was foreign to me. The Hispanic people always made me feel that they appreciated the effort I put into learning their language. This period during which I was unable to speak with comprehension proved to be a time of great grace as I was plunged into perpetual humiliation. This did not hurt me, even if it was the most difficult skill I had ever worked to acquire. What most devastated me was God's hiddenness in my prayer life. God seemed to withdraw His affection from me. This was the beginning of an intense interior struggle to trust that God was with me even if I could only feel a gaping hole in my soul.

As I struggled with the emptiness of God's *seeming* absence, I felt the allure of the flesh in a powerful way. During this time, I had made a retreat at the Cenacle, located in Chicago's Lincoln Park only a few blocks from Lake Michigan. For days, I was tormented and seduced by the desire for things that were contrary to the boundaries imposed by my religious vocation.

As I walked through the neighborhoods of Lincoln Park and strolled along the beach, I felt a weight bearing down on my emptiness. It came at the sight of people bathing in the sun. It came at the sight of families at play or lovers walking arm in arm through the park. I imagined myself living in one of the beautiful brownstones that neatly line the streets of Lincoln Park. There I could feel myself enjoying a quiet evening in the privacy of my own backyard. I could almost picture myself in the company of family and friends gathered around the barbeque.

This longing and at times lusting for such good things went on for a few days until I was stopped dead in my tracks when I heard Our Lady gently say to me, "But this is not for you." In that moment, I was jolted back into reality and desired anew the sacrifices being asked of me for the fulfillment of God's plan in my life, namely, to walk in intimacy with Jesus — to claim the hidden treasure. But, despite my desire to sacrifice, Jesus remained hidden and silent.

It had been perhaps eight months since I arrived at St. Stanislaus Kostka Parish. By the following April, I was convinced that God had abandoned me, that my vocation to the priesthood and religious life had been, perhaps, my own creation. If, indeed, God had once wanted me, it seemed now He no longer did. No matter how much I begged for some relief from the interior torment, God kept silent. I recall vividly celebrating a Sunday Mass and, at the elevation of the Host, silently crying out, "My God, You are killing me. You are literally killing me."

Days later, on the verge of despair, I called Fr. Bob Sears, a Jesuit priest who had given a retreat I had attended a month earlier. Providentially, when I called, he answered the phone. An hour later I was sitting in his parlor. Before I could begin to speak, I began to cry profusely. Through the weeping, I recalled my experience at the elevation of the Host, and I managed to blurt out those same words. I was sure that God was through with me. He was done. It was over. I truly felt God was killing me.

In a moment of calm, the priest finally spoke. He told me that, yes, God was killing me and that, yes, He allowed His own Son to be killed for our sake, and that, yes, I would have to die. He assured me that God was by no means done with me, but was only beginning with me. Those words liberated me. I think in that moment I began my descent into nothingness.

GRACE ABOUNDS IN GOD'S HIDDENNESS

God's silence in my prayer life would continue for nearly ten years. This desert offered only dry dirt to satisfy my thirst and hunger for God. Amid the desolation, it was only in the

Holy Mass that I felt strangely consoled and sustained by the crucified Jesus. The altar became for me a haven — a place where I felt protected and understood. It would become an increasingly lonely place, but nonetheless the place I preferred to any other. At the altar, I burned with the desire to be nothing, so that Jesus could be everything.

Admittedly, I am not a particularly gifted speaker. My homilies are at times unrefined and perhaps too long and scattered. I often experience a great deal of fatigue when celebrating the Mass. I try to overcome these defects, but with little success. In any case, at Mass, I know myself to be in union with God and I know that He is there, close to me.

Even while I suffered constant aridity in prayer, I experienced nonetheless the pull of God into rather heart-wrenching tragedies. There are so many stories to illustrate this, but one in particular would suffice to make the point.

On the morning of September 15th, the Feast of the Holy Mother of Sorrows, I was driving our secretary of 50 years to work. We were listening to the news on the radio. The breaking news filled me with horrific fear. Five children had just died in a fire in Cicero, Illinois. I heard that and immediately shut off the radio, feeling deeply connected to the family. I had no idea who they were, but I somehow knew that I would become intimately involved in this tragedy.

Throughout the day, I could not shake this thought from my mind. Around 7:00 in the evening. I received a call from Ann Martin, a parishioner at St. Hyacinth's Church where I had been previously assigned. She asked if I would assist the family of Colleen Poull in the funeral and burial of her five children. Tony, Colleen's husband, was lying unconscious in a hospital with smoke damage to his lungs. Colleen had been at work when the fire occurred. I recoiled at the thought of reaching into such horrible pain, but I knew I couldn't say no.

In that moment Jesus filled me with the strength of His presence and He began to lead this sorrowful mother not only through the death of her children, but also through the death of her husband. Two days after the funeral Mass of the children, Tony died suddenly and unexpectedly. The burial of the children had been delayed a few days until his health would have allowed him to be present. Instead, he joined them as his body and their bodies were returned to the dust of the earth. The burial took place on the Feast of the Archangels — a clear reminder that the immortal God has destined us to share in the infinity of His presence and that the sorrows of this life will eventually give way to an abiding joy when the veil of God's hiddenness is forever lifted.

While I waited for the lifting of that veil in my life of prayer, my sojourn through the desert found me immersed and vacillating between the joys and sorrows of people's lives. As with any priest, I find myself surrounded by grief at the violent death of a young person and an hour later witnessing the joy of a man and woman vowing their lives to each other in marriage. On the very same day, another woman arrives inconsolable at the infidelity of her husband. Abandoned and left with three small children, her family is destroyed.

A hurting parishioner catches me in front of the church and accuses me of catering to the Hispanic parishioners at the expense of other groups within the parish. At the very same time, visitors are watching this spectacle while entering the church, perhaps passing through those doors for the first time in many years. The roof is leaking, and I'm wondering whether there will be enough money to pay the bills. I have yet to prepare for the evening's homily, and Mass is due to begin in fifteen minutes.

The day is over, the doors are shut and locked, and I go to my room. Then I go to the chapel. Again I go to my room and again I go to the chapel. Jesus is silent. In God's seeming absence, I feel again, in a powerful way, the allure of the flesh — the desire for the passing things of this world, but again Our Lady repeats, "This is not for you." Maybe I have misunderstood. Maybe she is trying to tell me the priesthood is not for me. These thoughts are replaced when I am consumed again by the ideal that just will not die — the total and undivided consecration of my life to Christ.

FROM THE DESERT TO THE DARK OF NIGHT

It wasn't until the fifteenth anniversary of my priesthood that I was delivered from the dry of the desert and invited to drink from the fountain of The Divine Mercy. It was then that the Rosary became anew the chain that bound me to God. As I shared in my initial reflections, this led me to St. Louis Marie de Montfort and the total consecration of my life to Jesus and Mary as their slave. It was during this time that Our Lady asked me to give her the parish — that is, to make her mother and queen of the parish. She has been manifesting herself ever since. She is here.

Having been lifted from the desert of spiritual aridity, I found myself immediately vacillating between interior consolations and desolations. I have enjoyed deep experiences of intimacy with God on one hand, and endured dark experiences of God's absence on the other.

The darkness eventually grew to such a point that I was losing nights of sleep agonizing over a loneliness that gave me a first-hand experience of hell. Previously, I had coped with the dryness of my prayer life by straddling the fence between the narrow road to holiness of life and the wide road to taking pleasure in the superficial things of this world. I now found no escape from the darkness.

The world and every good thing in life became a source of grief to me. The thought of anything that once brought me pleasure only left me feeling nauseous. I would liken the experience to someone who naturally enjoys good food, but, when the stomach is sour, even the mere thought of one's favorite dish can be repulsive. I even doubted the very existence of God, and, without God, I could not live.

In 1999, after celebrating the Masses of Christmas and greeting parishioners in the back of the church, I again found myself totally alone and in darkness. It had been three months since my consecration to Our Lady. The loneliness was devastating. I sought Jesus, but He was nowhere to be found. I went to the adoration chapel at the parish of Our Lady of Lourdes and knelt before the Blessed Sacrament. I suffered a deep longing to be delivered from my misery. I remember thinking that if anyone should step into the chapel and put a gun to my head, I could have given my life freely. I would have done so not for any noble purpose, nor in defense of the faith. I just wanted the pain to go away. And yet, the darkness persisted.

One night in February, I couldn't sleep. Again, totally alone and feeling the darkness of God's absence, I went to the chapel sometime between 2:00 and 3:00 in the morning to beg God's deliverance. I didn't have the strength to kneel. I wanted to know what was happening to me. While I would normally do nothing to manipulate a response from God, I was desperate. I took the Bible into my hands and cried to God that to whatever page the sacred Word would open, I would take as His word to me. My eyes closed, I opened the book and received for my reflection the lament of the prophet Jeremiah.

> Woe to me, mother, that you gave me birth! Tell me Lord, have I not served you for their good? You know I have. Remember me, Lord, visit me. Because of your long suffering banish me not; know that for you I have borne insult. When I found your words I devoured them; they became the joy and the happiness of my heart. Because I bore your name I did not sit celebrating in the circle of merrymakers; under the weight of your hand I sat alone. Why is my pain continuous, my wound incurable, refusing to be healed? You have become for me a treacherous brook, whose waters do not abide! Thus the Lord answered me: If you repent, so that I restore you, in my presence you shall stand; if you bring forth the precious without the vile, you shall be my mouthpiece. I will make you toward this people a solid wall of brass. Though they fight against you they shall not prevail, for I am with you (Jer 10a; 11a; 15-20).

Still wallowing in darkness, at least I knew that God had heard my cry. I was in the good company of the prophet Jeremiah, whose words resonated with the state of my soul. God had heard me. He was asking me to trust and to understand that I had to be purged of the vile — to suffer the interior purgation.

I was on the narrow road to holiness of life. God was asking me for courage in this sojourn through the dry of the desert and into the dark of night. Christ was with me, He wanted me, and He would instruct me. He would configure me to Himself for love of His people. Jesus, knowing well the sorrows of this life, burns with the desire to satisfy the thirst of His people for mercy and to bring light to those in darkness. Holiness is synonymous with mercy, with compassion, and with empathy. This is God's greatest work in the life of a priest. To be configured to Christ is to be effective in responding to the cries of a broken, wounded, and hurting people.

Recalling what is written in the Letter to the Hebrews, I understand that I would do well "...not to disdain the discipline of the Lord for whom the Lord loves, He disciplines; He scourges every son He acknowledges... At the time, it seems a cause not for joy but for pain, yet later it brings the peaceful fruit of righteousness to those who are trained by it" (Heb 12:5b; 6; 11).

It is true what Mother Teresa wrote to a priest, "You have said '*yes*' to Jesus and He has taken you at your word. God cannot fill what is full. He can only fill emptiness." And so I continue my descent into nothingness — into emptiness, there to be filled with the priceless poverty of the priestly Jesus.

5

THE CARNIVAL THAT
DROPPED OUT OF HEAVEN

September 2, 2001

I don't know why I so easily doubt the validity of all that is happening here. At times, I speak with firm conviction and utmost confidence about building the Sanctuary of The Divine Mercy, yet no sooner do I turn away than my mind and soul are besieged with doubt. I am at least consoled by the sacred Word of God that speaks of the deliberations of mortals as timid and filled with insecurity and that the corruptible body burdens the soul and the earthen shelter weighs down the mind.

We read in the Book of Wisdom that what is within our grasp we find with difficulty, and it is with great effort that we search out the things of heaven. On earth, our paths are only made straight by the Holy Spirit given from on high. It continually confounds me how, despite our human foibles, heaven works with such great clarity. And Our Lady continues to remind me that she should be trusted.

A week ago, knowing that the 18-foot Icon of The Divine Mercy was due to return to the parish on September 7th, I began to panic. The icon had been in pilgrimage through the Chicagoland area for a few months. Since the message of The Divine Mercy is at the heart of Our Lady's plan, it would seem more than appropriate to have a grand celebration on its return. Busy as ever, I began asking parishioners here and there to think about what we could do to welcome back the statue.

We had scheduled an evening of prayer for September 8th, the Feast of Our Lady's Birth. In my mind, I continued to wrestle with the thought that we should do more to celebrate the return of the icon. I felt guilty for not having made necessary preparations well in advance.

On the evening of August 28th, I was called to the office. A gentleman by the name of Roland Correa came to ask my permission to transfer a festival and carnival from Wicker Park to St. Stanislaus Kostka Parish. The space originally allotted for the festival was insufficient to accommodate the carnival, and so it needed to be relocated immediately. The festival had been scheduled to take place between September 13th and September 16th. He assured me that if we would grant him the permission, it would then become the parish's festival.

What normally takes a parish a year to plan has now been secured within a matter of days. Roland and his agency acquired the necessary city permits, insurance, security, clean-up, and so forth. Public relations people had already been hired to publicize the event. Musicians and various vendors had been scheduled to take part. In short, we were to have a ready-made festival, which would be dropped from heaven right onto our property.

At the center of the celebration would be the 18-foot Icon of The Divine Mercy. Only yards from the icon would be a tent where we would expose the Blessed Sacrament for 24-hour adoration during the days of the festivities. Roland and his crew would provide the tent for the adoration chapel as well as all-night security guards.

Our Lady, aware of my schedule and my limitations, had prepared her own celebration for the return of the icon. For our part, we have only to prepare ourselves to be disciples of The Divine Mercy. We are the churched and the un-churched — believers and unbelievers — converging on this holy ground. I wonder: Is this not already a premonition of what is yet to come?

6

IN THE SHADOW OF TERROR

September 20, 2001

The United States of America may have changed forever on Tuesday, September 11, 2001, when terrorists, using our own planes filled with people as weapons, destroyed the Twin Towers of the World Trade Center, leaving thousands of people dead in the aftermath of this and related attacks.

While in horror and disbelief the entire country and most of the world was fixated on this tragedy, the "carnival that dropped out of heaven" had arrived and was being prepared here at St. Stanislaus Kostka Parish. It was due to open the following day. At the heart of the carnival would be the Icon of The Divine Mercy and the prayer tent for perpetual adoration of the Blessed Sacrament. As I wrote in my previous reflections, I had no doubt that the carnival was the work of the Blessed Virgin Mary.

With the country now thrust into shock and grief, it seemed to me that the parish festival should be postponed until Friday, September 14th. As had been previously planned, we began the 24-hour adoration of the Blessed Sacrament on Wednesday morning. The adoration would last a full week, ending September 18th, the Feast of St. Stanislaus Kostka (as celebrated in the Polish Liturgical calendar). In addition to Eucharistic Adoration, I had scheduled the Holy Hour of

Great Mercy to begin each day at 3:00 in the afternoon. We had planned to pray the Rosary each evening at 6:30, followed by the celebration of the Mass. The opportunity for Confessions was also made available each evening.

Initially, I viewed the festival as a celebration to welcome back the Statue of The Divine Mercy with prayer at the heart of the festivities. Given that the attack on the United States of America had just occurred, the victims and their loved ones, along with an earnest plea for peace, became the focus of our prayer.

As the mayor of Chicago was calling for the cancellation of events throughout the city, I began to struggle with whether or not we should follow suit. I did not want to act in a way that would be interpreted as insensitive to the prevailing grief of a nation, nor did I want to bring the Archdiocese and the parish into conflict with the growing chorus of cancellations being heard throughout the nation. All sports events were being cancelled as well as parades and other celebrations throughout the land. All day Thursday I wrestled interiorly with the decision, knowing that it would ultimately be mine. Archdiocesan personnel as well as city officials confirmed that the decision rested solely with me.

I recall feeling that perhaps I had been premature in distributing my previous reflections, writing with the certitude of faith that Our Lady had sent the carnival. I wondered whether she had anticipated a catastrophe such as this assault, which paralyzed the entire nation.

UNCEASING PRAYER

While tempted to act in a politically correct way by canceling the festival, I decided instead that I should trust my own discernment, believing that the carnival was heaven-sent and should therefore proceed as previously planned. On Friday evening, after three days of unceasing prayer, the festival opened even as the prayer continued.

After the evening Mass had ended, the Blessed Sacrament was carried in procession to the tent. There we transferred Eucharistic Adoration from the church to this makeshift chapel. The tent, located only yards from the Icon of The Divine Mercy, was at the center of the carnival's activities. The outdoor ambience was one of subdued celebration under the colorful lights of the rides. The air was filled with the aroma of hot dogs and fried pastry as the festive song of the Mariachi faded into the night sky. As the procession made its way from the church to the tent, people who had come to enjoy the carnival stopped and watched, perhaps out of curiosity or maybe out of reverence or respect. After we gathered in the tent, everyone knelt in prayer as the Blessed Sacrament was enthroned for adoration.

Slowly making my way back to the church to change from my vestments, it became clear to me that I was wise not to cancel the carnival. The heaviness of the previous days' terrorist attacks was still evident, and so this diversion was welcomed as people converged on the grounds surrounding the church. People were approaching me from all sides. Fathers asked me to bless their families or to just touch the heads of their sons and daughters. Adults were not shy in telling me they had not been near a church in years. One man said it had been 35 years since he had been to church. Others thanked me for the carnival and began joyfully reminiscing about how the neighborhood used to gather for such festivals so many years ago.

All weekend people were coming and going. Nearly 800 rosaries were distributed as well as pamphlets on how to pray The Divine Mercy Chaplet. Even when there were no more rosaries to give, people were still asking for them. Continuously, people stopped in the church to soak in its beauty and to offer a short prayer. The adoration tent was never empty. At times, only a few people could be seen on their knees. Other times, perhaps a dozen or more people were wrapped in the silence of prayer before the Blessed Sacrament. Some spent only moments in adoration. Others spent hours.

In the aftermath of the terrorist attacks, it was said that the nation was brought to its knees in prayer and that many would be flocking to churches, synagogues, and mosques. From government leaders to clerics to laypersons on the street, the nation prayerfully grieved as never before in history.

Perhaps more people prayed than ever before. Still, I had doubts that people would actually flock to the churches. Over the past several decades, so many people have become increasingly estranged from the practice of religious faith and seemingly uncomfortable with any kind of institutionalized religion for a wide variety of reasons.

Whatever the reasons may be, it is evident to me that the Blessed Virgin Mary foresaw the tragic event and took the occasion to draw her children to the Church by way of the carnival. She used the superficial to draw her children to the sacred. Knowing the anxiety and the fear of a grieving people, she cleared the way for an epiphany. Heaven has the means to lure us into the inner sanctum — that dwelling place of God that is in all of us. The Church is the sacrament that mediates the grace to bring Jesus to us and us to Jesus. Today it is the message of The Divine Mercy. Humanity is living in a time of grace. In trial and tribulation, eyes and ears are opening to grasp some understanding of these mysteries unfolding before us and heaven is pleading, "Come to Jesus now ... have no fear."

To Live in True Freedom

It was no mere coincidence that the Gospel read throughout the Catholic world on the Sunday following the terrorist attacks was the parable of the prodigal son. How beautiful that on his return to his father's house after squandering his inheritance on decadent living, his father, full of compassion, greeted him with a kiss, and called for a celebration. His son who was lost had been found. His son who was dead had come back to life.

Encircled by the sounds of celebration from the carnival outdoors, inside the faithful listened to this moving story of The Divine Mercy. As crisis gripped the nation, there could not have been a more appropriate Gospel reading. The Gospel itself welcomed those who stepped through the doors of the Church for the first time in many years.

At the same time, the Sunday's first reading, taken from the Hebrew Scripture, offered a strong admonishment as God commanded Moses to go at once to the people who had become depraved and had turned from the way pointed out to them. He accused them of the sin of idolatry and of being stiff-necked in their refusal to adhere to the Commandments.

Our response to the attack on America has to go deeper than merely waving the American flag or singing patriotic songs or talking tough. We are being called to rekindle the character of a nation built on a Judeo-Christian foundation that holds principle and integrity, discipline, and sacrifice as virtues that make for the greatness of a nation.

The Judeo-Christian idea of freedom does not allow for a free reign of the flesh, which leads only to enslavement. As St. Paul reminds us, "Lewd conduct, impurity, licentiousness, idolatry, sorcery, hostilities, bickering, jealousy, outbursts of rage, selfish rivalries, dissensions, factions, envy, drunkenness, orgies, and the like proceed from the flesh" (Gal 5:19-21).

Rather than give free reign to the flesh, we submit to the Spirit, whose fruits are love, joy, peace, patient endurance, kindness, generosity, faith, mildness, and chastity. The flesh and the spirit are directly opposed to one another. We have been called to live in true freedom, placing ourselves at one another's service. True freedom lies in adhering to the Ten Commandments with a reverential fear of God, serving to stabilize society in genuine peace while upholding the dignity of all God's people.

The face of the demonic in the evil inflicted upon our society during the terrorist attacks should awaken us to the evil that pervades our own nation. Terrorism has filled our cemeteries with young victims of gang violence, drug abuse, and suicide. I have buried too many young people as a result of this domestic terrorism and have seen firsthand how it threatens our society. The unborn themselves are victims of terror. To combat international terrorism we have to obliterate domestic terrorism. We have to eradicate from our lives the evil that wrongfully calls the reign of the flesh "freedom."

As with the prodigal son, it would serve us well to return to our Father's house and there experience the embrace of a loving and merciful God who holds us responsible and accountable for the well-being of society. Only in submission to God and adhering to the Ten Commandments can we claim victory. The President alluded to this in his address to the nation when he said that God is not neutral, but on the side of justice and true freedom. The President also alluded to this when he called us to be a people of principle.

In the shadow of the war waged on America, a carnival dropped from heaven here at the parish of St. Stanislaus Kostka. Heaven offers the superficial as a means to draw us to the sacred. Life is so precious and yet so fragile, as we clearly understand these days. Only God can unravel the mystery of our life journey. The battle is not against human forces but, rather, against the principalities and powers, the rulers of this world of present darkness.

Some are calling this a holy war and rightfully so. It is a holy war, but not a war among Christians, Muslims, and Jews. There is the potential for evil in all religions because all religions are made up of people. Too often, too many people work against the God they claim to serve and perhaps do not serve God at all. At the root of terrorism is pride. Pride is the free reign of the flesh and by its nature, the flesh lusts against the spirit. At many levels and in different ways, then, war is waged. Until we submit to God's Spirit, the conflict will persist internationally, nationally, locally, and interiorly.

What happened on September 11, 2001, is not the fiction and fantasy of Hollywood. It is reality involving real people. One thing is certain: We need the outdoor sanctuary of The Divine Mercy and the chapel for perpetual adoration of the Blessed Sacrament now more than ever. Our prayer must be constant and persevering — it must be deep. The storm we saw on the horizon is now on us and may be with us for a very long time.

7

CALLED TO BE A PRIEST

October 13, 2001

Straddled between the dark of Good Friday and the light of Easter Sunday, I was born on Holy Saturday. I really don't know when I was first conscious of the desire to be a priest. It seems it was always just there in my soul. Perhaps, on the day of my birth, God planted the seed of my vocation to the priesthood.

Straddled as well between the northern and southern hemisphere, I was born in Cristobal, Panama. My father was a career man in the United States Air Force, and it was for this reason that my life journey began in Panama.

Now as a priest, I straddle heaven and earth, standing on holy ground where heaven kisses the earth at the altar of sacrifice in the Holy Mass. As with every priest, on one hand I am there in the person of Christ. On the other hand, I am there in the name of the people. It is there that the two become one. In a most mysterious way God is there, wedded to the Church, reproducing His life in the lives of His people. In the Mass, the marriage is consummated — it is sealed. The body is united to the head, the heart and soul are imbued with the Spirit, and the mind is impregnated with the desire to do God's will.

The Seed of My Vocation

I was raised in a good family, but not a religious one. I am the second eldest of eight children. Admittedly, we rarely attended Mass as a family. Perhaps for this reason I readily recall my first memory of the Mass. We were stationed at Ent Air Force Base in Colorado Springs, Colorado. I must have been about four years old. Even as I write this, I relive with clarity that first memory of the Mass. In a darkened church and in the midst of many people, all I see is the Sacred Host elevated and illuminated. I can hear the silence that envelops the church. The only spoken prayer etched in my mind was the first line of the "Salve Regina," probably prayed at the close of the Mass: "Hail, Holy Queen, Mother of Mercy." To this day, this is the first and only memory I have of the Mass until I was about eight or nine years old.

By the time I was eight years old, our family moved to Tyndall Air Force Base on the Florida panhandle. Soon after that, I began attending Mass regularly with friends who lived in our neighborhood. When I was ten years old, I became an altar boy and served my first Mass on Thanksgiving Day in 1965. I know the precise date only because I have a dated photograph of the event.

From the time I was ten until the age of thirteen, the desire to be a priest burned within me. After my father returned from the war in Vietnam, we were reassigned and moved to the Air Force Base in Dover, Delaware. While in Delaware, the family took its first vacation to Chicago to visit my grandmother. It was there that I felt the pull to the priesthood in the most intense way. I attended Mass with my cousins at the parish of St. Hyacinth. Having only attended the makeshift chapels of military bases, St. Hyacinth was probably the first and certainly the most beautiful Catholic Church I had ever been in. There are no words to describe what I felt at the time. The church was no church at all. It was to me a cathedral and more than that, it was heaven. I remember kneeling there and in my prayer visualizing myself as a priest in this church. I asked Jesus to please grant me this request.

Our family remained in Delaware another year before we moved back to Florida. Now in high school, I had lost the burning desire to be a priest. Nobody encouraged me to continue the practice of the faith. My family did not practice and remained indifferent to any observance of the Catholic faith. Religion and prayer simply had no part in the life of my family. Even so, I had good parents who were active in the lives of their children. They kept everyone active either through sports or similar activities.

Living now on the Florida panhandle where the environs were unofficially governed by Christian fundamentalists, I began to distance myself from any tendency towards religious adherence. The Catholic Church was in the throes of the reforms of the Second Vatican Council. Every beautiful thing I associated with the Church was seemingly discarded as pointless or meaningless to the practice of religious faith in the modern world. At the same time that statues, rosaries, and vigil lights were tossed into the garbage, priests and religious were in exodus. They divested themselves of the symbols and signs of their consecration and were being dispensed from their vows.

Having only seen the Church through the eyes of a child, my adolescent mind could not comprehend what seemed to be a desecratory spirit run rampant. I felt deceived. I felt I had been seduced by the fiction of Catholicism and needed now to move on. I ceased the practice of the faith.

While the seed of my vocation to be a priest was hidden and buried deep in the recesses of my soul, I joined the Civil Air Patrol with a desire to go into aviation. During adolescence, I kept busy with school, work, and extra-curricular activities. For five years I did not attend Mass and for all practical purposes had no affiliation with the Catholic Church. On occasion, I would attend religious services with friends of other denominations, but nothing tugged at my mind and heart the way the Mass had when I was a child.

COME INTO MY HEART

After graduating from high school, I began a spiral descent into an abyss of darkness as I began searching for some meaning to life. I was leaning in the direction of agnosticism — the belief that God could not be known and that if there was a God, He was distant and uninvolved in the lives of His people.

As I began my first semester in the local community college, I began to seriously investigate Catholicism in a way I had never done before. I had never attended a Catholic school and had only brief stints in catechetical studies in preparation for the Sacraments. As I began the private study of the Catholic faith, I assisted in the Mass for the first time in nearly five years. I had my mind and heart set on a young woman my age, but as much as I tried to get close to her, I was distracted by the fixation I had for the Christ of the Catholic faith.

I found myself going to Mass almost every Sunday, and I read profusely anything I could find about the faith of the Church. Every so often I would tire of what seemed an obsession for the Church, and I would back off a bit. For the most part, the Mass only bored me, but the pull was there nonetheless. I would consciously resist the urge to go to Mass.

Nearly two years into my search, I was tormented with my inability to accept the Catholic doctrine of transubstantiation, the belief that Jesus is wholly present in the bread and wine. The Church teaches that the bread and wine truly become the Body and Blood of Jesus, with only the accidents of bread and wine remaining after the consecration. At some point, I felt that I would have to renounce the faith of the Church based on my inability to adhere to this teaching. It seemed utterly absurd to me.

One day I had gone to school and then from school to work. I was feeling utterly alone and lonely. I was mentally tired of the interior struggle I had endured, trying to understand and accept the faith of the Catholic Church. God seemed hidden in His heaven beyond the beyond. The priests and religious were still leaving their vocations in droves. The superficial and secular seemingly held the Church captive. The whole idea of religion seemed to be a farce.

When I left my job that evening around 6:00, I began driving aimlessly, not knowing where to go. I wanted my life to be over then and there. The interior emptiness and pain I felt seemed to go deeper than ever before. I had the horrific thought of driving my car over the bridge and into the Gulf of Mexico. I felt there was simply no purpose to life.

As I drove past the parish church of St. John the Evangelist, I noticed that people were going into the church as if for Mass. It was Thursday. I parked my car and went in. As was my custom, I took my place in the last pew near the door. It occurred to me that it was Holy Thursday, the first day of the Holy Triduum.

What happened next would change my life forever. As the Mass began, even though people filled the church, I felt as if I was there alone. It was just me and the priest. I heard for the first time every prayer that was prayed. The readings from the Sacred Scripture spoke to me. Though I could not fully grasp their meaning, I felt nonetheless that they were directed to me and to me alone.

During the Eucharistic Prayer in which the bread and wine were consecrated, I knew with the certainty of faith that Jesus was on the altar. I was in awe. The priest was gone. That is, he seemed to disappear. Only Jesus remained.

At the conclusion of the Mass, the priest carried the Blessed Sacrament in procession to the tabernacle for nocturnal adoration. This tradition recalls the hour Jesus requested that the apostles Peter, James, and John accompany Him in the Garden of Gethsemane. This was the hour He suffered the sweat of blood before His betrayal and arrest. The apostles slept. Jesus suffered alone, sustained only by an angel.

As the procession came down the aisle toward me, I felt the gaze of Jesus penetrate my soul. As He passed me, I was overwhelmed with His presence. There are no words to describe the warmth, the peace, and the love that flowed through my soul.

After the Eucharist was reposed, I went forward to kneel before the tabernacle. I must have been there an hour. I couldn't say anything. I was totally at peace in the presence of the Lord. After some time, He spoke in the silence of my heart. Calling me by name, He clearly, distinctly, and gently said, "Tony ... Tony, this is what it's all about. This is the heart of the Church. Come into My Heart." In that instant, I was flooded with a deep desire to be a priest. Every beautiful affection I had as a child was resurrected in that moment. I could not contain the joy welling up inside me.

Mid-afternoon the next day, I anticipated a similar encounter as I went to the Liturgy of Good Friday. But the church felt empty and cold. There was a deafening heaviness in the air. Jesus was gone. He was nowhere to be found. I thought my experience the night before had been an illusion — a figment of my imagination. As I joined the procession to venerate the cross, I simply didn't know what to think of the emptiness milling within me. As I neared the cross, I saw with the eyes of my soul the Blessed Virgin Mary in sorrow. She didn't say anything. She simply looked at me. Her eyes pierced my heart as she slowly turned to the cross. It was then that I knew. Nothing needed to be said. Interiorly, I began to weep.

By Easter Sunday, I took my place at the Mass among the rest of the worshipers. I was not unlike them, only I knew I would someday be a priest.

Within a week or two, I approached Fr. Frank Phillips who, at the time, was serving as a deacon in the parish in preparation for his upcoming ordination to the priesthood. I shared with him my experience. He invited me to visit the seminary of the Resurrection Fathers and Brothers in St. Louis, Missouri, for the Feast of the Triumph of the Cross. The following September I did just that.

Honestly, from the moment I arrived I felt no attraction to the seminary, to the community, or to the priesthood. On the contrary, I felt repulsed. The months following my Holy Thursday experience had left me with conflicting emotions.

My soul was in turmoil. I was tormented when I was awake. I was tormented when I slept. At one moment, all I wanted was to be a priest. The next moment, my heart was held captive by the woman and by the passing things of the world. A war waged within me, and I was confused and in pain.

Three days into my visit, I had resigned myself to the belief that Jesus was not actually calling me to the priesthood. I was relieved. I would return to Florida and go on with my life. Once and for all, I would bury the idea of a priestly vocation. Then something happened. I was sitting alone, looking through material and vocational brochures pertaining to the Resurrection Order and their apostolic missions. Scanning through the pages, I was struck dead in my tracks when the parish of St. Hyacinth jumped from the brochure and into my memory. I was immediately taken back to Chicago and to that moment when I knelt in that very church at the age of twelve. I was there again and powerfully imbued with the most intense desire to be a priest and asking Jesus to be so good as to make me a priest in that church.

Nine years later, I was, indeed, ordained a priest in the parish church of St. Hyacinth, and it was there that I enjoyed my first six years in the priesthood.

Before I formed you in the womb
I knew you,
before you were born
I dedicated you,
a prophet to the nations
I appointed you.
"Ah, Lord God!" I said,
I know not how to speak; I am too young."
But the Lord answered me,
say not, "I am too young."
To whomever I send you,
you shall go;
whatever I command you,
you shall speak.
Have no fear before them,
because I am with you to deliver you,
says the Lord.
Then the Lord extended His hand
and touched My mouth, saying,
See I place My words in your mouth!

Jeremiah 1:4-11

8

BREAD FROM HEAVEN
THAT WE NOT COLLAPSE

October 30, 2001

As I wrote in my previous reflections, on Holy Thursday when I was 20 years old, the curtain of the sanctuary had lifted for a brief time. I was given the eyes to see and the ears to hear. My mind began to understand, and my heart burned within me. To this day it remains a mystery, but I have no doubt: The Eucharistic Jesus is the Christ of the Catholic faith. He is the Savior of all humanity for all ages and for all times.

I am not unlike the disciples of Jesus who could not grasp this teaching, but I thank God that unlike some of them I did not walk away. I persevered as I wrestled with the mystery of the Holy Eucharist. Jesus was so good to give me strength in preparation for a personal epiphany — a clear manifestation of Himself in what only appeared to be bread and wine. By the power of the Holy Spirit and through the words and actions of the priest, the bread and wine truly and wholly become the Body and Blood of Jesus. I had asked the question, "How?" He never answered. Jesus simply allowed me to suffer the question for nearly two years before showing me that it simply was.

It was only later as a seminarian that I found myself in John's Gospel. I was there in the person of His followers. I understood then who I had been and who I was becoming.

PLEDGE OF HIS PRESENCE AMONG US

In the Gospels we read that Jesus had looked with pity on the crowd, calling them sheep without a shepherd. Then, turning to the apostles, He said, "Feed them that they not collapse as they go on their way." At that He multiplied the loaves, and they all ate. Jesus acknowledged that they were satisfied, but added that they would die nonetheless unless they eat the bread He would give them. This would be the pledge of eternal life. He promised to give them His Flesh to eat and His Blood to drink. Some of His disciples asked how this was possible. Jesus did not answer the question. Responding to them, He simply repeated numerous times, "Eat My Flesh and drink My Blood."

Unable to grasp what seemed to be an absurd teaching, some of his disciples chose no longer to remain in the company of Jesus. They walked away. I can feel the sadness in His eyes and hear it in His voice as Jesus, looking to the apostles, asked if they, too, would walk away. Peter stood up and said, "No." Where would they possibly go? They had come to believe that He had the words of everlasting life. Indeed, Jesus would give them food to eat that they not collapse as they'd go on their way. They would follow Him even as His way would lead them through the doors of martyrdom.

On the eve of His death, Jesus established the covenant of His Body and Blood. This covenant was later ratified when He became the innocent victim, the spotless lamb, whose hands and feet were nailed to the cross. At the Last Supper, knowing that His death was imminent, Our Lord gave bread to His apostles and said:

> Take this, all of you, and eat it. This is My Body which will be given up for you. When the supper was ended, He took

the cup. Again He gave thanks and praise to the Father, gave the cup to His disciples and said, take this all of you, and drink from it. This is the cup of My Blood, the Blood of the new and everlasting covenant. It will be shed for you and for all men so that sins may be forgiven. Do this in memory of Me (Mt 26:26-29).

After this, Jesus led his Apostles from Jerusalem to the Garden of Gethsemane. He reassured them that He would not leave them orphans. In the garden, He was betrayed with a kiss and then arrested. Interrogated in the house of Caiaphas, Jesus was turned over to the Romans, condemned, crucified, and died.

On the third day, the Risen Christ would encounter two of His disciples on the road to Emmaus. They do not recognize Him. He asks them, "Why are you sad — why the downcast eyes?" The disciples tell Him how their hopes died in the death of the Nazarean. They thought He had been the one. He had given them identity. He had been their strength. He had been their peace. He had given them courage and filled them with joy. He loved them. They thought He was the Messiah, but in His death their hopes, too, had died. For this, they were sad. For this, their eyes were downcast.

Seemingly perplexed, Jesus asked whether they had forgotten what had been written — what had been told through the ages. Wasn't this the way it was to happen? Was He not to die in such a way? Didn't He say He would rise on the third day? Still they did not understand.

When they neared the village to which they were going, Jesus acted as if He were going farther. But the disciples pressed Him: "Stay with us. It is nearly evening — the day is practically over." So He went to stay with them.

When Jesus had seated Himself with them to eat, He took bread, pronounced the blessing, then broke the bread and began to distribute it to them. With that their eyes were opened and they recognized Him, whereupon He vanished from their sight. They said to one another, "Were not our hearts burning as He talked to us on the road and explained the Scriptures to us?" They got up immediately and returned to Jerusalem, where they found the eleven and the rest of the company assembled. They were greeted with, "The Lord has been raised! It is true! He has appeared to Peter." Then the two disciples recounted what had happened on the road and how they had come to know Him in the breaking of the bread.

Jesus, rising from the dead and returning to the Father, would leave the bread as a pledge of His presence among and within His followers. They knew that their hunger had been satisfied and that they would be sustained. They knew they would not collapse as they went on their way. And now, for nearly 2,000 years, the Church has fixed her eyes on Jesus, uniting her heart to His Heart in the Holy Eucharist. This is, indeed, the Christ of the Catholic faith. In Him, the Church has stood the test of time.

Jesus, giving Himself as bread for the journey so that we not collapse, is a truth deeply rooted in the Hebrew Scripture. After having been liberated from their slavery in Egypt through the blood of the lamb, our ancestors were led through the waters of the Red Sea. In their forty year journey through the desert to the Promised Land, they were sustained by the bread that fell from heaven. This prefigures and prepares humanity for its true liberation from the slavery of sin and death wrought through the Blood of the cross. The

Messianic people then are led through the waters of baptism and sustained by the Eucharistic Bread in their pilgrimage through the desert of life until they cross over the valley of darkness and into the light of heaven. The Eucharistic Bread is the bread from heaven — the Body and Blood, the Soul and Divinity of Jesus. This is the Christ of the Catholic faith.

AN INTIMATE ENCOUNTER

In the Holy Eucharist, there is a truth that does not deceive. Satan may seduce us, friends may betray us, parents may abandon us, and priests may disappoint us. The government may use us, the media may manipulate us, many who come in the name of Jesus may only confuse us, but Jesus in the Holy Eucharist can only love us. His purifying love in the Blessed Sacrament removes the masks we wear through the healing, sanctifying, and salvific power emanating from the Sacred Species. His love makes us like unto Himself, bringing us into our true identity as a people created in the image and likeness of God.

Being in the presence of the Blessed Sacrament, then, is the greatest assurance we have that we will not be deceived. Even when Jesus seems hidden in His heaven beyond the beyond, we know that we have nowhere else to go to find Him. He may show Himself in many ways and in many places, but in His Eucharistic presence there is no deception — there is no one to cloud the reality of who He is. Satan must flee in His presence. Here the enemy cannot present himself as an angel of light. If Jesus chooses to hide Himself, making Himself seemingly absent, at least we know there is nowhere else to await His return because in His hiddenness He is ever present in the Sacred Host.

Unlike the saints, I have to admit that at times I don't deal gracefully with what seems to be Our Lord's absence. Like the saints, I readily admit that, apart from God, I am wretched, miserable, and corrupt. But, unlike the saints, when Jesus seems far away, I find it difficult to trust that His presence in the Holy Eucharist is unchanged and His grace ever active. At these times, I may explode into interior tantrums for fear that He has rejected or abandoned me. Despite this, Jesus remains steadfast and consistent in His patience with me. If I need Him to unceasingly whisper in my ear that He is with me, it is because I prefer to be acknowledged than be ignored. Even if He should only acknowledge me with a reprimand, I would be kept content and quiet. The biblical call to pray unceasingly and perseveringly may be heaven's way of keeping me vigilant, so that I will not grow deaf to the whisper of God's voice when spoken in the deepest recesses of my soul.

Intimacy with God is the desired fruit of priestly celibacy, so I long for some perception of His indwelling presence and the same manifestation of love He showed to Peter and John. When I read how the Risen Christ took Peter aside and asked Him, "Do you love me more than the others," an unnamed yearning wells up within me. With attention, I listen for the question and, indeed, He has asked this of me. My insecurities, though, give rise to my need to hear the question addressed to me always and everywhere. Even though my actions may not always give perfect testimony to the truth of my undying love for Jesus, my life is a response to His call, and my "*yes*" is constant and consistent as I seek Him daily in the Holy Eucharist.

And so, alone before His Eucharistic presence, it is as if I have responded to a call. The chapel becomes the boat and we set out away from the crowd, just Jesus and me.

Sometimes the sea is quite calm. Other times a storm rages, and I feel that I am being tossed about while He sleeps. Though I may become unnerved, begging Him to wake up, my faith assures me that He is within reach.

At times, like Peter, I am walking on water towards Jesus, who seems to have stepped away from the boat. Like Peter, when I feel the strength of the wind, I turn my eyes away from Him and begin to sink. Jesus never fails to lift me from the turbulent sea, so that I am not swallowed into its belly.

Sometimes the call to pray is an invitation to ascend to the top of Mount Tabor and there to behold Jesus in His resplendent glory. Like Peter, I want to stay on the top of the mountain. It is good to be there, but I am quickly reminded that I am a man with a mission and I realize that I must descend into the valley of tears and continue my sojourn to Jerusalem, carrying the cross along the way.

The mission, at times, seems impossible until I remember that it is the work of Jesus and the victory is already secured. The mission is to make this victory known, even as the battle continues to rage. My prayer before the Blessed Sacrament may be likened to a soldier who ducks into the trench for a respite. There I am accompanied by Jesus, even as the sights and sounds of the battle hold my senses captive.

More often than not, my prayer before the Eucharistic Jesus is the interior groaning that St. Paul so eloquently articulates in his letter to the Romans. My body holds me captive as I hold to the tension, trying to balance the incarnate reality of the flesh with the spirit vying for harmony within my soul.

The interior groaning is a profound prayer, expressing the realism of exile. It is the wordless prayer of intercession as

I absorb the hurts and wounds of others and my suffering soul brings them before Jesus. Often the groaning is born from my own wounds. The Wounded Healer chooses not to take them away. I am compelled to gaze on the holy wounds of Jesus to understand the sacred in my own woundedness. Jesus' compassion and empathy compels me to walk in solidarity with broken humanity. In this, He safeguards me from the evils of Pharisaism, religious arrogance, or elitism. In exile, I find my peace in Jesus and say with St. Augustine, "I will not rest until I find rest in Thee."

BECOMING WHAT WE CONSUME

It is in the nature of the priest to be spent. Sometimes I give to the point that I give what I do not have. In times like this, Jesus fills up what is lacking in me. When my strength is depleted, I crawl to Jesus in the Blessed Sacrament, remembering the woman who suffered the flow of blood for 18 years. She wanted only to touch the hem of His garment, believing that she would be healed. When she touched Him, Jesus felt power go out of Him and the woman was healed. The power that emanates from the Blessed Sacrament replenishes my lost strength and rekindles my desire to eat His Body and drink His Blood at the altar of sacrifice. His prayer ruminates in the depths of my soul, "Give us this day our daily bread;" this, yes, that I not collapse as I serve Him and His Body, the Church.

I am a warrior whose only armor is the Blessed Sacrament. Jesus does not pamper me. Rather, He unceasingly drags me through the desert and into darkness. In His light I see the enemy on all sides, but the intimacy of His company sustains me in battle as He allows me a share of His mind and

Heart. I feel His pain at what our fears bring us to do to ourselves and to each other. His fire burns in my soul that mercy be received and justice be known. I experience His sadness and loneliness that so few respond.

Before the Blessed Sacrament, the seeming futility of the mission opens my ears to the cry of the Christ sounding through the ages, "My God, My God, why have You forsaken Me?" In the next breath, He commends His spirit to the Father. What appears to be defeat gives way to victory, as He passes through the dark of death to the light of resurrection. In defeat, my faith claims the victory.

As the Eucharist perpetuates the paschal mystery of Jesus' death and resurrection, my priesthood holds me in the tension of the ongoing battle between good and evil. I stand between the light and the dark. My only weapon is the Eucharist as I attentively guard against the prowling lion who only seeks to devour. Jesus promised to pray for Peter, that He, in turn, strengthen the brothers, because Satan meant to sift them all like wheat. As a priest, I feel so often like a warrior shepherd. We are under attack — the sheep are being devoured.

The older I get the more intense the war wages. Jesus cautions me not to compromise. He cautions me to turn a deaf ear to the voice of the world and to turn my ear to the sound of His voice. Even in silence when the voice is not heard, He speaks. Lying prostrate before the Holy Eucharist, I am in the company of the High Priest, the Supreme Prophet, the King of Kings, the Hero Warrior. I hunger and thirst for Him that I become the Flesh that I eat and the Blood that I drink.

My priesthood is a sham if I am not radically transformed into His likeness. My celibacy is to be pitied if I do not bond with Him in an intimacy that makes me a true priest, prophet, king, and warrior shepherd. The Holy Eucharist is the only hope I have of becoming what Jesus has called me to be. If at times I recoil from the suffering, I am quickly reminded that Jesus promised the cross for those who would follow Him. He warned that the road would be narrow and difficult. Indeed, it is.

The language spoken before the Sacred Species is different from what is spoken in the world. He neither pampers nor dotes. The Hero Warrior sustains me in battle to fight the good fight for the salvation and sanctification of souls.

9

SATAN'S TRAP

October 30, 2001

Soon after I began my assignment here in the parish of St. Stanislaus Kostka, Jesus made me understand the nature of the battle on which I would embark when three similar experiences took place in the course of one week.

One night I had no sooner gone to sleep when I was awakened and realized my body was in a state of paralysis. I could neither move nor audibly speak. My eyes, though, were open. I felt a horrific evil presence moving about my room. I was facing the wall, so I could see nothing behind me. A fear enveloped my whole being as I felt the destructive power of this evil presence. I imagined that I would be strangled or that my body would be subjected to assault by a weapon of some sort. The closer it came towards me the more intense the evil became. I wanted to jump from the bed, but the paralysis prevented me from doing anything.

I was overwhelmed with fear and preparing for the worst when Jesus spoke in the interior of my soul telling me that I had nothing to fear. I felt a shield come over me, and as the evil moved about the room, I simply repeated over and over, though inaudibly, "You have no power over me." I was confident that I was protected, but the horrible sensation continued to consume me. The whole ordeal may have lasted about two minutes.

The experience repeated itself two other nights during that week. On the third night, the enemy came so close that I felt his breath roll down the back of my neck. Each night the adversary seemed to leave as it came. It was just there, and moments later it was gone. The shield that protected me also seemed to just go away, and as it did, so did the paralysis. I was imbued with peace and an overwhelming sense of God's presence.

These occurrences have never repeated themselves as such, but soon after I began to understand the nature of spiritual warfare. There is, indeed, a force that works against the good that is God.

To Awaken Satan

Jesus was so good to have allowed me an experience of Satan's assault in preparation for the ensuing battle that would rage within me and around me. The Lord showed me that no matter how violent the enemy's attacks may be, God's shield of protection would keep me out of harm's way. Even so, I would have to learn to wrestle with the demons without compromising the will of God. Indeed, I have wrestled.

I understand why so often in Scripture an encounter with the Divine is usually preceded by the summons to not fear. To encounter God is to awaken Satan. We are living in his domain. Jesus calls him the prince of this world.

My experience teaches me that when I am lukewarm or complacent, I enjoy a reasonable amount of comfort and I find that life in this world proves to be a faithful friend. On the other hand, when I respond in a specific way to the specific call of God to do a specific thing, the devil and his adversaries use every means at their disposal to discourage, distort, and destroy the mission before me. More often than not, the war is waged in my inner life though often provoked by external circumstances. I get severely beaten down but have always had the strength to get up and to stay in the battle. This I attribute to God's grace.

My priesthood is a specific response to a specific call. If I had listened to the voice of the world, I would have left the priesthood a long time ago. The world does not accept the challenge to walk with a vision that is perpetually clouded, but as a priest, I see things through the eyes of God, humbly trusting that God's sight makes up for my blindness.

Also, celibacy militates against my nature as a man. If I listen to the voice of the world, I should revolt in rebellion against the shackles of what may be perceived as an archaic discipline that is at odds with man's nature and the cause of untold harm, hurt, and heartache. I know that from the deepest recesses of my soul, I have a longing and need for intimacy. Because it is from there that I live, I know that only Jesus can satisfy this hunger and satisfy this thirst for love. Satan forbids me to go down into that deep place in my soul, because he knows that there I will encounter the Christ and from there the Christ can effect change in the world, transforming the domain of Satan into the kingdom of God.

While Satan forbids me to go down into that inner sanctum, Jesus demands this of me. Jesus demands my full attention. He demands the surrender of my life. He demands my obedience and He demands my trust. It is no longer a polite invitation. It is a demand because I am a priest, and He has entrusted me with a mission. His demand, though, is cloaked in mercy and gentleness and has the irresistible attraction of love. Still, its pain can be excruciating. It is in the nature of man to recoil from the pain, and so the war is waged. Jesus reminds me that I enjoy His favor, that He will not pamper me and that I must be steadfast in the pursuit of Him who has already found me and believes more in me than I believe in myself. He wants my full and undivided attention.

The seductive, deceptive, and illusory tactics of the enemy are so subtle that unless I am steadfast and persevering in prayer, I run the risk of succumbing to his lies. I know I have fallen into Satan's trap when I am robbed of the inner peace that is Jesus' gift to those who follow Him. It is not without reason that Jesus calls the devil the Father of Lies.

It seems to me that my greatest defense against the enemy is to accept the existential loneliness that is in the nature of life lived in exile. Apart from God, the loneliness has no meaning and by its nature would yield to the devil's destructive designs to soothe the pains of life through inordinate attachment to the things of this world.

The inner sanctum — that place deep in the recesses of the soul — is the dwelling place of God. As with the Sacred Host, Jesus is there, known, but not fully perceived, so I feel the loneliness and the longing. I am assured that He knows me and serves me. Within the deep recesses of my soul He has intimate knowledge of what no one can know. Even I am known to myself only partially. His designs are indeed mysterious, but there is nothing superficial or shallow about the intimacy I experience in His hidden presence there in the inner sanctum. It is from there that He reproduces His life in mine. Apart from Him, I am nothing, I have nothing, and I can do nothing. To embrace the precious nothingness is to make Jesus all in all.

The invitation to descend into nothingness, and there to claim the hidden treasure, comes to all of us. Jesus knows the opportune time and so, in the interim, even as we wrestle with the thought of letting go, He never takes His loving gaze from us. Satan will do all in his power to keep our eyes from meeting the eyes of Jesus. There is no end to the obstacles the enemy sets between our hearts and the Heart of Jesus. If the devil can keep us comfortable, filling the emptiness with the things of this passing world; if he can keep us from embracing the bitterness of the existential loneliness within us, then his mission is accomplished. He then robs the Church of her passion to make Jesus known, loved, and served. The Church will thus be made impotent and bear little or no life, and we will not know solitude.

10

Our Lady's Intervention

November 15, 2001

It is toward solitude that the Blessed Virgin Mary guides us. Over two years ago, on the Feast of the Holy Triumph of the Cross, when I consecrated my life to Our Lady, I quickly learned that I was responding in a specific way to a specific call to do a specific thing. The Holy Mother of God entrusted me with the task of building a Sanctuary of The Divine Mercy, and she is stirring the hearts of others to bring this call to fruition.

I respond to the call from my own poverty and in sharing these reflections have opened the window of my soul to show the power of God acting in and through nothingness. If, in peering through the window of the soul, I disclose the pain of the desert and darkness, or the torment of longing and loneliness, or the sadness of selfishness and sin, it is because I see the Christ.

To see Jesus is to know the reality of exile. If not for this, I could never know the reason for my priesthood. If not for this, I could never know the reason for the sword lodged in my heart — a sword that for all the years of my life has never been removed. The sword brings me to take my place alongside the Blessed Virgin Mary at the foot of the cross and there to hear echoed through the ages the cry of Jesus: "I thirst" (John 19:28). His thirst for souls is satisfied at the altar of sacrifice in the Holy Sacrifice of the Mass.

In the Eucharist, The Divine Mercy is perpetuated in the Blood and Water flowing from the pierced Heart of Jesus to save, to heal, and to sanctify a broken, wounded, and hurting humanity. This is the truth I know each time I offer the Sacrifice of the Mass where I behold humanity's liberation from its slavery to sin and death.

My priesthood keeps the pain of the people before me. The superficial and shallow trappings of the modern world create the illusion that all is well with humanity and that there is no need of God — certainly not a suffering God. Perhaps God may be accepted at best if He is kept at the level of the superficial and shallow. This is why the Eucharistic Jesus is so little appreciated today. He is too deep. He is too intense.

Even priests who put their hands to the Sacred Host may no longer feel its fire because too often they resist the descent into their own nothingness, to feel their own pain and behold Him who is their deliverer. Satan forbids the descent into the inner sanctum because it brings defeat to his reign. The enemy offers the superficial and the shallow to keep the priest at least lukewarm, or at best cold and indifferent to the sacred and sacrificial nature of his priesthood. The warrior shepherd, then, sleeps within him because He has relegated the Supreme Shepherd to the Garden of Paradise. Meanwhile, the sheep are alone in the Garden of Gethsemane awaiting the kiss of death.

SEEK REFUGE IN GOD

Our Lady intervenes. The Holy Mother of God remains as steadfast and true to her apostolic mission today as she did nearly five hundred years ago when the Indians were forced in fear to accept the faith. They chose death rather than accept the Christ of the Catholic faith. She intervened. The Blessed Virgin Mary appeared on the Hill of Tepeyac and immediately loved millions into conversion. She undid the wrong that had been done.

Again, she intervenes. Her request for a Sanctuary of The Divine Mercy is a mother's plea to her children to seek refuge in God. To this end, she prepares holy ground where sacred silence gives way to the sound of God's voice. She will not permit the cacophony of the world to interrupt or distort the voice of the living God. She will provide the means to draw the pilgrims to the Sanctuary of The Divine Mercy and into the silence of the adoration chapel where Jesus will give to drink from the fountain of mercy.

The Blessed Virgin Mary knowingly and consciously prepares this holy ground to draw to the fountain of The Divine Mercy both sinners and saints, the poor and the rich, the healthy and the sick. A friend who shares the vision for the sanctuary writes:

> Here in the heart of Chicago, where hundreds and thousands of people move along an expressway named for a slain president, "the Kennedy," a new spiritual oasis anchored by a Woman must be built. As the Statue of Liberty stood watch in New York Harbor to receive millions of immigrants with the plea to "give me your tired, your hungry, give me all those yearning to breathe free," now, in twenty-first century Chicago, another Lady will stand tall and ready with a touch of mercy for millions. This woman, however, is REAL. She does not live as an artist's imagining or as an historical symbol, but as our true Mother. She points to her slain Son who is not dead but lives to wash humanity in the Blood and Water that flows from His wounded side. To His open Heart, the Savior invites all to draw water in joy from the springs of salvation. Our Lady will seek out the tired and hungry and those yearning to breathe free, especially during rush hour traffic! While the Statue of Liberty was used to build a nation, Our Lady will build a kingdom for her Son.

11

THE FOUR O'CLOCK APPARITION

December 15, 2001

It is a pity that so many Christians have all but relegated the Blessed Virgin Mary solely to the pages of Sacred Scripture, as if to deny her a share in the Lord's resurrection. The inexhaustible testimony of Our Lady's presence within the Church over the course of 2,000 years should bear witness to her participation in the ongoing work of redemption. After the ascension of Our Lord into heaven, we find Mary in the novena of prayer. She is there praying with the apostles, interceding for nine days until the gift of the Holy Spirit is conferred, giving birth to the Church. It is wise to remain in the company of the Holy Mother of God. As with the Risen Christ, she indeed lives and remains with us.

To this end, I entrusted a litany of petitions to the Blessed Virgin Mary as the parish began a novena in preparation for the celebration of her feast on December 12th. The novena to Our Lady of Guadalupe began on December 3rd. It was then that I placed in her heart the spiritual and material needs of the parish.

The parish serves the faithful in three different languages and spends around $100,000 each year to maintain a school with a student body that is as diverse as the global community.

The challenge to survive from one month to the next leaves no doubt as to why the prayer of petition is at the center of a day's activity and would naturally weave its way into the heart of the novena.

Included in the petitions was a request for the $5 million needed to build the sanctuary and adoration chapel, install the parking lot, and restore the interior of the church. I asked as well for the $50,000 needed to secure the architectural plan for the overall project.

On the last day of the novena, I experienced an emptiness that kept me in a darkness that has become all too familiar to me. The darkness persisted even as the doors of the church opened Wednesday morning at 5:00. Nearly a thousand people came to serenade Our Lady of Guadalupe and to initiate the celebration of her feast day despite it being a weekday.

Under the serene eyes of Our Lady, the faithful quietly and prayerfully laid flowers at the foot of her image. Many were donned in the traditional dress of an era long gone. Marking themselves with the Sign of the Cross, they lit candles, as did their ancestors of past ages. Fathers and mothers lifted their infants before the icon in a gesture of hope and trust that their children would remain safe under the watchful eye of the Virgin of Guadalupe. As she was serenaded, more than a few tears were shed. As always, her feast day began as it would end. The faithful would return later that day in the dark of night to assist in the celebration of the Mass and bid her good night.

I was deeply moved by the sincere manifestation of faith, but continued wallowing in darkness as if consciously removed from the experience of the day's festivities. At 3:00 in the afternoon, I entered into the hour of prayer, as is my custom. The interior void persisted. I concluded the hour with the Sorrowful Mysteries of the Rosary, asking Our Lady of Guadalupe to grace me with $50,000 on this, her feast day. It was a request made in pure faith. Perhaps heaven put it in my heart to be bold. I needed a sign, and I humbly asked for one.

DISCIPLES OF MERCY

At 4:00, I ended the holy hour and moments later went to the office. The secretary, Rose Pistanowich, handed me a note to call Sister Carol Marie Schommer from the Big Shoulders Fund. Big Shoulders is an agency of the Archdiocese of Chicago whose mission is to raise funds for the neediest of the inner-city Catholic schools. Sister Carol Marie is the Director of their Patrons Program, a Big Shoulders initiative designed to match individual donors with schools struggling to make ends meet.

Sister Carol Marie's call came through at exactly 4:00 as noted on the message. I returned the call immediately. Sister Carol Marie answered the phone with a word of congratulations, telling me that one of their donors had decided to become a patron for St. Stanislaus Kostka School and donate $75,000 each year for three successive years. In addition to this generous financial commitment, the donor was also making a personal three-year commitment to lend his expertise to assist the principal in writing a long-term strategic plan and establishing professional relationships within the business community to help guide the school toward a financially strong and academically competitive future. I was overwhelmed by the donor's generosity but, elated by the news, immediately began a litany of thanks for having been graced with what seemed a heavenly *apparition*.

I immediately called Sister Susan Curtin, who is principal of the parish school. She had heard the news of the donation and was elated, but tired. For eleven years, she has labored faithfully to keep the school alive and well. Her day begins shortly after 6:00 in the morning and the light burns in her office well into the evening. The donor had visited the school some weeks ago. His decision to financially assist the parish school is a testimony to the fine way in which Sister and her staff minister to the students. Sister Susan's prayers are heard above the chatter of more than 200 students who bear all the features of the peoples scattered throughout the world.

The parish is blessed to have other dedicated religious laboring in the apostolic mission of the Church. In addition to Sister Susan, Father Emil Stec has graced the parish as a gifted confessor. On his 80th birthday, still recuperating from surgery, he heard four hours of confessions. He is sought out by penitents who come from near and far. His fidelity to administer the Sacraments of the Church and to do so with great generosity shows him to be a devoted priest and disciple of The Divine Mercy.

The parish is also served by Sister Ann Schaffer, who has been operating a soup kitchen since it was dedicated by Joseph Cardinal Bernardin in 1986. In this corporal work of mercy, Sister Ann and her volunteers provide a source of much blessing to the parish as they feed over 150 needy people daily. Sister's trust in Divine Providence has been a source of encouragement to the parish during difficult times over the course of these past several years.

There is no end to the rest of the faithful who participate in the apostolic mission of the parish. It is through their generosity that the parish is sustained spiritually and materially.

They include anyone who passes through the doors of this church donned in the virtue of humility and walking in solidarity with others. To the extent that we submit to God's will, the parish is blessed. It is humbling that the Blessed Virgin Mary has graced us with her presence and made all of us part of her unfolding plan.

As with many priests, I believe Our Lady has me specifically in her plan. If Christ is necessary to my knowing the why of my priesthood and the reason for my celibacy, the Blessed Virgin is indispensable to understanding the bitter joy felt in the sacred and sacrificial character of my life as a priest.

Jesus has recruited me for the battle. I savor the moments from time to time when I rest my head against His chest and feel the beat of His Heart. Those moments may be few and far between, but they sustain me as I wield the sword of righteousness. Jesus has not spared me the discipline of discipleship. For this reason, I enjoy the privilege of being made worthy to walk in the intimate company of the Supreme Shepherd. If I die in battle, I trust that, as He lifts my dead body to Himself, I will hear and feel forever the beat of His Heart.

Our Lady, too, has graced me with her presence, and some months ago she assured me that she would continue to manifest herself. Indeed, she has. I am learning that the words of Mother Teresa of Calcutta ring true in my life: "Mary has a very tender love, a special protection also, for every priest, if he only turns to her."

The Blessed Virgin Mary does not permit me the solace of her home in Nazareth. Instead, she turns her eyes from me to embrace the rest of her children. The Holy Mother bids me farewell, as from afar Jesus beckons me to Himself. She prods me forward to fight for her children — for their salvation — for their sanctification.

As a priest and pastor, I would do a grave disservice to the Virgin of Nazareth if I should keep her frozen in the pages of Sacred Scripture. She is a mother ever active in the lives of her children and is indeed with us.

I do well to point the faithful to the Hill of Golgotha. There, strapped to the cross, in those last moments of His life on earth, Jesus gave His mother to the beloved disciple, John. As John received her into his home, so too, we receive her into our parish. We welcome her here and call her Mother and Queen, for so indeed she is. May she keep us faithful and trusting that the ongoing mystery of the Incarnation will unfold according to God's will. May Jesus, then, reproduce His life in this parish and in the lives of all who embark on this holy ground.

Remembering Mary's words to the stewards at the wedding feast at Cana in Galilee, we hearken to her command to "do whatever He tells us to do." Make us, then, disciples of mercy.

12

THE PROSTITUTION AND RAPE OF THE HOLY FAITH

January 12, 2002

I return again to the words of the prophet Jeremiah and make them my own: "When I found Your words, I devoured them; they became my joy and the happiness of my heart, because I bore Your name, O Lord, God of hosts. I did not sit celebrating in the circle of merrymakers; under the weight of Your hand I sat alone … ".

Indeed, so often I feel alone. At times, I feel as if I am passing into death with no one to mourn my departure, nor anyone to sing my praises. No doubt, having set myself against the standard of the Christ, praise would be unwarranted and undeserved. But in the dying, I am embraced by another reality. In this world, I know myself to be a stranger in a foreign land. Shall I ever again feel at home in a world that seems to turn a deaf ear to the voice of God?

Even within the Mystical Body of Christ, the Church, one may very well feel like a stranger in a foreign land. This, because too often the faithful — including her priests and religious — are guilty of prostituting the faith or, as misfortune would have it, have caused the faith to fall victim to rape. An impassioned love for Christ and His Body, the Church, is falling prey to the powers and principalities of this world.

Either the gift is being prostituted when it is squandered in a lust for all that is carnal, or raped when attention to the sacred is diverted by the conflicting chorus of popular opinion and political agendas. Even when cloaked in the veneer of religiosity, the faith is too often violated.

HOLINESS OF LIFE

I sit alone under the weight of God's hand as He brings me to death, making me one who is dead among the living or, would I dare say, one living among the dead. Jesus crucifies my flesh with the caution that I turn from the clamor of ego-infested religiosity.

I don't understand why there is so little passion for the Christ. Why is He so little known? Perhaps His followers keep Him hidden in the deep recesses of the soul because they regard the treasure as so precious — so beautiful, that to expose it would be to somehow contaminate the priceless jewel.

For my part, I would not want to leave this world having kept the priceless gift hoarded and hidden. As a priest, to do this would be a most grave sin and cause for condemnation. Through the shedding of His own precious Blood, Christ has paid the price and ransomed me from the slavery to sin and death. I feel compelled to make Him known. I pray, then, that the good God grant me the grace to be a living monstrance.

In the monstrance, His living presence is made visible. He is not hidden. He is exposed. It would grieve me greatly if I should ever obscure the reality of who God is, or cause others to remain indifferent or to abandon the faith. Too many have repelled others from the desire to embrace Jesus that it frightens me that I could do the same. I beg Jesus, then, to permit me the grace to soar to the heights of sanctity. In making this plea, I am plunged into the depths of darkness and forced to see my wretchedness. His light, though, dispels the darkness. Jesus fills me with a deep trust and joy that prompts within me the request for holiness.

I believe that the only solution to the Church's infirmity is holiness of life. Many of her members have so saturated themselves in the illusions of the world that the Church, too, has become afflicted with its every disease. The priesthood and religious life itself will not flourish until the sickness is acknowledged and healing is sought. Because priests and religious, in a distinct way, set the standard by virtue of a public profession of consecration, to consciously or unconsciously conceal the sacred is to hurt the mission of the Church. Until we recognize how low we have stooped, how selfish we have become, and how silly we look, we should not expect to be fruitful.

Many priests and religious boast that they are no different from other men and women. In what seems to be a newfound alliance with the secular world, many priests and religious have come to believe that they have somehow made Christ acceptable and lovable — a god among gods. Then there are those who, fearing their own shadow, don the trappings of religion and with rigidity demand of others a retreat from anything that threatens their zone of comfort. In either case, the Church's holiness is neither respected nor adhered to. Ego-infested religiosity robs the Church of her passion to make Jesus known, loved, and served. It extinguishes the light that dispels the darkness of sin and death.

I make my plea before the Lord that I not succumb to these tendencies. Perhaps I dance to the beat of a different drummer. I prefer to sit alone under the weight of God's hand, rather than to conform to a standard that militates against the authenticity of Christ's presence among us.

The holiness of Christ must be the standard I keep before me. When I peer into the Sacred Host, I behold Him in whose image I have been created. Only He can reproduce this image in me. The image is immortal and eternal. It has the aroma of dignity, grace, and nobility, but its fragrance is only savored in poverty, suffering, and death. I should hope to be so poor, to suffer so much, and to be so consumed by the sanctity of the Christ that in the end I would not even flinch at the assault of death's blow to my body.

Already, though, I daily feel an assault to my spirit and indeed I do flinch, betraying how young I am in faith. I look for someone to mentor me into maturity, and I am disillusioned and lonely. I peer into the Sacred Host and see Jesus there assuring me that He, too, is alone — a stranger in a foreign land. I am His disciple and He, my ever faithful friend. He is my mentor in a world that foolishly dances itself towards the brink of self-destruction, too often assisted by those who bear the name Jesus.

THE SACRED CHARACTER OF THE CHRIST

My fear is that we have so estranged ourselves from the sacred character of the Christ that Jesus has been reduced to the mere likeness of a good man, cloaked in every conceivable virtue, but kept alongside the stars of Hollywood or those who perform with prowess in the arena of sports. His sacred power to conquer the dark of the demonic has been relegated to the myth of an age long gone. It serves the world well to rest His image among those of other religious and secular leaders. And so, if there is little passion for the Christ, it is because He is viewed as a mere god among gods.

It is innocuous for the world to set itself against the standard of a good man. But to behold the Christ — to behold His sacred power to wield the sword that brings life out of death and separates heaven from hell — would expose the deep recesses of the soul. It would cause a sudden change in the beat of the world's song and cause the dancers to fall under the weight of their own feet. There is little passion for the Christ because He is little known, and this, at a time when the prophetic voice of the Church should ring with clarity for the sake of His salvific mission to lose no one.

A few years ago when the media exposed an avalanche of alleged cases of sexual abuse perpetrated by priests, someone, in a well-meaning gesture to boost the morale of priests, responded with a media campaign entitled, "Good Men Wear Black." In both the accusations of sexual abuse and the media campaign to assure the public that most priests were good men, I felt an assault on the sacred character and dignity of the priesthood. On one hand, aside from the horrific wound inflicted on the victims, certain members of the presbyterate had grossly and sinfully violated the integrity of priestly celibacy and chastity and abused sacred power. On the other hand, through the campaign to assure the public that priests were good men in spite of the failings of some in the presbyterate, faithful priests of good character were being coddled and pampered as if their recourse to the Christ would not, or could not, give them the backbone to bear with the suffering and persecution they needed to endure.

Like the Christ, the priesthood and religious life are not about good people doing good things. Priests and religious are not *professional good people*. They have made a public profession of consecration to be configured to the Christ. If the sacred power of the Christ to conquer the dark powers of the demonic and lift humanity into another reality is dismissed as a fiction of the past, then religious and priests will wallow in the sickness of their own self-absorbed disease. The sacred character of the priesthood and religious life will then be viewed as another aberration in the harlotry of the Catholic Church. The unjust accusation that she is the beast or Antichrist of the Apocalypse is then sinfully fed and her holy character further desecrated.

A healthy and holy Church depends, in large measure, on the sanctity of those who set the standard. Priests and religious have publicly surrendered themselves to Christ in a posture of self-giving sacrifice. In the footsteps of Jesus, they must indeed dance to the beat of a different drummer. They must make the lonely walk leading others to the solitude of the Christ who brings rest to the soul.

13

Upon This Rock

March 5, 2002

In Matthew's Gospel, Jesus says it would be foolish to build a house on sand. He says the rain comes, the wind blows, and the house falls because it has no foundation. On the other hand, he speaks of the wise who build their homes on rock. When the rains come and the winds blow, the houses do not crumble because they have firm foundations. In the discourse, we are cautioned that if Jesus is not the center of our lives, we will not withstand the trials and the tribulations of the pilgrimage of faith. He is the rock, and upon Him we build our lives.

As with others, my faith is forever tested in storms that seem to persist with few signs of a respite. But, by God's grace, my faith is firm in Jesus who, though hidden, is as persistent with me as the ever present storms. I trust that if I remain grounded in Him I will not collapse, and the call of the Blessed Virgin Mary will come to fruition. These trials of faith are real and must be endured as a test of my fidelity to perseverance in the adventure of this unfolding drama.

I began writing these reflections last May after attending a meeting I held with some officials from the Archdiocese of Chicago. I wanted to know how to proceed with the building of the Sanctuary of The Divine Mercy. When I was asked whether I had the backing of the parishioners for the project of the Sanctuary, I could not answer with a resounding *yes.*

The idea of the sanctuary began in August 1999 when the Blessed Virgin Mary asked that I give her the parish. I immediately consecrated the parish to Our Lady, and a few days later, I received an $850,000 Archdiocesan grant to begin immediate work on the church's badly damaged exterior. The damage was so serious that an additional million dollars was needed. This money was also secured in the gift of a grant. Since then I have never withheld the fruit of my prayer, and I have invited everyone to walk with me in this journey of faith, parishioners and non-parishioners alike. Some share my discernment and confirm the validity of the unfolding drama. Others are a bit skeptical. Many may be indifferent. Most are understandably cautious but hopeful.

The idea of the sanctuary was neither the decision of a committee or council, nor was it the decision of a group of like-minded individuals. Heaven planted the seed and is utilizing a wide variety of people to bring it to fruition. Our Lady has the plan, and she guides us in her own mysterious and unpredictable way.

When officials from the Archdiocese asked me to write a description of the sanctuary, partially in an effort to secure possible support for the project, I began to write Our Lady's story. It seems to me that she determined when and what I should write. Of this I am certain: Woven through the reflections is a mother's plea to reach her children and bring them to drink at the fountain of The Divine Mercy.

The idea of the sanctuary has received official support from Francis Cardinal George. He is happy to give his blessing to the project if I raise the several million dollars needed to make it a reality. Since the amount is well beyond the capacity of the parishioners or the Archdiocese to provide, the Cardinal has given me the authorization to seek out others who may be willing to assist in the project.

SHE WILL NOT ABANDON

A few weeks ago, I held another meeting with Archdiocesan personnel. At the meeting, I learned that I run the risk of losing a $135,000 donation, which is being held by the Archdiocese in a non-binding agreement. If it can be shown that the whole project can be financed and completed, the money would then be designated for the sanctuary. I was told that I have until May to secure the necessary funds.

I began wrestling with conflicting emotions. It is true that I enjoy deep confidence that the Blessed Virgin Mary directs the unfolding drama as she leads us down this exhilarating path that promises to rekindle faith and hope in the lives of countless persons. At the same time, I experience long moments of terror as I am plunged into doubt. I even question my sanity and quiver at the thought that I could be leading a parish down a treacherous road, only to be deceived in the end.

My integrity as a man of faith and as a priest is on the line. Worse still, I risk harming the faith of a believing people who have put their trust in me. They trust me because I am a priest — an instrument in the hand of God. They trust that I am in the company of the Supreme Shepherd. Indeed I am, but I, too, am a mere man and like the rest of humanity, I suffer the trials of faith and can easily succumb to the enemy's deceptions. I beg Jesus and Mary not to allow me to succumb to a lie. If I should lead the people of God astray, it would be better that I not remain a priest. If I should be the cause of harm to anyone's faith, I should be reprimanded immediately and my ways corrected.

In sincerity and honesty, I wrote that the Holy Mother of God asked me to give her the parish. Her request was clear. It was distinct. I see her and hear her only through the eyes and the ears of my soul. One evening last August, though, she came to me as if from outside the inner sanctum. I was eating dinner in the rectory kitchen. I was sad. I felt terribly alone, and I felt betrayed, rejected, and abandoned.

Our Lady came. She assured me that she would never abandon me. She made me understand that she was preparing to manifest herself. That's all she told me. More than her words, it was her presence that reassured me. Never before had I felt such love. It was deep and enduring — it was pure. I felt whole. I felt like a man. I felt totally free to continue this walk in faith. I was ready for the battle as Jesus again beckoned me to Himself.

STEERED TOWARDS SAFE HARBOR

Remembering Our Lady's visitation last August is itself a consolation as I suffer the trials of faith. At times, I have asked myself if the experience was either a figment of my imagination or the work of the devil to lead people into deception. I cannot, though, reproduce her visit. The truth will be known only in the fruit borne from this walk of faith.

After my meeting with officials from the Archdiocese, the trial of faith began. I did not want to lose the $135,000 donation that came to us in a moment totally opportune and unexpected, giving me the impetus to move forward with confidence that the Blessed Virgin Mary was at the helm. To this day, I still have no definitive donors for the millions needed to build the Sanctuary. It would be truly miraculous if I could produce at least $2.5 million in less than two months. Even my confidence that Our Lady had arranged for the holy rocks from the Hill of Tepeyac to adorn the sanctuary suddenly seemed to be merely words of my reflections written in faith. I wondered whether the Lady's plan was crumbling before my eyes.

As my feeble faith suffered the assault of the fierce storm raging within me, I begged Our Lady for a sign — a rest from the trials of faith. Our faith journey is a mystery forever unraveling toward the calm waters of safe harbor. St. John Bosco once described a vision in which the Pope, at the helm, painstakingly maneuvers a giant ship. The ship is being tossed about by the raging winds of the storm as the Holy Father steers it towards safe harbor, passing through two pillars, one with the image of the Blessed Virgin Mary and the other with a symbol of the Holy Eucharist. This image is a solace to me as I feel myself suffering in solidarity with the Church.

The Church is passing through a severe trial of faith. The severity of the trial is exacerbated from within her own body — caused by the infidelity of some of her own members. It seems the world watches from afar, gleefully awaiting the Church's demise. Or perhaps, in sorrow and expectant hope, a searching people want to believe that she will not self-destruct — that the Church can withstand the storm and bring herself into calm waters, guided by the mysterious grace of the Holy Spirit.

I saw many of these searching people among the nearly three million who attended the International Youth Celebration in Rome during the Great Jubilee 2000 of the Incarnation. Pope

John Paul II generated so much hope as his aged and broken body shed the light of grace over the multitude seeking a way out of darkness. He painstakingly manifested the strength to instill a resurgence of faith in the young who needed to be grounded and guided by the enduring truth of the Gospel message. They wanted to believe — and rightfully expected — that this message would be incarnated in the life of the Church.

The eyes of the world should have taken note that in the outskirts of Rome, several million young people were encamped like refugees. They kept vigil through the night in song, dance, and prayer as they awaited the celebration of the Holy Mass. Jubilee 2000 was truly a respite in the Church's trial of faith. As the Holy Father arrived in the early hours of the morning and the Mass began, the Church's 2,000 year sojourn of faith had indeed come to rest for a brief moment on calm waters. I could still hear the words Jesus spoke to Simon reverberating through the ages: "Simon, son of John, thou art Peter and upon this rock I will build My Church and the gates of hell shall not prevail against it" (Mt 16:18). As the successor of Peter, Pope John Paul II indeed steers the Church toward safe harbor.

THE ROCK IS THE CHRIST

There is no reason to believe that the Church can survive the severity of her trials except that her faith is built on solid rock. That rock is the Christ, and by His own authority, His sacred power was entrusted to Peter that as the rains fall and the winds blow, the Church will not collapse. She will not be swallowed into the belly of the tumultuous sea. I take solace in the heroism of the Church's presence among us, and I am strengthened knowing that her trials of faith have withstood the test of time.

On March 1ˢᵗ, feeling pushed to the brink of the precipice, I asked Our Lady for a sign in my own trial of faith. I did not want to believe that her plan was crumbling before my eyes. I did not want to lose the $135,000 donation designated for the Sanctuary. I prayed that all necessary funds be secured within a month. Also, since it had been months since I had heard anything of the rocks from the Hill of Our Lady's apparitions, I began to wonder if having the rocks was only the fantasy of my own personal reflections.

At noon that day, the Blessed Virgin Mary gave me the rest I needed as I received the word that the Archdiocese of Mexico had contacted the Archdiocese of Chicago. The holy rocks cut from the Hill of Tepeyac would rest on the grounds of St. Stanislaus Kostka Parish. Upon this rock, she, the Holy Mother of God, would build her sanctuary.

Only hours after we received the news that the holy rocks would form the foundation of the sanctuary, plans were being made for the sculpting of an 18-foot icon of Our Lady. Recalling the vision of St. John Bosco, the Icon of the Blessed Virgin Mary and the Icon of The Divine Mercy, which is the symbol of the Holy Eucharist, will stand inside the sanctuary on 11-foot pedestals on opposite sides of the Via Dolorosa. These pillars of our faith will serve as the door to the adoration chapel where pilgrims will rest on calm waters and drink from the fountain of The Divine Mercy. In safe harbor, the faithful will contemplate the Holy Eucharist where the Body and Blood, together with the Soul and Divinity of the Lord Jesus, is truly, really, and substantially contained.

On the rocks taken from the holy Hill of Tepeyac the sanctuary will stand as a sturdy sign that heaven is reaching out to humanity. On the rock of Peter we have the promise of

Our Lord that the Church will not collapse — she will not self-destruct. In wisdom, we make Jesus the rock foundation of our lives and thus become a holy people withstanding the trials and the tribulations of our faith journey.

I thank the Blessed Virgin Mary that in this respite in my own trials of faith, I feel the exhilaration of being led down a path that promises to rekindle faith and hope in the lives of her children. Indeed, the gates of hell will not prevail.

Take care, lest any of you have
an evil and unfaithful spirit
and fall away from the living God.
Encourage one another daily while it is still "today,"
so that no one grows hardened by the deceit of sin.
We have become partners of Christ
only if we maintain to the end
that confidence with which we began.
Today, if you should hear His voice,
harden not your hearts.

Hebrews 3:12-15

14

And He Wept

March 19, 2002

The gates of hell shall not prevail are words that imply struggle and conflict at the core of the Church's spiritual sojourn as she and her members make their way in exile toward the safe harbor of heaven. These words of Jesus warn us that indeed the war has been waged, but that the victory is secured. The victory, though, is realized only insofar as we make ourselves fit for the battle through constant and persevering prayer, through generosity in sacrifice, and through disciplined lives.

Somehow, somewhere, someone has foolishly led more than a generation of Catholics away from these truths, and we reap now what has been sown. We would do well to heed the words Jesus spoke to Peter when He promised to pray for Peter, that He, in turn, strengthen the brothers because Satan meant to sift them all like wheat (Lk 22:31).

Perhaps we underestimate the destructive power of the evil one, making ourselves victims of his deceptions. The dark and abiding power of Satan nailed Jesus to the cross. Those who lusted after the illusion of the self — seduced and deceived by the evil one — became the instruments who sought to silence the truth. This truth calls us to die to ourselves and to live in Him. They were not foreigners who crucified Jesus; they were not pagans who put Him to death; they were His own people, *the people Jesus loved.* They were His friends. What was true then is still true today.

Many times a day I ask Jesus to reproduce His life in me. I know well that left to myself I am nothing. I am not so foolish as to believe that I could become a saint without suffering the long and enduring death to the self. God has graced me with the wisdom to understand how I am nothing and that the something I think I am is only misery and corruption. A self-possessed ego is more destructive than constructive to the building up of God's kingdom. His Church is served to the extent that I decrease and He increase. To reflect His light requires the annihilation of my ego that I may arise anew in Him.

THROUGH THE PRISM OF HISTORY

Jesus prompts within me the request that He reproduce His life within me. *The Word was made Flesh and dwelt among us* is as true today as it was 2,000 years ago as He incarnates His life into mine. He allows me the grace to know and experience His interior life as He Himself made the journey through the hills and the valleys of the Holy Land so many years ago. It seems to me that Jesus chooses to reproduce in me His sadness. I believe I know some of His sorrow.

As He made His way through the cities and the villages, He suffered a deep sadness as He paused and contemplated the lives of countless people. In them, He peered as if through the prism of history and saw how few would respond to His call, choosing the darkness of the tomb and the stench of sin rather than the light of life and the fragrance of holiness. I believe it was this oppression that troubled Him so deeply and drew Him to His knees as He wept before the tomb of Lazarus.

After raising Lazarus from the dead, Jesus left Bethany and made the lonely walk to the holy city of Jerusalem. He knew what awaited Him. He would be received with the joyous shouts, "Hosanna to the King; blessed is He who comes in the name of the Lord; hosanna in the highest." Only days later, the cheers would turn to jeers and the joy of festivity to the sorrow of a mother's grief as the crowds raised their fists in condemnation, shouting for His Blood — the mutilation of His Body — His silence in death. Jesus knew well what awaited Him. He knew that He would be betrayed, rejected, denied, and abandoned, but His sorrow was not for Himself.

When He came within sight of the holy city, He paused and He wept. He lamented:

> If only you had known the path to peace this day; but you have completely lost it from view! Days will come upon you when your enemies will encircle you with a rampart, hem you in, and press you hard from every side. They will wipe you out, you and your children within your walls, and leave not a stone on a stone within you, because you failed to recognize the time of your visitation (Lk 19:41-44).

Jesus had a profound love for Jerusalem as He expressed the depth of His sorrow when He tenderly pleaded for her attention. "How often have I wanted to gather your children together as a mother bird collects her young under her wings, and you refused Me!" He wept then and He weeps now. What was true then is true now.

In deep sorrow, Jesus shed tears of Blood in the garden of Gethsemane. His agony over the loss of those who choose the dark of the tomb to the light of life continues. His Blood, mingled with the Water that flows from His pierced side, promises to deliver us from the stench of sin to the fragrance of holiness. The choice is ours.

THE TIME OF OUR VISITATION

This is the time of our visitation, but we don't recognize it as such. Jesus knows the destructive power of the enemy. He wants to gather us to Himself, but we refuse Him. We choose not to be bound to Him through constant and persevering prayer. We recoil from the mere thought of sacrifice and disdain the discipline of the Lord, giving free reign to the flesh. The spirit is crushed, but we seem not to care. In arrogance, we've chosen the darkness of the tomb. The stench of sin has become sweet to our senses. We destroy ourselves and our children with us. We have become the enemy.

What has happened? Why do we seemingly abhor the grace of sacrifice and the dignity of discipline in our lives? Why is unceasing prayer foreign to the fabric of our lives? What has happened to the family? What has happened to the priesthood and the religious life?

Why are we fixated on perverted behavior in talk and in action? Why is there so much vulgarity on the television, radio, bumper stickers, and billboards? Why do we so casually entertain ourselves on sex and violence at the expense of our future? How do we so selfishly clamor for individual rights, but deny the unborn their right to life? What has happened to reverence and decency and modesty and chastity? The litany of lament is seemingly endless.

Somehow, somewhere, someone has foolishly led more than a generation of Catholics away from the truths of the faith. Someone has failed to remind us that this holy faith is meant to cost us our lives. Jesus said, "Lose yourself and you will find yourself ... die to yourself and you will live." Our faith is about Jesus. It is not about us. It is about Him. We have no identity apart from Him. We are dust and to dust we return. Only He can bring life from death.

Our selfishness and sinfulness are making us a dead people. We would do well to rise from the tomb and drop the burial bands that bind us, free then to go with Jesus to Jerusalem. There, to die with Him so that we may live with Him.

We have been led away from the truth of our journey. Life in this world is not about us, and contrary to popular belief the Church is not and has never been the problem. In the clamor for change, her members may try to bind the Church and bury her, but they only bind and bury themselves. The Church cannot keep us from following the high calling to holiness of life. The Church is always holy and free. She is the means to genuine sanctification. Her members may obscure her holiness, but even when seemingly eclipsed, her sanctity is alive in Christ, her head. She is bound to Him and to Him alone.

Through the years of my priestly formation, and even to this day, by God's grace, I have painstakingly withstood pressure from those who try to bind me. Those on the right and those on the left, conservatives and liberals, the angry and the timid, the power hungry and the sex-craved, the rich and the poor — each in his or her own way runs the risk of losing sight of Jesus' vision and perhaps unconsciously tries to bind the Church and bury her. The Church is more than the sum total of all her members. She should not succumb to the agenda of interest groups. She cannot be recreated in the image and likeness of neither man nor woman. This would only falsify her identity as created solely in the image and likeness of God.

If I had not sought the refuge of Jesus in the Blessed Sacrament, I could have easily succumbed to the lies. The lies are so dangerously deceptive. My prayerful plea for humility serves me in submission to the universal vision of the Church, which far transcends the constraints of time. From the Pope in Rome to the people in the pew, we must humble ourselves. In humility, we love the Church as Jesus loved Jerusalem.

Jerusalem is the holy city no matter how much she is pillaged by those who live within her walls. She is a symbol of the covenant — the marriage between God and His people. The Church, too, is in the covenant of marriage. She is wedded to the Christ. She is His very body. She is without stain no matter how corrupt her priests may be — no matter how worldly her religious become — no matter how unfaithful her members are. These sins desecrate the Church's holiness, but they do not take it away. The desecration gives the appearance that she is bound and buried. Jesus, then, weeps in and through her.

As He wept for Jerusalem, He weeps for the Church because her members fail to recognize the time of their visitation. His body is deeply wounded, deeply divided, and smells from the stench of sin. Arrogance, avarice, apathy, and evil intent have made the Church appear no different from the other organizations and institutions of this world. Ego-infested religiosity indeed desecrates the Church's sacrificial and sacred character and hurts her mission.

The Gospels begin and end with the call to repentance and reform. Bishops, priests, religious, and laity would be terribly naïve, dangerously adolescent, or deeply steeped in sin not to recognize the need for reform. It is one thing to be renewed according to the standard of the world. It is quite another thing to reform to the standard of the Christ.

Our children deserve the fruit of our unceasing prayer and willing sacrifices — sacrifices made not for personal gain, but for the love of Christ who took upon Himself our sins and delivered us from the jaws of death. The young should see the discipline of our lives, as by example we make them fit for the battle.

REFORM TO THE STANDARD OF THE CHRIST

This is the time of our visitation, the time of grace. This is the time of mercy. The time is passing away. We do well to recognize the time we are in and not refuse Him. We are in conflict. The struggle is real — the war has been waged. If we turn to the Heart of Jesus, we are promised the victory.

As I continue my journey towards death, I make my plea before the Lord that He reproduces His life in me. If He allows me a share in His sadness or His loneliness, I accept. Nothing quite compares to the joy of knowing that He dwells within me.

I prepare myself for the long haul if God should choose to give me long years of life. I cannot continue my journey weighed down by the baggage of others. I will not keep company in the tomb of the ego nor smell from the stench of its sin. Jesus calls us into the light of day and to love His body, the Church. He calls us to suffer in her, with her, and for her. Only in holiness of life can we untie the burial bands of the sins that bind us. The old self is left to rot in the tomb; the new self lives to give witness to Jesus.

As time passes, I feel myself more and more bound to Jesus and His body, the Church. The conflict and the struggle, though, seem more intense, compelling me to spend hours a day in prayer for the mere sake of survival. At the age of 46, I feel it may have been easier to have become a saint if I had died at the age of 33. Even at this juncture in my life, after 16 years in the intimate company of Jesus, I still so often feel like a mere boy of 12, asking God to be so good as to make me a priest. If I should live a long life, I hope, like Simeon, one day to behold the Christ and ask the Master to send me to death in peace for having seen the salvation of those I love. At times I weep interiorly, but knowing God dwells within me is sufficient cause for a joy unsurpassed by sorrow.

Our Lady comes clothed in light to dispel the darkness of the tomb and the stench of sin. She comes to make us fit for the battle. She is our solitary boast, for in her we see clearly that the Church is indeed without stain. She is holy and immaculate. The Woman of the Apocalypse shows us that *the gates of hell shall not prevail.* She cautions us, though, that the ancient serpent has taken his place at the shore of the sea, there to wage war on her children, on those who keep God's commandments and give witness to Jesus.

15

AT THE LAST HOUR

June 7, 2002

Saint Peter says we may have to suffer the distress of many trials so that the genuineness of our faith, which is more precious than the passing splendor of fire-tried gold, may lead to praise, glory, and honor when Jesus Christ appears. Since the day I entrusted the parish to the Blessed Virgin Mary, my faith has indeed been strengthened through the distress of many trials. Even so, my faith still seems less than the size of a mustard seed, which leaves me humbled as I wonder at heaven's choice to use someone as weak as I am. That Our Lady has a plan for the parish does not surprise me: That I am an instrument in her plan does. This alone is a true testimony to the wonder of God's mercy.

As I wrote in previous reflections, in late February, I learned that the parish was at risk of losing $135,000. The money was being held by the Archdiocese in a non-binding agreement that stipulated that the funds would be designated for the building of the sanctuary on the condition that we could secure the financing by a given date. I had until May to secure the rest of the necessary funds to build the sanctuary. Since I had been introduced to two prospective donors, I was confident the money would be secured. I trusted that the Blessed Virgin Mary would inspire them to assist in the building of the sanctuary.

By mid-April, both donors backed away from the project, choosing to remain faithful to long-standing charities they had supported for many years. To say I was discouraged would be an understatement.

In the meantime, 2,000 copies of my reflections, *A Mother's Plea*, had been printed and distributed. The most recent printing included all but these last chapters. We had just completed the Spanish translation of all 14 chapters and wanted to print 2,000 in Spanish and another 2,000 in English.

On Friday, April 19th, at 5:00 in the evening, the printer came to the rectory to pick up the disks to format the texts for publication. I gave the disks to him, knowing I only had the money to pay for about 1,000 copies of books. I had no idea how I would pay for the additional 3,000 copies, but I felt compelled to print them nonetheless.

Two hours later, at 7:00, I began the celebration of the Mass. After Mass, I greeted people in the sacristy. I noticed a man standing off to the side, waiting patiently to speak with me. After everyone left, he came to me and handed me an envelope from a woman who told him to give it to me personally. I thanked him, locked the doors to the church, and went to my office. I opened the envelope and read a short note, which said: "I have just read your book, *A Mother's Plea*, and I believe Our Lady wants you to have this money." Enclosed was a check for $15,000 from Manuela Loyola. Speechless and elated, I was certain I now had the money needed to print 4,000 copies of the book. Indeed, I had no more and no less. This was another of Our Lady's mysterious manifestations and a lesson for me to put aside any feelings of discouragement. It was obvious that she would provide the means to bring her plan to fruition in her own way and in her own time.

As April rolled into May, I was anxiously aware that I had only a few thousand dollars for the sanctuary. I had no prospective donors who could even remotely enkindle the hope for $2.5 million more. All I had was faith, but faith that was less than the size of a mustard seed. Recalling Jesus' words that if your faith were at least the size of a mustard seed it could move a mountain, I clung to my faith in God's providence and Mary's intercession.

Well into May, I began wondering whether I would receive the dreaded call telling me that the $135,000 designated for the sanctuary would be withdrawn. I knew that the executors of the will could not wait indefinitely to act. I knew, too, that I didn't have the estimated $2.5 million to build the sanctuary. Sure enough, the call came the last week of the month, although I wasn't in the office to receive it. The executors and I played phone tag for a few days, but to no avail. Finally, on Wednesday, May 29th, I left a voice mail message. I thanked them for their patience with me and informed them that I had not received the $2.5 million. I also assured them that I understood their need to withdraw the allocation. Even if we lost the money, I had to remember that it came to us in an unexpected and opportune moment providing me with the impetus to move forward with confidence that the Blessed Virgin Mary was at the helm. I believed that even if we had lost the $135,000, she would still provide the means to build the sanctuary.

Late Thursday afternoon, May 30th, I missed a call from a gentleman I had spoken to over a year ago. At that time, believing the Blessed Virgin Mary wanted a sanctuary to The Divine Mercy, I frantically sought the means to make it happen. With a touch of shyness in my request for assistance,

I had called this gentleman to ask if he would help us financially. We spoke only briefly, and he told me he was not certain he could help the parish, but to consider the seed planted and to leave it to Our Lady.

I tried in vain to return his call Thursday evening. He had left town for the weekend, and I, too, had to leave early Friday morning to celebrate my niece's wedding in Florida. When I returned to Chicago Monday evening, I noticed that he had called again. Tuesday morning we finally connected. As we spoke, I could feel the pounding of my heart. I sat there almost paralyzed, and anxiously awaited another of Our Lady's mysterious manifestations. I knew I was in the last hour of hope in finding resources. The door to the month of May had just closed, and I had resigned myself to the loss of the $135,000. The gentleman on the other line spoke slowly and deliberately. The silence between his every word gave me the sense that Our Lady was the bridge between us.

Any lingering doubt I may have had vanished as the gentleman, who chooses total anonymity, said that he and his family, after much discernment in prayer, had decided to finance the building of the Sanctuary of The Divine Mercy. With those words, my soul transcended the confines of my body. For a moment, my spirit seemed completely free from the shackles of the flesh. I felt confirmed in my personal discernment and grateful to the holy Mother of God, whose faith made up for what was lacking in mine. In all honesty, I felt that my faith was still less than the size of a mustard seed. It is her faith that moves the mountain.

Immediately after the phone conversation, aware that I had probably lost $135,000, I called one of the executors of the will and asked whether he had received my phone message the week before. He said that he had and then expressed his sorrow that I did not get the $2.5 million needed for the sanctuary. I wasted no time in telling him that indeed I had received the money. At this point, he said that he and his mother believed in the unfolding miracle and wanted to wait awhile longer before withdrawing their pledge of money from St. Stanislaus Kostka. He assured me that they would begin the legal process to transfer the funds to be utilized in the building of the Sanctuary.

SPIRITUAL MATURITY

A teacher in the ways of faith and moving us toward spiritual maturity, the Blessed Virgin Mary again mysteriously showed herself. At the last hour of hope, it is clear that she was indeed at the helm.

There is no doubt that Our Lady is tilling the soil, enabling the roots to go deep. The seed of the self must die that Jesus be born anew and live in our midst in a perceivable way. As the foundress of the School Sisters of Notre Dame, Mother Theresa of Jesus Gerhardinger once said, "All the works of God proceed slowly and in pain; but then, their roots are the sturdier and their flowering the lovelier."

In solidarity with most of humanity, the pilgrim Church has fallen victim to the deceiving spirits of this age. With a contrite spirit, we humble ourselves in sincere repentance to atone for our sins. Only in doing this can we proclaim with authenticity the mercy of Jesus — a proclamation that must resound throughout the world. The Church's prophetic voice, announcing the coming of Jesus as the just judge, falls on deaf ears when the actions of the pilgrim Church betray her claimed identity as the beloved spouse of the most holy

Redeemer. Our Lady — the virgin spouse of the Triune God and the holy and immaculate mother of the Church — prods us to die to ourselves that Jesus live in us, transforming us into instruments of His mercy in this, the last hour before He comes to judge the living and the dead.

In the guise of light, the seduction and darkness of evil has gripped the Church and hurts her mission. From the College of Cardinals to the people in the pews, the call to wake from slumber comes as a plea from the Blessed Virgin Mary. Hers is a call to authenticity.

Through the eyes of Jesus, the Church would do well to see herself in the beloved disciple John, resting her head against the Heart of Jesus and feeling the fire of His love, consumed by its purifying heat. Unless she seeks refuge in His Heart, the Church will not have the means to ignite the fire to proclaim the incomprehensible love of Jesus for souls nor the capacity to satisfy His thirst before He comes at the end of time.

In the last hour, Our Lady awakens the Church to open the font, giving access to The Divine Mercy through the Sacraments of Reconciliation and the Holy Eucharist, reiterating the warning of St. Paul:

> There will be terrible times in the last days. Men will be lovers of self and of money, proud, arrogant, abusive, disobedient to their parents, ungrateful, profane, inhuman, implacable, slanderous, licentious, brutal, hating the good. They will be treacherous, reckless, pompous, lovers of pleasure rather than of God as they make a pretense of religion but negate its power (2 Tim 3:1-5).

In the presence of God and of Christ Jesus, and by His appearing and kingly power, St. Paul charges us to preach the word, to stay with this task whether convenient or inconvenient —

correcting, reproving, appealing — constantly teaching and never losing patience. Paul says, "The time will come when people will not tolerate sound doctrine, but, following their own desires, will surround themselves with teachers who tickle their ears. They will stop listening to the truth and will wander off to fables." As for us, he says, "Be steady and self-possessed; put up with hardship, perform your work, fulfill your ministry" (2 Tim 4:1-5).

Shortly before he died, Pope Paul VI said prophetically that the smoke of Satan had entered the sanctuary. In a June 29, 1972 homily, he lamented:

> The tail of the devil is functioning in the disintegration of the Catholic world. The darkness of Satan has entered and spread throughout the Catholic Church even to its summit. Apostasy, the loss of faith, is spreading throughout the world and into the highest levels within the Church.

Jesus himself warned us that in the end evil will increase and the love of most will grow cold, asking whether there will even be faith in the world when the Son of Man comes in His glory. Our response is *yes*. We say *yes* because we recall the words Jesus spoke the night before He was crucified. In His farewell discourse, He directed His words to His little flock and prayed to His Father on their behalf and on behalf of those who would believe on their testimony. He promised that He would not leave them orphaned.

A SHEER MIRACLE

Our Lady has asked for a sanctuary and has provided the means to bring it to fruition. The Sanctuary of The Divine Mercy, leading to the chapel of adoration of the Blessed Sacrament, testifies to the truth of our Lord's promise, "I will be with you always."

In the last hour, *we will suffer the distress of many trials that our faith, which is more precious than the passing splendor of fire-tried gold, may by its genuineness lead to praise, glory, and honor when Jesus Christ appears.* When the time of our dissolution draws near, we will say with St. Paul, "I have fought the good fight, I have finished the race, I have kept the faith" (2 Tim 4:7). In faith and good works, the Church merits the crown that awaits it. On that day, the Lord, just judge that He is, will award it to her — not only to her, but to all who have looked for His appearing with eager longing.

Yes, indeed, I knew that it would be a sheer miracle if I could secure $2.5 million within the short period of a few months. In the last hour, the miracle came through the faith and generosity of anonymous donors. My consecration to Jesus through Mary seems more permanent. Though still a slave and totally bound, I have never felt so free.

As for the exact day or hour,
no one knows it,
neither the angels in heaven
nor the Son,
but the Father only.
The coming of the Son of Man
will repeat what happened in Noah's time.
In the days before the flood
people were eating and drinking,
marrying and being married,
right up to the day Noah entered the ark.
They were totally unconcerned
until the flood came and destroyed them.
So will it be at the coming of the Son of Man.

Matthew 24:36-39

16

MURDERED OR MARTYRED?
THE DEATH OF MARY STACHOWICZ

November 2002

Recently, I waited for a cab on a cold and rain soaked day in downtown Chicago. I felt lost against the backdrop of the magnificent array of skyscrapers lining the street. I seemed invisible, even to myself, as I stood there among the frenzied movement of countless pedestrians. When I entered the cab, I was wallowing in that familiar darkness that seems to have befriended me these last few years.

After I shut the door, the driver turned to me and asked if I was Jewish. I answered him by saying, "kind of — my roots are Jewish, but I am a Catholic." He must have noticed the skullcap I wear as a personal sign of the consecration of my life to Jesus and the Blessed Virgin Mary. He said, "I can see you are a holy man. Your face is aglow with light." I smiled, knowing that in that moment, I neither felt holy nor bathed in light. But I said, "Yes, I am a man of God, and I see that you are, too."

Misery seeks company and so moments later, feeling comfortable in his presence, I began lamenting about the sadness I felt for the ills of society and the prevailing godlessness that seems to be growing. I may have sounded a bit pessimistic. The driver turned to me with a wink and a sparkle in his eye and said, "Ah, but the prophets longed for these days." His words and the manner in which he spoke them sent shivers up and down my spine.

I listen intently for the voice of the prophet to bring some sense to the chaos that runs rampant in the world and in the Church these days. Even non-religious people have a keen intuition that something is terribly wrong. God put the cab driver in my path that day. Unknown to him, he was a consoling and calming presence to me.

I was suffering grief at the tragic and untimely death of my friend, Mary Stachowicz. I met Mary nearly 18 years ago, only days after my ordination to the priesthood. Many years later, she had assisted me in the editing of these reflections and was preparing to review the journal upon its completion. Instead, she was taken by force and brutally murdered on November 13, 2002. November 13th is the Feastday of St. Stanislaus Kostka. I shall speak about Mary shortly.

For now, suffice it to say that there is no end to the escalation of violence that plagues a world just embarked on its third millennium. It seems to me this violence is symptomatic of the world sitting on a keg of dynamite whose flickering flame is ever so close to igniting devastation unlike anything ever known since the dawn of creation. As the Holy Father mentioned when he consecrated the Third Millennium to Our Lady on October 13, 2000, "Mankind can turn this planet into a garden or a pile of rubble." Every day that passes we seem to choose the rubble. The victims of violence are thrown into the darkness of grief, loneliness, and confusion through the words, misdeeds, and sickness of a people no longer grounded in God. In other places and at other times in history, prophets sounded the alarm in an attempt to bring people to their knees before it was too late.

With unprecedented advances in technology, our global community continues to grow smaller and more sophisticated. The Gospel has now been preached throughout the world to the north, south, east, and west. The prophets lived and died for these days. More than a few prophets caution us that in the end, when hearts would grow cold and the faith of the Church is repudiated, to watch for the appearance of the Luminous Woman, wrapped in silence and clothed in the strength and the power of humility. Just as she preceded the first coming of Jesus, she would prepare the world for His Second Coming. I believe that Our Lady may now be in the belfry, marking the hour and pleading with us to return to sanctuary.

ON THE FRONT LINES

Since the day I consecrated the parish of St. Stanislaus Kostka to the Blessed Virgin Mary, I have felt weaker, stronger, more peaceful, and more anxious. These are welcome signs from God of the narrow road that I must travel in doing His will. The intense spiritual warfare that I experience makes me acutely aware that this parish is on the front lines. On one hand, Our Lady has requested the Sanctuary of The Divine Mercy and has provided the means for its realization. On the other hand, yielding to her will has thrust me into a perceptible battle — for my soul, for the soul of the parish, for the very soul of Christianity. This is something I was not prepared for during my formation in the seminary. Spiritual warfare was never a serious topic for study in the 1980s. My walk into this uncharted territory makes for an arduous adventure. Trust, patience, and persevering prayer help keep me in the heat of battle, clinging to the knowledge that in the end truth alone will prevail.

As the war wages, I find my strength, my sanity, and my solitude in sanctuary. Because I see the world shackled by evil and living in the shadow of death, sanctuary is the sure means to my survival and sustains me as I accept the burden of the cross. I know I am configured to the Christ when the weight of the cross keeps me crawling to my own Calvary. It is not so much my own cross I carry. It is that I so clearly see and sense the sufferings of others who seek their own solace. A world that is increasingly under the influence of evil is in dire need of sanctuary, and I tire of so many who downplay the power of the evil one or go so far as to deny his existence. For them, sanctuary is a frivolous need because they give little attention to suffering and therefore show shallow concern for the sacred.

How can I shut my eyes to evil when I am called to console a family and bury their daughter? Jasmine was only 14 years old when her boyfriend fired bullets into her head. I felt deep sadness as I arrived for her wake, only to see her body clothed in the beautiful white dress and veil she wore for her First Holy Communion just a few months earlier. As mourners laid fresh cut flowers over her coffin, I noticed that her rosary had been gently woven through the fingers of her hands.

I arrived only moments after Karina's body was removed from her home. The belt that she had used to hang herself still hung from a ceiling beam in her bedroom. Her parents had been making final preparations for Karina's Sweet Sixteen birthday party scheduled for the next day. Instead, I helped them plan her funeral. Nine days later, Karina's boyfriend, unable to comprehend what had happened and consumed by the hopelessness that evil feeds, decided to join Karina in death. He hanged himself in his parent's garage.

Abandoned, Rebecca's dismembered body was found neatly packed away in a footlocker. It had been discovered behind a furniture store just blocks away from the parish. She was only 14 years old.

Marianne and three of her children perished the day before Thanksgiving. The windows facing the alley had been bolted shut for fear of intruders, giving them no exit from the raging fire. Her husband, Ignacio, and another son watched in horror as the rest of the family was consumed in flames.

A mother and father came to me in fear and shock at discovering their daughter's addiction to drugs. An intelligent and gifted musician, the 16-year-old had been given heroin — it didn't cost her a dime. The neatly dressed drug dealers waited for her as they daily await other naïve victims. Across the street from her high school, they preyed on her and lured her into addiction. She was hooked and became a hooker.

THE FLAME IN HER HEART

And then there is the story of Mary Stachowicz. Just hours after I began writing this chapter, I received a phone call from Mary's daughter Angie. Her voice told me that something menacing was unfolding. She was crying. Her words rang with fear as she said, "Mom is missing. We don't know where she is. Her coat and purse are there. Her car and the keys are there, but she's gone. Something has happened." In that moment, I was overcome with a queasiness and dizziness that brought a paralysis to everything I was doing.

Mary was a graceful and compassionate woman. She was strong-willed but humble. She was without malice. Her faith in Jesus Christ, her love for the Virgin Mary, and her defense of the Catholic faith and Catholic spirituality were simply integral to her personality. When she spoke about Jesus and Mary — when she spoke about Teresa of Avila and a few other saints close to her heart — you could see in her eyes and hear in her voice that she enjoyed intimacy in her relationship with those in heaven. Concern for the faith of her family was the flame that perpetually burned in her heart, and that fire spread well beyond the walls of her home. Her only agenda was to make Jesus and the Church known and loved.

Not too long ago, at Angie's wedding, I was privileged to observe Mary Stachowicz in the company of her husband and four children. Her head slightly tilted, her shy smile radiated the joy of a life seasoned by sorrow but totally content in the moment. Her deep and luminous eyes seemed to gaze in every direction. They were turned to the labor of the past and looked with hope to the future. They seemed to peer upward to that mystical place beyond the beyond, and yet inward to the inner sanctum — to the deep recesses of her soul.

On the Feast of St. Stanislaus Kostka, Mary assisted in the Holy Sacrifice of the Mass, consumed the Sacred Host, and crossed the street to begin her work as a receptionist and translator in a funeral home. Unknown to her, her reception of Holy Communion that morning was preparation for her death. This was her viaticum, the Sacrament proper to the dying Christian — food for the passage through death to eternal life. It is the completion and crown of a Christian life on this earth, signifying that a person follows the Lord to eternal glory and the banquet of the heavenly kingdom.

Moments after crossing that threshold from the church to the funeral home, Mary Stachowicz ascended the "Hill of Golgotha." She was kicked, brutally beaten, and repeatedly stabbed with a knife. The killer then wrapped her head in a garbage bag and strangled her to death. According to his confession to police, he did this because she had befriended him. With the instinct of a mother, she had invited him to embrace the faith and reflect on his lifestyle. In his own words, the 19-year-old stopped beating Mary only after he had become too tired to continue. He not only "crucified" a holy woman, he "crucified" her entire family and all her friends as well. I can only wonder about the demons released in the life of the young man who committed this heinous crime.

It is inconceivable that after beating Mary to death, he discarded her body in a crawl space, and then spent the next few days consoling and praying with her family as they fearfully and frantically sought information about their mother's disappearance. On the third day, her body was found.

On November 13th, Mary crossed the threshold from this world into the next. Taken by force, she walked from one kingdom into another — from the paradise of the proud to the halls of the humble. The proud strut about in the sickness of their own disease, compelled to extinguish anyone who gets in the way of their illusory kingdoms. Only the Father of Lies supports the perversion of their power. Jesus calls him the prince of this world.

The Kingdom of Heaven Suffers Violence

While the Church in recent decades has been almost silent to an extreme regarding the devil, Sacred Scripture is not. Saint John the Apostle writes that the "whole world is under the power of the evil one" (1 John 5:19). Satan and his adversaries are at home this side of the grave. Their war is waged against the children of light who give testimony to the faith and remind the world that the reign of God will endure into eternity unencumbered by the dark and destructive power of evil.

Tormented by the horrific manner of Mary's death, I wondered what thoughts raced through her mind when she was taken by force. I wondered what she suffered. I wondered about her being so isolated and so alone as she ascended the "Hill of Golgotha." Those thoughts remained with me as I celebrated the joyous Feast of Christmas — the peace-filled Feast of the Incarnation.

My consolation came the day after Christmas, a day when the Church wisely celebrates the Feast of St. Stephen, the first Christian martyr. The martyrdom of St. Stephen incarnates the words of Jesus that "the kingdom of heaven suffers violence and violent men take it by force" (Mat 11:12). These words of Jesus echo the prophecy of Simeon. While gazing on the Virgin of Nazareth as she held the Infant close to her heart, Simeon said to her, "This child is destined to be the downfall and the rise of many ... a sign that will be opposed — and you yourself shall be pierced with a sword so that the thoughts of many hearts may be laid bare" (Luke 2:34-36).

When the world first set its eyes on the Babe of Bethlehem, the Herods of the world awakened. Their illusory kingdoms were threatened, and their consciences were disturbed. They set out to destroy the tiny Infant wrapped in swaddling clothes. In an attempt to ensure that Truth Incarnate be obliterated from the face of the earth, countless innocent infants were slaughtered in search of the Infant Jesus.

Heaven's protective shield preserved the Christ Child until the appointed time when, at the age of 33, Jesus finally met His fate as He was silenced in death and His Spirit released. The fire that had been ignited would eventually spread to all four corners of the world. It was no longer a question of silencing one man. For Jesus was very much alive and actively reproducing His life in the life of His followers.

Sacred Scripture tells us that one of Jesus' followers, Stephen, who was filled with grace and power, was working great wonders among the people. Those who opposed Stephen debated with him, but their arguments could not stand up against the wisdom and the spirit with which he spoke:

> As they heard the things he said, they were cut to the heart and gnashed their teeth at him. But he, being full of the Holy Spirit, looked up to heaven and saw the glory of God, and Jesus standing at the right hand of God; and he said, "Behold, I see the heavens opened, and the Son of Man, standing at the right hand of God." But they cried out with a loud voice and stopped their ears and rushed upon him all together. And they cast him out of the city and stoned him … And while they were stoning Stephen he prayed and said, "Lord Jesus, receive my spirit." And falling on his knees, he cried out with a loud voice, saying, "Lord, do not lay this sin against them" (Acts 7:54-60).

On the Feast of St. Stephen, I realized that as Mary Stachowicz ascended the "Hill of Golgotha" the heavens opened and she, too, beheld the *glory of God and Jesus, standing at the right hand of the Father.* Jesus had reproduced His life in the life of this woman. She was no stranger to the evil that lurks to silence the good that God does. What actually went through Mary's mind as she suffered the blows to her body remains a mystery to all of us, but undoubtedly God's favor was with her.

In the deep sorrow of Mary's wake, her family remained as poised and as dignified as they had been during the exuberant joy of her daughter's wedding. They were noble and grace-filled. On both occasions, my heart whispered ever so softly, "Mary, you did well." At her wake, I recalled a comforting passage from the Book of Revelation: "Happy now are the dead in the Lord! Yes, they shall rest from their labors, for their good works accompany them" (Rev 14:13).

When Mary crossed the street from the church to the funeral home, she crossed over from one world into another. Separated only by several yards, the doors of the church and the doors of the funeral home face each other as if to remind us that indeed life in this world is passing away. We are on a journey. At a given moment in time, we shall pass through the door of death and, one by one, behold God who will render judgment on the manner in which we lived our lives. The passage through the door of death will be a walk from one kingdom into another — indeed, from the paradise of the proud to the halls of the humble.

There can be no doubt that something is terribly wrong these days. Something has gone awry. The Luminous Woman is in the belfry marking the last hour. The call to sanctuary is a call to return to the burning bush. Just as God called out to Moses from the bush engulfed in flames, He calls out to us from the fire that burns within us. As in the time of Moses, so now in our time, God sees the affliction of His people and knows what they suffer. He wants to set them free. Moses was sent in his time and we are sent in our time. This is the only time we have and the time is running out. The very soul of Christianity depends on our response to being fully consumed in the fire of God's love. What we bring to the world is not ourselves. We bring Jesus.

If Christians remain spectators — if they do not enter into the drama of God's ongoing revelation of Himself in history — they deprive the world its right to the truth. If Jesus has become an afterthought and if we show no passion for the sacred mysteries of our faith, then we have dishonored and betrayed our ancestors, the prophets and the saints, upon whose blood the Church was built. The world deserves to see that we are who we claim to be — disciples of The Divine Mercy. The world has the right to embrace Jesus or to take Him by force.

Our way is not an easy way. Jesus promised only three things to those who follow Him. He promised the cross. He promised peace. He promised light. This side of death, the cross alone remains our perpetual companion. The call to sanctuary is a call to grow in the knowledge and experience of His peace. It is a call to come into the light. It is a call to be His peace and His light as the world struggles to be set free from confusion and darkness. The peace and the light always suffer the assault of evil. Their perfection and their brilliance will be fully realized only after we pass through the door of death.

17

BRING BACK THE ANGELUS

December 2002

As preliminary plans for the building of the Sanctuary of The Divine Mercy get under way, I remain attentive to the hidden presence of the Blessed Virgin Mary as I listen to her prophetic voice heard so often in silence. In the year 2000, after some years in disrepair, the bells of St. Stanislaus Kostka rang only for a brief time. The miraculous ringing of the bells marked the arrival of the Icon of The Divine Mercy and in the same moment the death of Ray Garza. Ray had been the custodian of the statue during its sojourn through the city of Chicago. Shortly, thereafter, the bells ceased to ring.

Now, three years later, after receiving a donation for a new bell system, I wasted no time in purchasing it and having it installed. Even before the Sanctuary is constructed, I have obeyed Our Lady's request for its immediate opening. She calls us to unceasing and persevering prayer. The bells ring, then, in response to her summons to pray. Daily, they announce the commencement of the morning and evening Masses as well as the evening Rosary. At 3:00 in the afternoon, the *Profundis* rings in commemoration of the death of Jesus with the call to observe the Hour of Great Mercy. The bells also ring at 6:00 in the morning, 12:00 noon and 6:00 in the evening to mark the Angelus. The bells, then, not only mark the movement of time, they are a call to prayer. We are in a time of grace, and this is the hour of mercy. In the dark of night, when the clock strikes 12:00, judgment will be rendered.

HER SUMMONS TO PRAY

The day after the installation of the bells, I awoke with thoughts of the Angelus milling through my soul. Naturally, when I celebrated Mass that morning for the children of the parish school, I spoke about this ancient prayer which honors the mystery of the Incarnation of Jesus Christ in the womb of the Blessed Virgin of Nazareth. In her consent to the angel's announcement, Mary conceived, and the eternal Word was made Flesh.

I told the children that since the sixteenth century, church bells throughout the world have tolled the Angelus in the morning, at noon, and in the evening. All activity ceased during those moments, as humble reverence for God was observed. I instructed the students that when they hear the toll of the Angelus, they should pause and prayerfully remember that God has not hidden Himself in His heaven beyond the beyond. He became one of us and remains with us.

After Mass that morning, I returned to the sacristy only to behold the glowing face of Patricia Orona. Pat is a quiet, unassuming woman who has worked in the parish for more than a quarter of a century. That morning her eyes were wide open and danced with joy as she excitedly said:

> You may not believe this. When you were speaking to the children about the Angelus — this caught my attention. Two days ago as I passed under the picture of Our Lady outside the chapel, I heard as clear as day, the beautiful voice of a woman say, 'Bring back the Angelus.' I didn't even know what the Angelus was. I've said nothing to no one, but I

couldn't shake that voice and those words from my mind. And, then, as I'm thinking about that voice and those words, there you are, Father, speaking to the children about the Angelus.

THE ULTIMATE ACT OF HUMILITY

Our Lady's words to Pat only confirmed what was stirring in my soul. The emphasis on the Angelus is her response to a world that has so arrogated itself that it refuses to contemplate with any seriousness the mystery of God who condescended and in humility clothed Himself in our humanity.

Her call to build the Sanctuary of The Divine Mercy on parish grounds is heaven reaching into the world to remind us that Jesus is the single most important figure in human history. He is the Christ. He is humanity's salvation and the means to its sanctification. His conception by the Holy Spirit in the womb of the Blessed Virgin Mary and His crucifixion and death are gestures that express the ultimate act of humility. God humbled Himself. He threw Himself into the face of evil, knowing that He would be taken by force, His power manifested in humility.

In humility, God showed Himself in the nakedness of a child when the light of a star illuminated the dark of night, and Jesus was born of the Virgin Mary. In humility, God's nakedness was wrapped in His own Blood, as with an eclipse of the sun darkness covered the earth in the light of day. There, atop the Hill of Golgotha, Jesus, unashamed to call us brothers, took upon Himself our sins and offered His life in expiation. Battered, beaten, bruised, and bloodied, Jesus' crucified body lay in the arms of His grieving mother before being banished to the dark of the tomb. He walked us from one kingdom into another when on the third day He rose from the dead. We draw our strength, then, from the mighty power of the Risen Lord. It is in this power that we brace ourselves to fight for the very soul of Christianity.

Jesus is the very soul of Christianity. He is the Incarnate God. The sacred mystery at the heart of sanctuary is God becoming Flesh and Blood. This is the Holy Eucharist — the Blessed Sacrament — the Body, the Blood, the Soul and the Divinity of Jesus Christ in the appearance of bread. The Holy Eucharist is the Holy of Holies — the hidden treasure — the *pearl beyond price*. This is the heart and soul of Catholic spirituality. The Holy Eucharist is heaven reaching out to humanity. In the Sacred Host, we behold the mysteries of Incarnation and Redemption. We lie prostrate in adoration before the humble manifestation of God, and we behold our strength in His humility.

18

THE SEARCH FOR SANCTUARY

February 2003

The realization that we are truly known, loved, and served by God lies at the heart of Catholic sanctuary, but we too often avoid the holy encounter through the proliferation of noise. Soothing songs are sung, wonderful words are written, and powerful preaching is performed but seemingly only to placate Jesus and keep Him forever at a comfortable distance. We consciously avoid stepping into the silence of sanctuary in order not to suffer the sword that pierces the soul and the spirit and penetrates the joints and the marrow.

In the silence of sanctuary, we are not hidden from Jesus. We are naked and exposed to the eyes of Him to whom we must render account. It is the infiltration of excessive noise within the sacred space of sanctuary that has obscured the mystery of mercy and made a mockery of the Church's mysticism. The purity of the Church's prayer and ritual is cloaked in the clamor of sound, shielding the surest means to sanctification in the silent search for solitude in the Sacred Species.

DISPOSED TO THE HOLY ENCOUNTER

It is my search for sanctuary that has led me to seek the sacred in places near and far. From the peasants in Poland to the mystics in Mexico, I have found the jewel of Catholic spirituality incarnate in the faith of a people whose simplicity and humility make them disposed for the holy encounter.

When I was a seminarian, I spent four months in Poland studying the language and culture at the Jagiellonian University in Kraków. While I was there, I traveled alone through the country and absorbed a strong spirituality nurtured through centuries of long suffering. I also visited my grandmother's family in the villages of Swiecany and Widac. I was so humbled by the sincerity of their piety that I could not bring myself to tell them I was studying for the priesthood.

During this visit, I came to understand the faith of my saintly grandmother, Ludwika Depczynska. During her periodic visits to our family home, my grandmother sowed the seeds of my spirituality. The Rosary and the Holy Eucharist were the pillars of her faith. It was no wonder to me that she, who was born on August 15th, the Feast of the Assumption of the Blessed Virgin Mary into heaven, died September 8th, only days after I had returned to the United States. September 8th is the feast of the birth of the Virgin Mary.

In Mexico as in Poland, I experienced the mysticism of a deep Catholic spirituality. Prayer was as natural to these people as breathing. They spoke of the Virgin and of the Christ with the familiarity that one speaks of a best friend or a dearly loved member of the family.

On one occasion, I was deeply moved by the humble faith of a family suffering grief at the death of their patriarch. I had joined the family in the novena of prayers offered for the repose of the soul of this *anciano*. We gathered each evening to pray at the *tapete*, a beautiful carpet made from painted sand, bearing the colorful image of Our Lady. The *tapete* marked the spot where the patriarch had died.

Surrounded by the fragrance of freshly cut flowers and the warm scent of burning candles, there was a stillness and silence that permeated the softly spoken litany of "Ave Marías" as the mysteries in the life of Jesus were contemplated. The nine days of prayer culminated in the celebration of the Holy Mass followed by a procession to the cemetery where the *tapete* was laid over the grave of the deceased. Afterwards, a quiet fiesta was celebrated in the home of the patriarch as a gesture of transition from the pause demanded by the death of a loved one before returning to the rhythm of life's labor.

REVIVAL OF CATHOLIC MYSTICISM

During the Great Jubilee Year 2000 of the Incarnation, I had the privilege of leading pilgrims on three different occasions through the Holy Land and Rome. I also spent three weeks in a private pilgrimage with a friend, Christian Lubinski. We traveled to various sanctuaries in Portugal, France, Spain, and Italy.

By the time the Jubilee 2000 had begun, it had been a few months since I had formally consecrated my life, making myself a slave to Jesus through the Blessed Virgin Mary. I gave Jesus and Mary the absolute freedom to do with me as they wished. I had reached a point in my life where I knew a change was needed. I simply could no longer straddle a fence in the debate between the secular and the sacred, or between the conflicting spiritualities and the ecclesiologies unofficially dividing the Church.

I was determined no longer to wallow in the crisis of priestly identity being fomented by groups propagating their own agendas. Having been raised in a family that quietly respected the opinion of others as almost superior to its own, I seemed always to yield to the counsel of my elders. Internally, I suffered the opinions of so many intelligent and well-spoken priests and religious whose words seemed only an attempt to extinguish the flame of Catholic mysticism that flickered in the inner sanctum of my soul.

Admittedly, at the time I lacked the wisdom of an old man, but at the age of 46, I had seen and heard enough that I would no longer be stifled. Neither would I allow the passion that burned within me to be repressed. There would no longer be any question as to who I am, what I am, or how I am to live. With confidence, I would embrace the truth I had always known and with integrity claim my identity as a priest — the custodian of sanctuary.

As I traveled through the sanctuaries of Europe and Israel, I struggled with a growing desire to abandon my responsibilities as pastor of St. Stanislaus Kostka in order to delve more deeply into my priesthood. I wanted to serve God free of all obstacles. I wanted to rid myself of the pettiness of parish life that too often seemed only to cloud the vision of God's kingdom. I was tired of an endless barrage of meetings that never seemed to accomplish anything, other than to put people at odds with each other.

The task of administration and the burden of finances consumed my energy during the day. Too often, these themes disrupted my sleep, reemerging in my dreams. I was disheartened that so few people really seemed to respond to the invitation to actively participate in the life of the parish.

Stability in the neighborhood had been severely disrupted, as parishioners were being priced out of their homes due to the unjust escalation of property taxes.

Everywhere I turned, I was confronted with a multitude of opinions about what I should be doing or what I was not doing as pastor and priest. Although six Masses were being celebrated every Sunday in three different languages, too often the people in the pews could not see beyond the limits of their own hour of worship to appreciate the complex reality of an inner-city, multi-ethnic, financially poor, and socially diverse parish. And all this, housed in a most beautiful 19th century Romanesque temple that begged for millions of dollars of much needed repair.

After I consecrated my life to Our Lady, I began to imagine that God was inviting me to leave the parish and its problems behind. I wondered whether He was calling me to be an itinerant preacher, a roaming pilgrim priest or, better still, that I would spend the rest of my life in the solitude of a hermitage. I secretly hoped one of these would be the gift He offered me. Instead, He offered me the parish of St. Stanislaus Kostka.

While in Europe and the Holy Land, it was quite clear to me that God was schooling me in the spirituality of the Church. The Holy Eucharist, the Blessed Virgin Mary, and sacred silence would deeply define the unfolding will of God for the tasks that lay ahead. These tasks included my personal sanctification, the sanctification of the parish, and the building of the Sanctuary of The Divine Mercy.

With a discerning spirit, my friend Christian and I never deviated from the holy ground of sanctuary. Even when traveling made the celebration of the Mass impossible, God provided us with holy food for the journey. Once we left a train with only moments to spare and jogged to the nearby bus station for an awaiting connection. Passing a church along the way, we were both compelled to step inside. We had just laid our bags down when, to our delight, we saw that the line of communicants approaching the sanctuary was dwindling down. We were able to receive the Holy Eucharist and within moments boarded our bus to continue our pilgrimage.

Everywhere we went — Fatima, Lourdes, Sacre Coeur, Borgus, Never, Rome, or Assisi — we met others like ourselves. The connections were heartwarming. In Paris, at rue du Bac, the shrine of St. Catherine of Laboure, a small group of newly formed Franciscans approached us. With a certain shyness, they said they had watched us praying at Sacre Coure and, in a whisper, they asked if we were in the reform. I thought for a few brief seconds, wondering what they meant, but wasted no time assuring them that yes, indeed, we were. The reform they spoke of is the regeneration of the faith and spirituality of the saints — the revival of Catholic mysticism. Weeks later, the band of Franciscans found us again in Assisi. Hope is generated by those who seek only to belong to Jesus with the desire to feel His fire burn deep in the recesses of the soul. This light shines in the darkness of the confusion and the complacency gripping the Church these days.

FROM THE CENACLE TO GETHSEMANE

From the sanctuaries of Europe, we traveled to the holy ground of Israel. There we joined more than 40 teenagers in Nazareth to begin a two-week pilgrimage through the places where, 2,000 years ago, the Incarnate God had walked the earth. Every so often I was able to secure some time away from the crowd. While in Jerusalem, I took advantage of a couple of spare hours to return to a recently excavated road that had mesmerized me in a previous visit. This time, as I stood alone alongside that road, I was drawn into a prolonged epiphany. The road begins just outside the wall of Ancient Jerusalem not far from the Cenacle where Jesus celebrated the Last Supper on the eve of His crucifixion. The road passes the house of Caiaphas, the High Priest, and winds its way down a valley to the foot of the Mount of Olives, which is very close to the Garden of Gethsemane.

Arriving at the courtyard of the house of Caiaphas one early afternoon, the heat of a sunlit day turned suddenly to a cool, dark night as I saw Jesus walking down that road flanked by His disciples. He was a free man. Instantly aware that I had just supped with Jesus, I found myself on the road and in the intimate company of the apostles as Jesus shared with us His farewell discourse. He assured us that we would always be a little flock and that He would not leave us orphaned. In Gethsemane, I did not sleep like the rest. Instead, I watched Jesus from a short distance as He suffered alone in prayer. I felt the painful sting of betrayal as Judas branded a kiss into the Blood-stained face of the Master. Then, in horror, my eyes fixed on Jesus, I watched as He was shackled in chains and led back up that road, interrogated in the home of Caiaphas, and held captive until being turned over to the Romans the next morning. Within hours, He was sentenced to death and shortly thereafter carried His cross to Calvary for crucifixion and death.

As I contemplated the events that took place on and alongside that road, I became acutely aware that Jesus had cornered me into a response. He held a choice out to me and only I could make the decision. It seemed to me that He was taking the consecration of my life to the Blessed Virgin Mary with a seriousness that sent fear through my veins. I had to decide whether to continue offering my life in cooperation with Our Lady's plan for the parish. I knew that in doing this Jesus wanted me bound, so that He could be set free. He wanted me dead to myself that He could live.

Having allowed me to walk that road from the Cenacle to Gethsemane, I knew that to refuse Jesus would be to betray Him. I would return to the parish of St. Stanislaus Kostka and resume my walk through the desert's night. I would walk in faith, continuing to feel the assault of evil — forces all around me that consciously or unconsciously worked against the unfolding drama of God's will for the parish.

The greatest battle, though, was fought in the interior of my mind and in the recesses of the soul. Feeling inadequate and incompetent, I so easily succumb to a propensity to laziness or a natural inclination to egocentricity. Rather than lose myself in God, I yield too often to distraction and discouragement as I fight distortions of the mind and the deceptions of the heart. Even so, by God's grace, I have never shirked my responsibilities as a priest and a pastor. I have never taken my eyes away from Jesus, even though He so often makes Himself imperceptible to the senses. All the while, and in spite of me, Our Lady has been consistent and constant in bringing her plan to fruition.

Sowing the Seeds of Sanctuary

Our Lady's request for a sanctuary on the grounds of St. Stanislaus Kostka Parish is in perfect harmony with the desire of my soul. As I am intent on hearing the voice of the prophet, I naturally and restlessly seek the solitude of sanctuary. There can be no prophet without sanctuary. To find one is to find the other. Without sanctuary, my priest-hood would be a farce. Simply speaking I would be a fraud, at least to myself, if not to others.

Our world, so inundated with noise and distraction, creates its own need for sanctuary. The masses, though they claim that they want peace, have no idea where to find it. It is not surprising, then, that peace draws innumerable people to the sanctuary of Medjugorje. A small village in Croatia, Medjugorje, is the place of the alleged apparitions of the Blessed Virgin Mary. I was there in July of 1989 and recall vividly the experience of peace I enjoyed when praying on the Hill of Podbrodo. The hill was the sight of Our Lady's first apparitions to the young people, beginning on June 24, 1981.

There were perhaps a dozen people from my group praying that evening, including Mary Stachowicz. Each one was there on the hill as if alone. From the hill, I could see the church of St. James securely anchored in the small village below. Inside, the worshippers were packed like sardines, while hundreds of others who prayed outdoors snuggled close to the church. In those days, before the war in Bosnia, this was a daily ritual.

It was about 6:30 in the evening, the hour when the young people claim to see and speak with the Holy Mother of God. As I was praying on the hill, I was suddenly aware that a stillness had come over the entire village. The wind didn't blow. The dogs didn't bark. The birds didn't fly. Nothing and no one moved, and there was no noise to be heard anywhere from anyone. Everything and everyone and seemingly time itself stood still. As I pondered the eeriness of it all, from nowhere the soft scent of flowers filled the early evening air and an indescribable peace had enveloped the Hill of Podbrodo.

There was no question that the Blessed Virgin Mary had arrived. She was neither seen nor was she heard. She was just there. Nothing more was needed. Her departure was signaled by the phenomenon of the sun gyrating in the sky, covered by what had the appearance of the Sacred Host, emanating the colors of the rainbow from around its side. Immediately thereafter, life resumed as normal in the village, although the fragrance of her peace remained to varying degrees.

After a few days, I left the holy ground of Medjugorje with a little sadness, knowing that my experience there would be quite a contrast to the rudeness of the world's clamor for attention and the carelessness of its activity. At the same time, I had an intuitive sense that God would sprinkle the world with similar sanctuaries for the tilling of the holy ground that lies hidden within all of us. Sanctuaries like Medjugorje are heaven's way of sowing the seed of God's life in the sacred soil of our interior sanctuaries — sanctuaries buried in the depths of the soul.

Custodian of the Sanctuary

Soon after I returned to Chicago I was devastated as God seemed to withdraw His affection from my life. That is when I began the long sojourn through the dry of the desert. Ten years later, after making myself a slave to Jesus and Mary, I would leave the desert and walk into the dark of night, there to be guided only by His light. Heaven's call for a Sanctuary of The Divine Mercy is the fruit of the desert's dryness and the night's darkness. Saint Stanislaus Kostka is destined to be an oasis of life-giving water — illuminated by the light of the Risen Lord and wrapped in the silence of Our Lady's prayer.

As I continue my spiritual journey, it becomes increasingly clearer to me that as a priest I am principally the custodian of sanctuary. I believe the health and holiness of the Church depends on sanctuary. A people's thirst for God deserves to be satisfied and those in darkness should have access to light. In order for God's voice to be heard, silence must prevail. Sanctuary is that place where heaven kisses the earth in a most unique and profoundly mystical way. It is the place where we encounter the Incarnate God. Sanctuary is the holy ground where the strength and power of God's humility arms us to confront a world whose dangerous lack of humility sounds the death knell to humanity.

19

AWAKENING THE SLEEPING GIANT

March 2003

The world today is caught in the grip of evil's seduction and drowns in its poison, lusting after the illusion that self-adulation supercedes reverence for God. A world deceived into believing that God is not a reality to be reckoned with is a world that breeds sickness. Even within the hallowed halls of the holy Church, the perversion of the power of this lie has seduced her members and obscured the sacred domain of sanctuary. Perhaps, unconsciously, we've shrouded the sacred in an impenetrable veil through secularism or sheer laziness, or worse still, we've consciously desecrated the sacred, gouging the eyes from the holy face of God that we not be exposed to Him to whom we must render account.

When sanctuary is disturbed, Jesus exercises the passion of a warrior, as shown repeatedly in Sacred Scripture. He vehemently admonishes the Pharisees and the Scribes for their hypocrisy, for their lack of compassion, for their arrogance. Jesus exposes their malice and their deceit. He shows them to be superficial and unwilling to submit to the sacred authority of the living and true God. Rather than foster the kingdom of God, which they embody, they serve only themselves. Their pride makes them most destructive to the opening of the sanctuary to those seeking to be free from the grip of the evil one. As it was then, so it is today. The merciful mission of God is most disturbed by the very people who bear His Holy Name. The throne of God must be accessible to all, and its custodians must be ambassadors of the kingdom of God and disciples of The Divine Mercy.

HIS LIGHT EXPOSES THE DARKNESS

Within weeks of receiving word that the Sanctuary of The Divine Mercy would be financed, I followed the promptings of the Spirit and readjusted and reprioritized the pulse of parish life. A parish once oriented around programs would now become a parish oriented around prayer. At first glance, I seem to be stating the obvious. But in reality, priests are so pressured into sustaining and participating in a multiplicity of programs, meetings, services, committees, and councils that the Sacraments and prayer run the risk of being relegated to an afterthought. It is as if the institution of the Church has created its own tools to distract and divert attention from the sacred character of the priesthood and the primary purpose of the parish to worship God, to save, to sanctify, and to heal.

As I bound myself and made the daily ritual of prayer and the celebration of the Sacraments a priority, I quickly began to experience the beginnings of a newfound freedom. Having made myself a slave, I knew I was being formed in the spirituality of the Blessed Virgin Mary. I felt free to no longer keep hidden what I always knew to be true. Namely, the complexity of opinions and activities in the Church today either overwhelm us into paralysis or keep us scurrying about from one agenda to another, one psychology to another, one spirituality to another, one ecclesiology to another, or one moral thought to another.

My consecration and subsequent call to sanctuary would free me to give less attention to the voices of the masses and full attention to the simplicity with which heaven speaks. Simply stated, heaven also confirms the pain I feel in my soul. The road is narrow, and the kingdom is taken by force. The soul's most dangerous and destructive enemy comes from within. Too often, hidden beneath the guise of sheep, are wolves that, perhaps unknown to themselves, devour the sheep. Pride, pomposity, sloth, egocentricity, and arrogance do more harm to the mission of the Church than those in the world who profess to be unbelievers or with honesty show their disdain for the Christ.

Having been invited to walk in the intimate company of Jesus and Mary, I am keenly aware of my own propensity to egocentricity. This frightens me so much that I beg daily that God not permit me to get in the way. I understand clearly how Peter dropped to his knees when for the first time he saw and heard the words and deeds of Jesus. Peter's lament that Jesus should go away from him often rings true in my soul, as I seem to behold the Master each day as if for the first time. Just as Simon Peter had, in the holiness of the Christ, I perceive the depth of my own sinfulness. The humility of God is humbling because His light exposes the darkness.

THE VIRTUE OF DISCIPLESHIP

The marvel of God's perfection is that He extends His hand to sinners, not only to clothe them in mercy, but also to make them sharers in His mission to redeem, sanctify, and heal a sinful, ailing, and despairing humanity. As Jesus lifted Peter from his knees to make him a fisher of men, He has so graciously called me and countless others into the same mission. The Holy Father himself, the successor of Peter, has expended every ounce of his God-graced authority and strength to awaken the Church to this very specific call — to set aside all fear and to claim and exercise the virtue of discipleship in Christ.

The heroism of Pope John Paul II has given me the courage to lose everything for Jesus. His own slavery to the Blessed Virgin Mary gives me the strength to stand firm against those who dismiss the humble and the pious as somehow synonymous with littleness and weakness. These virtues of the Holy Mother of God hold within themselves the very power and authority of God. Through these virtues, heaven will manifest itself and indeed confound the wise and mighty of this world. Oh, that the sleeping giant would awaken to her call!

20

JESUS IS KNOCKING

April 2003

In the belfry, marking the last hour, the Blessed Virgin Mary calls us to sanctuary. Ultimately, sanctuary is the inner sanctum that is deep in the soul — the dwelling place of God within all of us. There she calls us to pray constantly, perseveringly, and attentively. There the flame flickers, waiting to be rekindled.

In the Gospels, Jesus says He comes to light a fire on the earth. He shows zeal, that it be already ignited, forewarning us that in the last hour evil will increase and the love of most will grow cold, but He says, the good news of the kingdom will be proclaimed throughout the world as a witness to the nations. Following the example of the Virgin of Nazareth and the witness of countless others who precede her and come after her, we give our consent to God's free use of our lives. In the company of the prophets and the saints who burned with desire, we too permit God to ignite within us that same desire to be sent.

With urgency, the Blessed Virgin Mary has requested that a sanctuary be built on the grounds of this parish and is sprinkling the world with similar sanctuaries.

In sanctuary, the Blessed Virgin calls us back to Nazareth to the room of the Annunciation. Wrapped in the silence of her prayer, we are called to imitate her steadfast attention to

God and to surrender our lives in obedience. In doing this, we give our consent to God's free use of our lives.

AWAKENED TO THE SOUND OF GOD'S VOICE

In sanctuary, we return to Bethlehem to adore the Prince of Peace. There, He offers us the gifts of gold, frankincense, and myrrh. He makes us priests, prophets, and kings. He clothes us in dignity, grace, and nobility. He receives our sacrifices. He sends us to be lone voices in the desert calling for the repentance of sin and the conversion of hearts.

In sanctuary, we follow Jesus, Mary, and Joseph to Egypt. There we find refuge from the world's Herods who seek to destroy us — refuge from the assault of evil — refuge from the lion that endlessly prowls, ready to devour its prey.

In sanctuary, Our Lady calls us to Cana and Capernaum. There we listen to Jesus, and we do whatever He tells us to do. There we witness His power to give sight to our blindness and to set us free from what holds us captive. There we are delivered from the dungeon of darkness and set free from the oppression of the devil.

The Blessed Virgin calls us to sanctuary. She invites us to follow Jesus into the lonely places of the desert, the wilderness, or the top of a mountain. There we are nurtured in the intimate love of God who knows us, loves us, and serves us. There we discern His divine will. In sanctuary, we return to Gethsemane and Golgotha to contemplate the Suffering Servant. We are consoled in our loneliness, and we find empathy when we have been abandoned, betrayed, or rejected. We unite our sufferings to His, and rest in His compassion.

The Virgin Mary calls us to the empty tomb, to see beyond the cross, and to behold the glory and light of the Risen Christ. She assures us that we are not condemned to the sorrows of suffering or the grief of the grave.

In sanctuary, Our Lady opens the door to the Cenacle where Jesus has reserved a place for us at the altar of sacrifice — the table of the banquet. In her company, He feeds us with His Body and Blood and fills us with the Holy Spirit. He transforms us into disciples of mercy, making us instruments of His peace and carriers of love. Where there is despair, we become beacons of hope. Where confusion paralyzes, we become pillars of truth.

In the belfry marking the last hour, the holy Mother of God awakens us to the sound of God's voice. As with the young boy Samuel who slept in the temple where the ark was, she prods us to open our ears, our eyes, and our mouths — to wake from sleep. She is the ark holding within her the Holy of Holies. As Eli, the priest instructed Samuel, she is instructing us. Wrapped in the silence of her prayer, we listen. In sanctuary, Jesus calls us by name and we respond, "Speak Lord, Your servant listens." Our Lady is marking the last hour. She will not permit the cacophony of the world to shout into silence the voice of the living God. She calls us to sanctuary.

The Blessed Virgin's call to build a sanctuary of The Divine Mercy is a defense against the rude noise of a world that behaves as if God is not a reality to be reckoned with — a world that breeds social, psychological, and spiritual sickness. Rather than drown in the spewed poison of the evil one, we humbly surrender our lives to Jesus — we drink at the fountain of His mercy. We seek refuge in God who humbled Himself and shared in our nature in all things but sin. He threw Himself into the face of evil, knowing that the kingdom of heaven would be taken by force.

We brace ourselves to fight for the very soul of Christianity — the full realization of God's mercy as revealed in Jesus Christ to bring salvation and sanctification to all. The call to sanctuary is a call to be armed against the ensuing battle and to be made warriors in the image and likeness of Jesus. Saint Paul warns us that on the day of evil, we shall do all that our duty requires and hold our ground. The transforming grace that flows from Jesus, the jewel of Sanctuary, will clothe us in the armor identified by St. Paul.

> We stand fast, with the truth as the belt around our waist, justice as our breastplate, and zeal to propagate the gospel of peace as our footgear. Always we hold faith up before us as our shield and we take the helmet of salvation and the sword of the Spirit in defense against the fiery darts of the evil one. (Eph 6:14-17)

IN HIS IMAGE

To be donned in these weapons of the Holy Spirit is to be made to act in the imitation of the Christ. It is true that the prophets lived and died for these days. The prophetic voice of the Church needs to resound loud and clear throughout the world in this our time. The saints of old have cautioned us to watch for the signs. Their voices echo through the ages that, as the Blessed Virgin Mary preceded the first coming of Jesus, she will prepare the world for His Second Coming. She is now in the belfry marking the last hour and calling us to sanctuary. When the clock strikes 12, judgment will be rendered.

As we embark on holy ground and approach the throne of God to be washed in the blood of the Lamb, we wrap ourselves in silence. We remove our shoes and cover our heads. We beat our breasts and bow our bodies. Because we have sinned, we are beckoned to the bath of blood. We come to sanctuary in our names and in the name of humanity to atone for our sins and those of the whole world. The hour is penitential.

In St. John's apocalyptic vision, he describes seeing a multitude of innumerable people from every nation, race, culture, and tongue. They stand before the throne and Lamb, dressed in long white robes and holding palm branches in their hands. They cry out in a loud voice, "Salvation is from our God, who is seated on the throne, and from the Lamb" (Rev 7:10).

One of the elders asked St. John, "Who do you think these are, all dressed in white? And where have they come from?" (Rev 7:13). The Apostle responded, saying to the elder, "Sir, you should know better than I." The elder replied, "These are the ones who have survived the great period of trial; they have washed their robes and made them white in the blood of the Lamb" (Rev 7:14).

Christians are indeed suffering a great period of trial as the Church enters an era of bloodless martyrdom. The faith of the Church is being taken by force from without as well as from within. The mass apostasy that St. Paul describes in his letter to the Thessalonians is upon us, as faith is repudiated by those who by virtue of Baptism bear the imprint of Christ.

The living and true God, who condescended and in humility clothed Himself in our humanity, offers us an opportunity to be transformed into His own image and likeness. In humility, we repent of our pride and arrogance and we reverence God, who holds our destiny in the palm of His hand. The prophets warn us of the consequences of our choice to not pay Him homage. Sooner or later, left to ourselves, we discover our wretchedness, corruption, and misery. When the illusory kingdoms pass away, only His kingdom will endure.

TO SPEAK TO OUR HEARTS

The Blessed Virgin Mary exercises her prophetic office in her request for a sanctuary on these grounds. She echoes the words of the prophet Hosea, calling us into the desert in order to speak to our hearts. She asks that we come as in the days of our youth, when innocence made the heart receptive to the breath of God's Spirit. She wishes to espouse us forever in right and in justice, in love and in mercy. She will espouse us in fidelity that we come to know, love, and serve the Lord.

Jesus is at the door knocking. In our reluctance to respond, the Blessed Virgin Mary points to her Immaculate Heart, opens the door, and invites us to behold our victory. She is the ark holding within her the jewel of sanctuary, inviting us to adoration. She is the fountain that brings forth life-giving water, inviting us to drink. She is the altar which bore the sacrifice of Him in whose Blood we are redeemed.

Every generation has its time, and this is our time. This is the only time we have.

Remember I am coming soon! I bring with Me the reward that will be given to each man as his conduct deserves. I am the Alpha and the Omega, the First and the Last, the Beginning and the End! Happy are they who wash their robes so as to have free access to the tree of life and enter the city through its gates! Outside are all those who love false-hood. It is I, Jesus, who have sent My angel to give you this testimony. I am the root and offspring of David, the Morning Star shining bright. The Spirit and the Bride say, "Come!" Let him who hears answer, "Come!" Let him who is thirsty come forward; let all who desire it accept the gift of life-giving water. Amen! Come Lord Jesus! Come! (Rev 22:12-17; 20).

21

MEETING WITH THE CARDINAL

May 2003

The day of the long-awaited meeting with the Cardinal Archbishop of Chicago had finally arrived. I awoke in the morning with excitement and anxiety, already eagerly anticipating an end to the new day that would bring joyful rest in the knowledge that the sanctuary would carry the Cardinal's affirmation and blessing. Instead, I would lie down to a sleepless night suffering what seemed to be a strong reprimand from the Cardinal, softened only by the ever-so-faint, but consoling presence of the Holy Mother of God.

The day before the meeting, Fr. Seraphim Michalenko, MIC, had arrived along with others who formed a consultative body for the design of the Sanctuary of The Divine Mercy. Father Seraphim had been the vice-postulator for the cause that investigated and promoted the canonization of Maria Faustina Kowalska. The canonization took place on April 30, 2000, making her the first person raised to sainthood in the new millennium. Through her diary, the message of The Divine Mercy had been inaugurated as a sign of the times we live in.

By 9:00, we were gathered in the rectory at St. Stanislaus Kostka for a preliminary session to prepare for our meeting with Francis Cardinal George. We were scheduled to meet the

Cardinal at 2:00 in the afternoon in the chancery. Our morning deliberations went well, with everyone animated and eager to start a new chapter in the unfolding story of The Divine Mercy at St. Stanislaus Kostka.

After arriving in the chancery, we waited about a half an hour for the Cardinal, who had been delayed due to a previous meeting he had attended. As we waited, out of nowhere, voices from the most recent and distant past began to harmonize in a chorus of lament that accused me of fraud, fanaticism, naiveté, and neglect — as if to negate the integrity and credibility of the Sanctuary of The Divine Mercy. I started to feel as though *A Mother's Plea* might be a mere fable. I was under attack and seemingly without the armor and weapons needed to defend myself. It never crossed my mind that in these moments, I may have been the victim of a vicious assault of the devil. The longer we waited, the more anxious I felt and the more nervous I became. The weight of my insecurities began to overwhelm me at the thought of speaking before a man of such authority, bearing, and intelligence.

My level of confidence was plummeting at a pace I could not control as I thought about what I was about to do. I, a mere priest, was about to present to the Cardinal Archbishop of Chicago the conceptual plan for a sanctuary that I claimed was under way at the request of the Blessed Virgin Mary. In retrospect, I wish that in that moment, I had recalled the Gospel story of Peter walking on water enveloped by the wind of a fierce storm. If I had, I may have spared myself one of the most embarrassing and humiliating experiences of my life.

> Immediately after feeding the five thousand, Jesus dismissed the crowd and insisted that the disciples get into the boat and precede Him to the other side. When He had sent them away, He went up on the mountain by Himself to pray,

remaining there alone as evening drew on. Meanwhile the boat, already several hundred yards out from shore, was being tossed about in the waves raised by strong headwinds. At about three in the morning, Jesus came walking toward them on the lake. When the disciples saw Him walking on the water, they were terrified. "It is a ghost!" they said, and in their fear they began to cry out. Jesus hastened to reassure, them: "Get hold of yourselves! It is I. Do not be afraid." Peter spoke up and said, "Lord if it is really You, tell me to come to You across the water." "Come," He said. So Peter got out of the boat and began to walk on the water, moving toward Jesus. But when he perceived how strong the wind was, becoming frightened, he began to sink and cried out, "Lord, save me!" Jesus at once stretched out His hand and caught him. "How little faith you have!" he exclaimed. "Why did you falter?" Once they had climbed in the boat, the wind died down. Those who were in the boat showed Him reverence, declaring, "Beyond doubt You are the Son of God" (Mt 14:22-33).

I had indeed faltered in my faith and turned my eyes away from Jesus. After the Cardinal arrived, I began a presentation on the conceptual design of the sanctuary. I started to further sink as I felt my mouth go dry and my head begin to throb, followed by an inability to speak in any intelligent and coherent way. The Cardinal began to react strongly to my poor presentation, which only exacerbated my already exaggerated sense of insecurity. I was caught in a place from which I could not escape and began to despair as I watched my vision of the Sanctuary of The Divine Mercy explode into oblivion before the eyes of my soul.

As the embarrassing ordeal came to an end, the Cardinal, looking disturbed and racked with fatigue, departed in seriousness. His last words to me as he walked through the door were, "I want the Sanctuary and I do believe it will be a place of pilgrimage." While the Cardinal's words lifted me from the depths of the darkness of total despair, I remember thinking that if indeed it was God's will that there be a sanctuary, He certainly had chosen the wrong person to help make it a reality.

I left the chancery feeling a sickening humiliation. I was determined to get as far away as possible from the things of God. I wanted no part in this plea of the Holy Mother, which seemed in the moment only to be a frightening figment of my imagination.

After returning to the rectory, I immediately went to the chapel to pray while the donor and another member of the team, Oscar I. Delgado, held a private meeting about matters unrelated to the Sanctuary of The Divine Mercy. In prayer, the spirit groaned in the depths of my soul. I didn't know whether it was my spirit or the Spirit of God. Even though the Cardinal had expressed his desire for the sanctuary, I felt nonetheless that four years of painful discernment had just been thrown into the garbage.

Suddenly, in my desolation, on the threshold of despair, a ray of hope welled within me. The Blessed Virgin Mary would give me a sign. Despite this hope, I left the chapel embarrassed and depressed over all that had happened. I reassuringly told the donor and Oscar that Our Lady would give us a sign. I needed to regain my strength and to restore my confidence. I needed heaven's assurance that I was not losing my sanity.

THE FIRST SIGN

After a brief discussion, the donor left the rectory to begin his long trip home, and Oscar and I went to Greek Town for dinner. I had no appetite and was in no mood to talk to anyone. I wanted to distance myself from all things that resembled anything religious. After four years, I wondered whether I had been duped by the trappings of religion, or again, whether the Sanctuary of The Divine Mercy had been the fantasy of my own imagination. So, while I rarely go out for dinner, that evening I was desperate for a respite from the holy ground of St. Stanislaus Kostka Parish.

The drive to Greek Town is a mere five minutes from the parish. I have an affinity for ethnic places because in a time like ours, when people seem so disconnected, an ethnic ambience expresses continuity with the past and the preservation of identity. The Greek Islands Restaurant was no exception. Although I am not Greek, just walking through its doors that night lent some solace to the somber sense of the lingering limbo engulfing my soul.

After we were shown to our seats, it was only a few moments before the waiter approached our table. He took our order, paused a moment, then looked me in the eye, and asked if I was a priest. I told him I was. He proceeded to ask whether I believed in the Second Coming of Christ and the Last Judgment. Feeling more than disposed for a quick end to the misery of the day, my voice rang with a tinge of arrogance in my quick response to his question. I answered, "Yes, I do believe and hope it would come soon." At that, animated with passion, the young waiter eagerly described being mesmerized from the days of his boyhood by the apocalyptic vision of St. John the Apostle.

I immediately perked up. Beneath the sound of his words, I could almost hear the whisper of a woman's voice promising to rescue me from what seemed the demise of defeat and to rekindle hope that victory had been secured. Without knowing it, this waiter had suddenly become an agent of God's mercy.

I had just spent several days pondering the apocalyptic vision of St. John in preparation for the meeting with the Cardinal Archbishop of Chicago. From the saint's vision, I had drafted a written rendition of the religious iconography that would adorn the Sanctuary of The Divine Mercy. It was no coincidence that now, less than an hour after leaving prayer, enveloped in doubt and believing the conceptual design for the sanctuary was dead, I should be listening to a complete stranger expound on the Book of Revelation.

Our waiter was born and raised in Greece. From his home, he enjoyed a bird's eye view of the rocky island of Patmos, where St. John had been sent into exile as punishment for adhering to his Christian faith. According to tradition, it was on the island of Patmos that the apostle experienced and recorded the apocalyptic vision that forms the Book of Revelation, the last book of the Bible.

His vision shows the ultimate victory that will be fully realized at the end of time when Christ comes in His glory. Saint John describes the final battle that will bring irrevocable defeat to the kingdom of Satan and describes an end to the enduring struggle the Church suffers in her mission to be the holy sacrament that mediates the perfection of God's grace.

My heart burned as the waiter spoke, because I knew that the religious art of the Sanctuary of The Divine Mercy was being designed to portray the apocalyptic vision of St. John. And so, I had no doubt that indeed I should not lose heart. As the waiter left with our order, I looked to Oscar and said, "This is the sign."

THE SECOND SIGN

And, if this wasn't enough, when the waiter returned with our dinner, with full liberty, he sat down beside me. With his chin resting in the palm of his hand and his eyes again illuminated with enthusiasm, he described himself as a man lacking religious depth but deeply intrigued by the writings of Aristotle and Plato as a foundation and preparation for Christian philosophy. Again, I was stunned because, along with the apocalyptic vision of St. John, I had always been keenly interested in the typologies of the Old Testament for the same reason he was attentive to the pre-Christian philosophers.

The full realization of the history and prophecies of the Hebrew Scripture in the story of Jesus and the subsequent birth of the Church shows the wisdom of God's Spirit as ever active in human history. This, too, would be shown in the interior design of the sanctuary. It was precisely in this that my poor presentation before the Cardinal had created confusion and provoked a strong response against the furnishings of the Eucharistic adoration chapel. I again felt confirmed by the discourse of the waiter, who had reminded me of the importance of perceiving the constancy and consistency with which God reveals Himself.

It is from the perspective of the Christ that all history should be read and understood. Indeed, there are degrees and elements of truth to be found in all peoples and in all times, all of which are destined for purification and full realization in the Christ. While the Church may boast of the privilege she enjoys as guardian of this truth, she nonetheless should be humbled by the gross deviations of some of her members, which too often only serve to cloud the vision of God's kingdom and the truth of who Christ is. Deeply grounded in history from the *fiat* of Abraham, and as custodian of truth, the Church's strength and authenticity are known only in humility. The flowering of biblical history is woven through the lives of the humble, and its solitary boast is the Blessed Virgin Mary and the Fruit of her womb.

In the Virgin of Nazareth, we see the constancy and consistency with which God moves through history. The Jewish Mary is the bridge that links the Old and the New Covenants. From a nation specifically chosen by God, God's full revelation of Himself in Jesus Christ came through this humble handmaid of the Lord. Keeping in mind the promise God made to Abraham, that Abraham's descendents would be more numerous than the stars in the sky, the Blessed Virgin's *yes* to the Incarnation was spoken on behalf of her people as well as in the name of all generations to come who would call the Virgin blessed.

From the sojourn of the Israelite community to the catholicity of the Church, God has acted with utmost continuity. In the *yes* of Abraham, the Church was conceived and would gestate in the lives of her ancestors. For centuries in hiddenness, the seed of truth — the seed of God's life — had germinated. The pain of labor began with Mary's *fiat* to the announcement of the angel Gabriel that she had been chosen to conceive and bear the Messiah. The birth was realized 33 years later, when the lance pierced the side of the dead Jesus and Blood and Water gushed forth.

All it took was a few words from the waiter to ignite within my soul the fire of passion for union with the God of history and a connection to all people and to all time. As in Mary's Magnificat, the Sanctuary of The Divine Mercy expresses solidarity with the promises made to our ancestors.

Its realization brings hope that all generations to come will call us blessed for having been faithful to God, who is ever present and active in the here and now.

THE THIRD SIGN

For a third time, towards the end of our meal, the waiter returned and again sat down beside me. As if fulfilling a command, he shared the brief story of the weeping icons. As in his previous two visits, he spoke and I listened. He knew nothing of the journey of faith I had been walking for four years, nor had I spoken about the day's deliberations with the Cardinal. Seemingly out of nowhere and as a matter of fact he said, "Father, nearly 200 years ago pirates came into my town in Greece and robbed the jewels from all the icons of Our Lady. The icons all wept, and to this day, the people of my village weep when they tell the story." Having said this, the waiter's eyes opened wide with sadness, showing shock and grief at such a sacrilege. He stood up and walked away, and I left Greek Town with an image of weeping icons etched in my soul.

That night I lay down to a sleep that would not come. I was grateful that Our Lady had sent the signs, which rescued me from the demise of defeat, but I was bothered by the humiliation I had inflicted upon myself and my potential loss of credibility with the Cardinal. My pride was so strongly felt that I would not allow myself to benefit from the grace of humiliation. Internally I fought to save face, but I didn't know how. I tossed and turned all night, thinking about the people I had misrepresented in the ill-prepared presentation I had made before the Cardinal.

I finally fell asleep, but only moments before I had awakened to greet a new day. In those brief moments I dreamed of the weeping icons of Our Lady. In the dream, I understood the sadness and grief heaven suffers at the loss of faith of so many who claim to be Christians. In the assault of secularization, the Church is being robbed of the jewels of her spirituality — a spirituality deeply rooted in the sacred silence of the Virgin's prayer and the sacrificial mystery of the Holy Eucharist. These two pillars of Catholic spirituality are the soil that breeds a people clothed in the Beatitudes.

The Blessed Virgin Mary's obedience, humility, and trust brought forth the Christ who gave Himself as the sacrificial offering for the salvation and sanctification of sinful humanity. With Mary, we offer our lives in union with Jesus so that He will reproduce the same sacrificial offering in our lives. Transformed and clothed, then, in the Beatitudes, we become true disciples of The Divine Mercy because we have been washed clean in the bath of Blood and Water flowing from the pierced side of Jesus — from His wounded Heart.

The Blessed Virgin Mary is the fountain that brings forth the life-giving water, which is the Christ. She is ever-present in the celebration of the Holy Eucharist and in adoration of the Sacred Species. She is the *altar* that bore the sacrifice of him in whose blood we are redeemed. She is the *ark* of the New Covenant, holding within herself the *Holy of Holies.* Her Son is the jewel of the Church and is perfectly and most mysteriously perceived in the Sacrifice of the Mass. She beckons us to approach the Sacred Mysteries properly disposed, imitating the humility of St. John the Baptist. We decrease that Jesus increase. We lose ourselves that He be found. We die to ourselves that He live. We become, then, what we consume. As with Mary of Nazareth, our souls magnify the Lord.

The sadness and the grief of the weeping icons bewail the loss of faith as symptomatic of a deviation from a Catholic spirituality that is deeply Marian and deeply rooted in the sacrificial nature of the Holy Eucharist. The lives of Mother and Son are so woven together that to see one is to see the other. To know one is to know the other. To love one is to love the other. To serve one is to serve the other. Theirs is the perfect symbol of the marriage between God and His Bride the Church.

TO SERVE AND NURTURE CATHOLIC SPIRITUALITY

Very much at peace with heaven's confirmation of the Sanctuary of The Divine Mercy, I did not hesitate to hand deliver a letter to the Cardinal, expressing my apologies for the inarticulate way I presented the conceptual design of the sanctuary. I left the letter at his office, with a request for further critique of the theological and biblical correctness of the design. I assured the Cardinal that the purpose of the sanctuary is to serve and nurture Catholic spirituality — not to obscure or confuse it. I firmly believe that the sanctuary will assist the faithful in the deepening of their spirituality. Catholic spirituality is grounded in solid tradition and therefore deeply connected to the whole history of God's self-revelation, as finally and fully realized in Jesus Christ.

The Cardinal called me the following day and again assured me of his support for the sanctuary. After reading my written rendition of the conceptual design of the sanctuary, he expressed his approval and said that he would continue to reflect on some areas that may need to be refined. His voice resonated with optimism and kindness. For my part, I breathed a sigh of relief, feeling that I had just been graced with a share in the resurrection of the Lord.

22

THE DEMISE OF THREE MILLION DOLLARS

A Letter to the Parishoners, Friends, and Benefactors of St. Stanislaus Kostka Parish

November 1, 2003

Dear Parishioners, Friends, and Benefactors,

With deep peace and great sadness I wish to share with you my decision not to accept a donation of three million dollars. This donation was designated solely for the building of the Sanctuary of The Divine Mercy and was given as a gesture of faith in the sincerity of my writings as read in the book, *A Mother's Plea*. The donors believe the writings are inspired by the Holy Mother of God and through prayerful discernment, gave the three million dollars in response to her personal call to them.

Despite sincere and genuine efforts and a deep desire to follow Our Lady's plea, the donors, the parish of St. Stanislaus Kostka, and many others who have walked with me in discernment have been caught in a quagmire of confusion and strife so contrary to the spirituality of the Blessed Virgin Mary. I firmly believe that influences beyond my control would compromise the integrity of the vision and threaten to destroy the virtue and credibility of the sanctuary. In conscience, I cannot allow this to happen.

For this reason and aware of the conditions placed on the three million dollars, I currently cannot accept the designated donation. To protect the character of the people involved, I choose not to expound on this matter. My decision not to accept the money is supported by personnel of the Archdiocese of Chicago as well as my spiritual and theological advisors.

I wish to make it clear that we are proceeding with plans for the sanctuary. The spiritual battle we are fighting only strengthens my resolve that this Sanctuary of The Divine Mercy will be built. After a difficult meeting many months ago, the Cardinal assured me that he indeed believes there will be a sanctuary and that it will, indeed, be a place of pilgrimage. Countless others have expressed similar sentiments. The question is not whether or not there will be a sanctuary, rather when and how it will happen. And so, the story of this miracle of The Divine Mercy continues to unfold through most unexpected twists and turns. The Woman and dragon are indeed in battle.

Together, then, let us move forward in faith, and let the good work begun in us come to fruition in due season and due time. May Our Lady truly form us into disciples of The Divine Mercy.

In Christ,

Fr. Anthony Buś, CR

Indeed, the story continues to unfold through the most unexpected twists and turns. After a year of endless struggle, I finally made the decision I had tried prayerfully to avoid making for several months. That I walked away from three million dollars did not grieve me as much as the fact that people were confused, offended, and hurt in what had become a war of wills.

After so many months of struggle and a final meeting that left me convinced that something had definitely gone awry, I understood that the integrity and the credibility of the Sanctuary of The Divine Mercy was at stake and along with it, the integrity and credibility of numerous persons, including the parishioners of St. Stanislaus Kostka and the Archdiocese of Chicago.

I had left the meeting while the heated deliberations continued. I had to prepare for the evening Rosary and Mass. As I prepared for prayer, what most disturbed me was the total lack of regard shown with respect to the ongoing discernment that has consistently confirmed, defined, and refined the sanctuary. From the advice of the Cardinal Archbishop of Chicago to the enthusiasm of the Archbishop of Puebla, Mexico, from theologians to religious and liturgical artisans, from spiritual advisors to the faith of innumerable lay people, *A Mother's Plea* and subsequent preparation for the sanctuary had received the affirmations I needed to proceed with confidence in doing the will of God.

At 6:30, I led the Rosary as I do every evening. As I prayed, in my anger and anxiety, I turned my eyes to Jesus in the Blessed Sacrament and felt the peace of His ever-abiding strength. I was suddenly inundated with all the signs that God had given and all the people who had confirmed the unfolding drama of Our Lady's request that a sanctuary be built according to her design.

Still, peace and harmony had been irrevocably disturbed. I simply could not submit to influences well beyond my control, influences that are contrary to my understanding of the proper discernment of God's will and the exercise of mature spirituality. I could not in good conscience compromise four years of painfully exhilarating discernment. Under current conditions, I would have to say *no* to the gift of three million dollars. Indeed, I did so in deep peace but with great sadness. The purification I undergo daily gives me profound insight into the power of pondering and persevering prayer.

If Our Lady had asked that I distance myself from the donation it was because the devil had gained an authority and a power that he did not deserve through the confusion and unrest he had sown in all of us. Although declining the money under these circumstances was a major set-back to the project that caused me and the parish much grief, I clearly understood that there could be no compromising the sacred in the Virgin's request for the Sanctuary." If heaven has indeed requested the sanctuary, *the gates of hell shall not prevail.*

Since the consecration of my life, and that of the parish, to the Blessed Virgin Mary, I have come to understand how Sacred Scripture and religious verbiage can curtail or hamper the unfolding truth of God's will if not embraced with genuine humility. The Psalms clearly teach us that pride and deceit, being the antithesis of humility and truth, are despicable before the eyes of God.

No matter how many Masses we attend, Rosaries we pray, or Holy Hours we make, if we do not die to ourselves, we may unknowingly become instruments in the hand of the devil, who seeks only to destroy the good that God is and the good that God does. I would be wise not to allow myself to be deceived into thinking that the devil cannot pervert my good intentions. How easy it would be to allow him or to allow myself delusional control over the mysterious movement of God's Spirit.

Pride and deception may have stifled the full flowering of God's kingdom from the beginning of creation, but they cannot stop it from happening. These are the sins that divide the Church, destroy families, wreak havoc on religious orders, and basically perpetuate the devil's domain of darkness. Every war that is waged has its roots in pride and deceit, and the seed of such sins is idolatry.

The sickness of narcissism can bring down a nation, but it cannot destroy the kingdom of God. This is the battle that is written through the pages of history since the beginning of time. It is the story of our lives — the battle against the self that seeks to exalt itself as supremely chosen above all others or, so wounded, that the exaltation of the self is its own perverted preservation.

The healing of the destructive influence of the messianic complex can be learned in the life of Jesus. He, the true Messiah, is the only one who is supremely chosen, and yet He defers to the Father. When in Mark's Gospel, a rich man knelt down before Jesus and asked, "Good Teacher, what must I do to share in everlasting life?" Jesus answered, "Why do you call Me good? No one is good but God alone." Jesus' whole life was a lesson in truth and humility, and all of us chosen in deference to Him would do well to heed His example.

Knowing how obstinate our egos can be, we ask God to save us from ourselves and not let us get in the way of His divine will. In a word, we ask that He save us from the sin of Pharisaism. Failing in their attempts to trip and trap Jesus, some of the Pharisees finally crucified Him. Their pride made them appear successful in their desire to silence Him — at least for three days. As we are people of faith so, too, the Pharisees were men of faith. As we seek to do God's will so, too, they sought to do the will of God. There seems to be so fine a line between the sanity and insanity of religious faith that from the cross Jesus is compelled to beg the Father to forgive the Pharisees for the sickness of their sin. In the end the seeming success of their desire to silence Jesus proved only to serve the divine will of God.

My fervent prayer is that the service I render God be born from truth and genuine humility rather than deceit and pride, whether it is my pride or the pride of others, whether it is my own self-deception or the deceit of others. If I should get in the way or become an impediment to the fulfillment of His divine will, I trust His light will expose the darkness. God, who knows my heart and the stirrings of my soul, will show mercy. I persevere in obedience to Him.

You may for a time
have to suffer the distress
of many trials;
but this is so that your faith,
which is more precious
than the passing splendor of fire-tried gold,
may by its genuineness
lead to praise, glory, and honor
when Jesus Christ appears.

1 Peter 1:6-7

23

THE STATUE OF THE DIVINE MERCY
GOES TO THE CONTINENT OF AFRICA

November 28, 2003

On the evening of November 2ⁿᵈ, feeling severely faint with fatigue, I marked myself with the Sign of the Cross as I began the last Mass of the day. I had been donned in the vestments of the Sacred Liturgy since early morning in what seemed like an unusually long and busy day. As so often happens when drained of all energy, I dreaded hearing again the sound of my own voice. Like a babbling parrot, I would repeat with pain and prudence my decision to decline a three-million-dollar donation. Also ruminating in my mind was the eventual explanation I would give for the departure of the Statue of The Divine Mercy. Both the money and the statue were key symbols in the story of the sanctuary requested by the Blessed Virgin Mary. My faith assures me what seems like loss will prove to be gain in the scheme of God's mysterious movement through this unfolding story.

The grace I have to be passively active affords me the ability to write as I pray and to pray as I write. In these moments of grace, God speaks with a clarity that needs no explanation. They become moments of manifestation with God ever present in epiphany. And so, it seems providential that the day I announced to the parishioners my decision to refuse three million dollars, the Statue of Our Lady of the Millennium would arrive and remain on the grounds of the parish for three weeks. I knew then as I write now that this was no mere coincidence. The statue came that Sunday evening, the Day of All Souls and the birthday of Carl Demma, as if to bid farewell to the Statue of The Divine Mercy and to reconfirm Our Lady's request that a sanctuary be built.

The Statue of Our Lady of the Millennium was the inspiration of Carl Demma, who died nearly four years ago on the Feast of Corpus Christi, only hours after leaving St. Stanislaus Kostka. He had come to pray late in the evening on the day we formally received and blessed the newly sculpted statue of The Divine Mercy and was prepared to begin touring the statue through the Chicagoland area the following day.

The Statue of The Divine Mercy was a gift given to St. Stanislaus Kostka several months after the parish was consecrated to the Blessed Virgin Mary. Sculpted in Mexico by Gogy Farias, the statue became the window that opened the eyes of so many to the vision of a sanctuary, which seemed to be designed by Our Lady herself. Four years ago, it never would have crossed my mind that the statue would go anywhere, except the parish of St. Stanislaus Kostka. It remains a key symbol of the consecration that Our Lady requested when she asked that I give her the parish and make her Mother and Queen.

Her request still conjures up my earliest memory of the Mass and hearing for the first time the words of the *Salve Regina*. I may have been about four years old. I was in a darkened church and recall the sound of people's footsteps against the hard floor. This was the only sound that broke the stillness of the silence that made me know I was in a place unlike any other. The darkness was pierced by the illumination of the elevated Host. The only spoken words I recall were the first words of the "Salve Regina" — "Hail, Holy Queen, Mother of Mercy." This is my first memory of Mass. Probably spoken at the close of the liturgy, the profound impact of this prayer slept secure in the deep recesses of my soul until awakened by the Blessed Virgin Mary, who clearly and distinctly asked that I give her the parish — that I make her Mother and Queen.

The Mother of Mercy's request for a sanctuary shows her maternal concern for her children as she longingly lures us to Jesus in this dangerous time in history. As Queen, she wields the sword that pierced her heart. She is in battle against the enemy, whose lust seeks only to destroy her children. Her weapon of war, the sword that split her heart in the spilled Blood of her Son, is the victory of the cross.

On November 2nd, the two statues would greet each other as they had four years ago. Only this time, it would be for the last time. The statue of Our Lady arrived as I celebrated the last Mass of the day. It had begun to rain and would continue to rain almost non-stop for two days.

Trying to explain prudently my decision to walk away from a monetary gift designated for the Sanctuary of The Divine Mercy was not easy. Up to this time, I had been excitedly optimistic in spite of the struggles that led to my decision. But now, while we had come so far and had hoped to begin the construction of the sanctuary in early Spring, my decision not to accept the funds left me bewildered as to when and how I would proceed with the project. The money had come to us at an opportune moment through the prompting of the Holy Spirit and the donors' generous response to what they perceived to be a call from the Blessed Virgin Mary. Indeed, it was Our Lady calling, and, indeed, they had acted in sincere faith.

In declining the donation a year and a half into the project, I also acted sincerely in obedience to the strong soul-felt stirrings of the Holy Spirit. Such seeming contradiction is not surprising if understood in the light and darkness woven through the pages of Sacred Scripture. In my personal journey, I understand more clearly what I have so often heard: It is a narrow but crooked road that leads to the fulfillment of God's will.

After Mass, tired and hungry, I went to my room on the third floor to bring closure to the end of a stressful day. Obedient to the ritual and rhythm of my daily schedule, I sat down in my rocking chair. I would quietly spend the last hour of the day reading, reflecting, and praying before going to sleep. As I sat down, I looked up and saw, perfectly framed by the window, the serene face of Our Lady of the Millennium. Illuminated against the backdrop of night's darkness, her countenance reflected that unique blend of sorrow and joy. The rain rolling down her cheeks gave the impression that she was crying. I was compelled to go outside.

As I stood alone before the 33-foot image of the Blessed Virgin Mary, I felt a deep consolation. Overlooking the ground that would one day be the Sanctuary of The Divine Mercy, it was as if, in power and in strength, the Lady had come in the appointed time to defend and to claim what belonged to her. For our part, we are the characters in her story, and we would do well to be patient and at peace as she turns the pages.

SHRINE OF OUR LADY OF KIBEHO

The following day, Fr. Leszek Czelusniak, MIC, a missionary priest from Africa, arrived to make preparations for the transfer of the 18-foot Icon of The Divine Mercy from the grounds of St. Stanislaus Kostka to the Shrine of Our Lady of Kibeho.

Kibeho is a small village in the Diocese of Butare, which is in Rwanda. From 1981 to 1988, Our Lady appeared to six school-aged girls in the parish of Kibeho and to an illiterate young pagan shepherd who converted to the faith and was baptized in 1983. Father Leszek had served on the Vatican commission that investigated and scrutinized the apparitions of Our Lady in Kibeho, which were deemed credible in June 2001. Even before the Vatican approved the authenticity of the apparitions, Kibeho had already become an international sanctuary and a place of pilgrimage.

In Rwanda, Our Lady, exercising her prophetic office, forewarned that if her call was not heeded there would be the slaughter of a multitude. She said that the rivers would flow with the blood of the dead. In May 1994, the *Chicago Tribune* ran a front page news story claiming that 40,000 corpses had been pulled from the rivers of Rwanda. By the time the genocide ended, over a million lives had been lost.

The central message of heaven's visitation in Rwanda is a call to prayer and penance for the conversion of sinners. Our Lady asked that she be recognized as the Holy Mother of God and that the Rosary be prayed in preparation for the return of Jesus.

Several months ago, while making a retreat in Poland, Fr. Leszek learned about our sanctuary and the Icon of The Divine Mercy. Negotiations and prayerful discernment began, eventually leading to the confident decision that the Statue of The Divine Mercy would go to Africa. The decision to relocate the statue from Chicago to Rwanda was made in view of another statue being sculpted and enthroned on a pedestal ascending from a fountain. Overlooking the Kennedy Expressway and the Chicago skyline, the new statue would rise like a beacon, marking the Sanctuary of The Divine Mercy at St. Stanislaus Kostka.

After having traveled for nearly four years through the Chicago area, it is in the plan of the Blessed Virgin Mary that the statue of The Divine Mercy would rest permanently in its new home overlooking the Shrine of Our Lady of Kibeho. The connection between the Sanctuary of The Divine Mercy at St. Stanislaus Kostka and the sanctuary in Kibeho confirms and clarifies the apocalyptic urgency in the call of the Blessed Virgin, whose plea resonates through the whole world for those who have the ears to hear.

As the Statue of The Divine Mercy is transferred to Rwanda, the message of Our Lady of Kibeho is transferred to the holy ground of St. Stanislaus Kostka. This transfer seals the meaning and purpose of the Blessed Virgin Mary's request that the parish of St. Stanislaus Kostka be consecrated to her and a Sanctuary of The Divine Mercy built. In her apparitions in Kibeho, the Holy Mother of God said, "If I am now turning to the parish of Kibeho or to the Diocese of Butare or to Rwanda or to the whole of Africa, I am concerned with and turning to the whole world."

Each day, as I look at and listen to the details of the lives of people, I wonder whether a genocide has begun in our own land. The shedding of blood is hidden from our eyes, as in secret, the unheard cry of the unborn succumbs to this slaughter. Their deaths are symptomatic of a culture that has turned away from God and seeks to fill the void in the wrong places, with the wrong things, and through the wrong people. The rejection of God and the subsequent renunciation of responsibility for the work of life through the nurturing of faith and family have led to the convenient repudiation of the unborn.

Today the philosophy of life emphasizes the fulfillment of all desire in the reign of the flesh and the exaltation of the self. It is as if the pearl beyond price can be purchased in the sloth of a superficial and shallow idolatry of the things of this world.

The dignity of life's labor has been lost, leaving in its wake a bleeding loneliness that longs for connection in love. If the eyes of the soul do not open themselves to God, the longing for love only leads to a lust at the allurement of the devil, who promises to fill the void. His lies are the deceptions and seductions that create the illusion that the holy work of God can be renounced. The result is the victimization of an entire nation that in turn shows no regard for the jewel of God's creation in the conception and life of the human person.

The shed blood of the unborn reflects the interior dying that happens in the soul of man who suffers his own slaughter when his life is severed from God. The dignity, nobility, and grace of a people are thus lost in addiction and enslavement to the flesh and the passing things of this world. The unborn and, indeed, innumerable people only get in the way. Therefore, they must be silenced in death. The killing may be inflicted in a multiplicity of ways sparing the actual death of the body, but leaving the living to suffer a profuse inner bleeding hidden from the eyes of all. The religious and non-religious share in the suffering because all are victims in a society that shows little or no reverence for God.

This blood being shed is not hidden from the eyes of the Blessed Virgin Mary. The sanctuaries of Kibeho and St. Stanislaus Kostka are signs and symbols of the solicitous care the Holy Mother of God shows for her children. She shows her passion to rescue them from the grip of the evil one. In calling them to sanctuary, she transfers her own concern for souls into the lives of her children, making them zealous disciples of her Son. Having been to the heart of sanctuary, they become *monstrances* of the Real Presence mediating The Divine Mercy. They become *icons* illuminating the grace of God.

Centered, then, in Jesus Christ, the urgent plea to assist and participate in the holy work of redemption for the salvation and sanctification of souls is heard in the wailing of a Mother whose children are being ripped from her womb. She anoints us with the sword that pierced her heart, and she sends us into battle. The call to sanctuary being heard throughout the world is a call to arms, and the weapon for war is the victory of the cross.

You know the time
in which we are living.
It is now the hour for you
to wake from sleep,
for our salvation is closer
than when we first accepted the faith.
The night is far spent; the day draws near.
Let us cast off deeds of darkness
and put on the armor of light.

Romans 13:11-12

24

DEFENSE OF THE
ICONIC MONSTRANCE

December 8, 2003

Then God's temple in heaven opened and in the temple
could be seen the Ark of His covenant. There were flashes of
lightning and peals of thunder, an earthquake, and a violent
hailstorm! A great sign appeared in the sky, a woman clothed
with the sun, with the moon under her feet, and on her head
a crown of twelve stars. Because she was with child, she wailed
aloud in pain as she labored to give birth. (Rev 11:19; 12:1-2).

As long as the sacrifice of the Cross is perpetuated in the celebration of the Holy Eucharist, the Blessed Virgin Mary is in
the pain of labor and with her, the whole Mystical Body of
Christ. The labor of birth and the labor of battle are the
unfolding drama of God's active presence in the world. Even
if, in the view of the world, man is eventually silenced in
death, in the eyes of God, he is awakened to life.

That God becomes man to save humanity from the
darkness of sin and death is an expression of God's humility in
condescension. Conceived of the Holy Spirit and born of the
Virgin Mary, He would die on the Hill of Golgotha to bring
humanity through the threshold of death to the fullness of
life. Even so, having been saved from sin and death, humanity

in pilgrimage continues to sin in the wait for death. Therefore, the salvific and sanctifying grace of the sacrifice of the cross is perpetuated in the celebration of the Mass, that hope be ever enkindled in the victory of the Resurrection of Jesus and the promise that humanity is destined to share in the same Resurrection.

In the interim, in sojourn through the domain of Satan towards the full realization of God's kingdom, the Church is in battle as she births and sustains her children. In the apocalyptic vision of St. John the Apostle, the Church recognizes herself in the sign that appears in the sky. She sees herself in the woman with Child, wailing aloud in pain as she labors to give birth. In a most singular and perfect way, the woman is the Blessed Virgin Mary who, along with her Son, remains ever present and ever active in a world suffering from the assault of evil. They themselves passed through the threshold of death and away from the devil's darkness. Their lives are so intricately woven into the pilgrim Church that they are made defenders in the war waged on their offspring.

As with the ancient Ark of the Covenant, like Mary, the Church holds within herself the *Holy of Holies* and is commissioned to safeguard and show forth the jewel of her faith. She does so with the clear knowledge that Jesus will be taken by force and along with Him, His Body the Church.

COURAGE IN BATTLE

Courage for perseverance in the battle compels the Church to look to Mary, her sister, who by God's choice and by God's authority becomes not only Mother of the Christ, but also Mother of the Church. Only in imitating the Blessed

Virgin's steadfast fidelity to the will of God can the Church effectively and gracefully bring forth the Christ and claim victory in the war waged on her offspring.

Appropriately, the Blessed Sacrament, that is, the Sacred Host, enveloped by one of the most ancient icons of the Blessed Virgin Mary, will be at the heart of the Sanctuary of The Divine Mercy. The icon, which dates back to the earliest centuries of the Church and is commonly called Our Lady of the Sign, evokes the prophecy of Isaiah and the apocalyptic vision of St. John the Apostle. Their prophecies recall the onset of man's salvation in the sign of the woman bringing forth the Child. The monstrance bearing the image of Our Lady of the Sign safeguards and shows the jewel of Catholic spirituality which is the Body, Blood, Soul, and Divinity of Jesus Christ present in the consecrated Host. Both the image of Our Lady and the Blessed Sacrament are symbols of the victory in battle and together define the Sanctuary of The Divine Mercy.

The Virgin of Nazareth remains the solitary boast of the Church because she cooperated with the will of God in absolute perfection and with steadfast fidelity. In the name of her ancestors, the descendants of Abraham, and in the name of all generations who came after her, the whole of humanity, she said *yes* to the mystery of the Incarnation. She, who acted on our behalf 2,000 years ago, remains ever active in history to make Jesus known, loved, and served and to remind a hurting humanity that God knows, loves, and serves His creation.

As word began to spread that at the center of the Sanctuary of The Divine Mercy would be an Iconic Monstrance of Our Lady of the Sign, holding within itself the heart and soul of Catholic spirituality, I was almost immediately inundated with strong objections to this image. The objections came from Catholics who view the image as an impediment to Christian ecumenism. Criticism also came from Catholics strongly devoted to Our Lady and the Holy Eucharist, who expressed opposition on the grounds that the image takes away from the centrality of Christ as the supreme truth of Christian faith. In some cases, even priests were among the critics. They seemed to confirm the concern that, while theologically an argument can be made for the Marian Monstrance, it would reek of hyperbole, that is, exaggerated piety.

Defending the Iconic Monstrance of Our Lady of the Sign gives me the privilege of *anointing* for the cause of the Woman of Sorrows who, wedded to her Son, is solicitous in her concern for the salvation of her children. The Monstrance of Our Lady is a symbol of the Church, whose mission it is to show the Word Incarnate truly born of the Virgin Mary.

At the Annunciation, when the Angel Gabriel greets Mary with the new name, *Kecharitomene* — Full of Grace, the angel testifies that in her and through her there is no obstacle to the full manifestation of the Incarnate God because she is without the stain of sin.

In the ancient covenant, the cloud overshadowed the Ark to signify the presence of God in the midst of His people. Likewise, in the Annunciation, the Holy Spirit overshadows Mary so that God be made present and visible to His people. If 2,000 years ago God, who is ever constant and consistent, showed no shame in fully revealing Himself through the humble Virgin of Nazareth, He would show no shame today. The *shekinah glory* then is the *shekinah glory* now. Mary's consent to actively participate in the will of the Father to send the Son is symbolized in the Marian monstrance as an invitation to all people to share in the same mission. With Mary in the Annunciation, in faith and trust, the Church says *yes* that the Incarnation happen and Jesus be made known.

His Holiness, Pope John Paul II, expressed in his encyclical *The Eucharist and Its Relationship to the Church* that "Mary anticipated, in the mystery of the Incarnation, the Church's Eucharistic faith. When, at the Visitation, she bore in her womb the Word made Flesh, she became in some way a 'tabernacle' — the first 'tabernacle' in history — in which the Son of God, still invisible to our human gaze, allowed Himself to be adored by Elizabeth, radiating His light as it were through the eyes and the voice of Mary" (*Ecclesia de Eucharistia*, Chapter 6, "Woman of the Eucharist").

When the kings and the shepherds prostrated themselves in adoration before the newborn Babe of Bethlehem, Mary did not scurry away for fear she might be the mistaken object of their adoration. In humility, she received the homage due her Son and the veneration shown His mother.

Simeon, vigilant in patient and persevering prayer, awaited the Ark's return to the temple. When his eyes beheld the *Holy of Holies*, his words rang with praise and prophecy. Directed simultaneously to Almighty God and the Woman with Child, he rejoiced for having seen the Savior held so close to the heart of the mother. Rather than blush in embarrassment that attention had been directed away from Jesus, the Virgin of Nazareth pondered the sword sworn to slay both mother and Son.

The Iconic Monstrance of Our Lady of the Sign recalls both the praise of the woman described in Luke's Gospel who rejoiced in the womb that bore Jesus and the breasts that nursed him as well as Jesus' response that "blessed rather are those who hear the Word of God and keep it" (Lk 11:28). Mary is blessed because she bore the Babe of Bethlehem but, most especially, because she acted in perfect obedience to the will of God to the benefit of all God's people. The Monstrance is an expression of the adoration given to the Son and joy in the faith of the woman who trusted that the Lord's promise to her would be fulfilled.

In the Monstrance, as at the wedding feast in Cana of Galilee, we behold in Mary the virgin bride and we adore Jesus, the groom. At the wedding feast, the celebration of marriage has begun. It is consummated at the long awaited hour when, on the Hill of Golgotha, the lance pierces the side of Jesus. The Water and Blood that pour forth give life to the Church. At the foot of the cross, the Mother of Sorrow suffers the pain of labor as her children are birthed. She is the altar that bore the sacrifice of her son through whom she and her children are saved from the slavery to sin and death. Over her heart, the Blood of Jesus is spilled. To adore Jesus in the Iconic Monstrance of Our Lady is also to kiss the altar upon which His Blood was shed.

From the cross, when Jesus looks to his Mother and says, "Woman, behold your son," and to the beloved disciple John, "Son, behold your mother," He calls all disciples into relationship with the Virgin of Nazareth (Jn 19:26-27). He calls us to communion in family. At Pentecost, this communion is evident, as Mary is seen in the Church and with the Church, as the Church, after nine days in a novena of prayer, is empowered. The power that emanates from the Sacred Host in the Monstrance of Our Lady of the Sign is the same power that ignited the flame of the early Church with a passion to live and die in Jesus, with Jesus, through Jesus, and for Jesus. In the Iconic Monstrance of Our Lady, the Church expresses union with Mary in the surrender of its life to Jesus. With Mary, the Church — vigilant and pondering — perseveres in prayerful preparation for the coming of the Christ in the splendor of glory at the end of time.

WOMAN OF THE APOCALYPSE

Unwarranted fear that the Iconic Monstrance of Our Lady of the Sign would be offensive to God serves only to perpetuate the admonishment to Ahaz. When the Lord spoke to Ahaz, he said:

> Ask for a sign from the Lord your God; let it be deep as the nether world, or high as the sky! But Ahaz answered, I will not ask! I will not tempt the Lord! Then the Lord said: Listen, O house of David! Is it not enough for you to weary men, must you also weary God? Therefore the Lord Himself will give you this sign: the Virgin shall be with child, and bear a Son, and shall call Him Emmanuel. (Is 7:11-14)

The fear that the Iconic Monstrance of Our Lady of the Sign will distract from the Christ is wearisome indeed. From the ancients of old to the disciples of the third millennium, the preservation of God's desire to be wedded to His people is expressed in the mercy of God's condescension in the mystery of the Incarnation. Such preservation requires cooperation that humanity be restored to its rightful identity, as conceived and created in the image and likeness of God — an identity clothed in dignity, nobility, and grace.

In the biblical image of the nuptial, the Church is the virgin bride wedded to the Christ who births her children through the waters of baptism. The Church nourishes them at the altar of sacrifice in the banquet of the Holy Eucharist. Only in Jesus and Mary of Nazareth can the Church boast of being without the stain of sin, and only through Jesus and Mary is the Church's offspring truly born in perfect fidelity to the covenant ratified by the Blood of the cross.

At the cross, the marriage is consummated and the children are born. Isaiah's prophecy is fulfilled as the Virgin Mary, she, the Daughter Zion, suffered the pain of labor and in a moment's time gave birth to children she never conceived. Today, still at the foot of the cross, the urgent plea is heard in the wailing of this mother whose children are being ripped from her womb.

The ancient serpent of Genesis, the dragon of the Apocalypse, in a word, Satan, seducer of mankind, has waged war on her children. In this Woman of the Apocalypse, who is our sister before she is our Mother, the Church sees itself and is thus awakened to its mission to save those who are lost and to sanctify those suffering the assault of desecration to their identity as conceived and created in the image and likeness of God. Mary of Nazareth is the perfect and most immaculate symbol of all that the Church is called to be. She embodies the Church's mission and the Church's destiny.

The Iconic Monstrance of Our Lady of the Sign is a symbol of the union of Jesus with His bride, the Church. It expresses the immutable bond between the Mother and the Child. It shows the complementary union between the Man and the Woman and the sacred power of God's reign in the mutually shared authority of the King and the Queen. Subject to the Christ, the Virgin Mary is exalted and thus the whole of humanity is donned in dignity, nobility, and grace.

The Marian monstrance, then, expresses the gracious humility of God, who condescended in order to lift humanity from the darkness of death to the light of life and from despair in the domain of the devil to hope in the hallowed halls of heaven. The monstrance is a symbol of victory in the battle against the powers and principalities of this world. By this victory, evil, eventually and eternally, will succumb to the irrevocable death that will bring forth the full realization of the reign of Christ.

What seems like common sense to me has proven to be a point of controversy and consternation for so many. I am surprised that the Iconic Monstrance of Our Lady of the Sign should elicit such strong sentiment against something so certain to bring solace to a hurting humanity. When asked why I won't waver in my decision concerning the Marian Monstrance, my response is simply that this is what Our Lady wants, and I will defend her desire because I believe it brings blessing beyond anything anyone can imagine.

To suggest that somehow the Marian monstrance will distract attention from Jesus is to imply that there is competition in heaven between the Son and His Mother, between the King and the Queen.

To suggest that the Marian monstrance creates confusion and gives the impression that Catholics adore the Woman as opposed to the Man, is to betray a spirituality void of relationship and, therefore, creates a dangerous disconnect between the head and the body. Christ is the head of His body, the Church. The Blessed Virgin Mary, in a singular and most perfect way, symbolizes the Church. Of all the Church's members, she alone is without the stain of sin. In her, the Church can confidently boast of the excellence of its holiness and show the Christ unencumbered by the veil of sin that clouds the vision of God's kingdom.

To suggest that the Marian monstrance is an impediment to Christian ecumenism is to deceive non-Catholics by being less than honest about the truth of Catholic dogma and devotion to the Holy Mother of God.

To suggest that prudence dictates a diminished Marian representation, rather than one intricately woven into the Holy Eucharist, is to expose a lack of faith in Jesus to teach the mysteries of the faith through the supreme power emanating from the Sacred Host. To behold the Mother leads to adoration of the Son and to worship the Son leads to imitation of the Mother.

To suggest that Mary's humility would militate against such a visible manifestation in the Marian monstrance, would be to deny the Virgin the exercise of her apostolic mission to bring forth the Christ as she did 2,000 years ago. As with the Christ, Mary is not frozen in the pages of Sacred Scripture. She is alive and ever active in the life of the Church.

The New Evangelization

One afternoon, after listening to such criticism against the Marian image in the monstrance, I went to pray at the Hour of Great Mercy, as is my custom. With a heavy heart, I entered the holy hour. My mind was spinning with doubt as I wondered whether I was acting with an obstinate pride in my unwillingness to deviate from the very prominent image of the Blessed Virgin Mary in the monstrance. The hour of prayer ended as it began. The question hovered over me, as if awaiting an answer to what had become the cause of much anxiety.

After the Holy Hour, I was preparing to hear confessions when a man stopped me and introduced himself. The past May

I had been in the Chicago Loop to speak to a gathering of Catholics on the topic "Mary in the New Evangelization." The gentleman, coming to St. Stanislaus Kostka for the first time, offered me the gift of a sacred image. Together we walked to his car, parked only steps from the entrance to the church. As he opened the back door, I was overwhelmed as my eyes beheld a bold and beautiful image of *Our Lady of the Sign*. It was indeed the ancient icon whose very image would adorn the Sanctuary of The Divine Mercy. In that instant, feeling the momentary presence of the Holy Mother of God, the heaviness was lifted from my heart and my mind was put to rest.

From the days of my youth, the Blessed Virgin Mary has stood watch as if from a distance, waiting for the appointed time and the appropriate place to enslave me so that I more fully respond to the specific will of God. She does not give me solace in the comfort of her home, but keeps me marching in cadence to the movement of the Holy Spirit, in the company of her Son. The battle is real and is being fought on many fronts. If it weren't for the many signs Our Lady gives, I don't think I'd have strength for perseverance. In spite of the struggle, she especially sustains me through the faith of humble people who daily remind me that God, indeed, comes to the help of His servants.

In her request that a Sanctuary of The Divine Mercy be built, the Blessed Virgin Mary exercises her prophetic office and shows herself as the Woman of the Apocalypse, clothed with the sun, with the moon under her feet and on her head a crown of twelve stars. The Iconic Monstrance of Our Lady of the Sign expresses the sentiment of St. Louis Marie de Montfort and, indeed, the deep-felt sense of the Church — that knowledge of Mary leads to knowledge of Jesus as He ought to be known.

If then, as is certain, the knowledge and the kingdom of Jesus Christ are to come into the world, they will be but a necessary consequence of the knowledge and the kingdom of the most holy Virgin Mary, who brought Him into the world for the first time, and will make His second advent full of splendor *(True Devotion to Mary, Preliminary Remarks 13)*.

No apologies are needed, nor do we diminish our affection for and devotion to the Blessed Virgin Mary. "If you wish to comprehend the mother, comprehend the Son, for she is the worthy Mother of God. Here, let every tongue be mute" (St. Eucherius).

THE CANTICLE OF THE
BLESSED VIRGIN MARY

My being proclaims the greatness of the Lord,
my spirit finds joy in God my savior,
for He has looked upon His servant in her lowliness;
all ages to come shall call me blessed.
God who is mighty has done great things for me,
holy is His name.
His mercy is from age to age on those who fear Him.
He has shown might with His arm;
He has confused the proud in their inmost thoughts.
He has deposed the mighty from their thrones
and raised the lowly to high places.
The hungry He has given every good thing,
While the rich He has sent empty away.
He has upheld Israel His servant,
Ever mindful of His mercy;
Even as He promised our fathers,
promised Abraham and his descendants forever.

Luke 1:46-55

JESUS I TRUST IN YOU

25

FROM THE EYE OF THE STORM, SHE GUIDES US

December 20, 2003

Well into Advent, and in preparation for the great Feast of Christmas, I paused to reflect on the seed that germinates through steadfast and persevering faith. This process continues to be painfully purifying while, at the same time, the cause of inner joy. The seed that I write about is seed that will bear fruit in the realization of the Sanctuary of The Divine Mercy. Like the ancients of old, I salute what I see from afar, though only through the eyes of my soul. By the grace of God alone, I am steadfast and persevering.

What some call a mere fantasy of my own making remains the conviction of my soul; namely, that the Blessed Virgin Mary has requested the sanctuary. At times, I have to admit I tire of the battle, which, more often than not, is fought in the midst of a storm. This season of Advent brings deep consolation as I contemplate the enduring faith of the *Anawim,* that is, the poor of Yahweh, who walked perseveringly in eager and hopeful anticipation of the light that would pierce the night's darkness in Bethlehem on that first Christmas morning.

The Sanctuary of The Divine Mercy is destined to be a *Bethlehem* whose ambience, wrapped in the silence of Our

Lady's prayer, will bring to birth the Christ conceived in the souls of the Church's offspring and will conceive Christ in the hearts of non-believers, bringing them to conversion. The seed that now germinates will bear fruit, in due season and in due time, not only in the realization of a perpetual adoration chapel and the grounds adorned with religious iconography, but also in the manifestation of the Church's catholicity. As with the pilgrims of Bethlehem, the Church's catholicity will be expressed in people of different ethnicities, races, ages, and creeds who will find their way to this sacred ground for the holy encounter.

I had a premonition of this when two weeks ago on a Saturday morning I observed the richness of the Church's catholicity as various persons passed through the doors of the parish. As I attended an early morning meeting, I was animated by the passion and enthusiasm of about 30 people — White, Asian, African, Hispanic, Irish, and Polish. An hour later, rushing from the meeting, I hurried to the vestibule to receive the body of Tom Bezak as it was carried into the church, flanked by grieving loved ones. The funeral cortege, which consisted of hundreds of Polish-Americans, arrived as Fr. Eduardo Garcia led 300 Hispanics in procession from the church to the school for a day of recollection.

While I celebrated the funeral Mass in the upper church, newborn babies were being baptized in the lower church. Concluding the Funeral Rite and leading the mourners to the vestibule for a final blessing, a 15-year-old arrived in the company of her family and friends for the celebration of her *Quinceañera* — a religious rite in the Latin-American tradition that marks a girl's passage into young womanhood. Tom Bezak's family and friends left for St. Adalbert's Cemetery as I began another procession that would lead the young girl to the altar for the dedication of her life to God. And all this was only the start of a new day.

There is no doubt that in anticipation of the building of the Sanctuary of The Divine Mercy, the parish must nurture the seed of God's life in the lives of those who pass through its doors. Our lives should reflect hope for those who celebrate life and grieve death, no matter who they may be. Imitating the Blessed Virgin Mary, we hold Jesus close to our hearts, showing Him forth that all people find here, Him whom they seek.

Only in the transformation of our lives can we give testimony to the authenticity of the sacred that is revealed in and through religious iconography. The prayer of the parish, then, wrapped in the silence of Mary's humble contemplation of Jesus, allows the work of the soul to happen. Money or no money, this labor is crucial to the building and nurturing of the sanctuary. It requires much faith and steadfast perseverance from those who seek to do the will of God in bringing Our Lady's call to fruition.

REORIENTATION OF THE SANCTUARY

After I declined the three million dollars in obedience to the strong soul-felt stirrings of the Holy Spirit, my faith and trust were again put to the test. It was only a matter of days, though, before the sanctuary project began to experience, quite miraculously, an interesting reorientation. Knowing that I now had absolutely no money, the religious iconographers from Spain nonetheless wasted no time in scheduling a meeting. Within three weeks, they had returned to Chicago to assist in the redesign of the sanctuary. They had asked that I have an architect present for the meetings.

The following day, providentially, two architects, Paul Straka and David Zeunert, were knocking on my door. Having read the reflections, *A Mother's Plea*, they showed enthusiasm for the project and offered their assistance. At the same time, Diane Wilder came to me and expressed her desire to assist in the development and the promotion of the "vision" as written in the reflections. She was willing to leave her current job in order to utilize her skills full-time on the sanctuary. All this was unfolding, much to my surprise. I was far too busy with my parochial duties even to wonder where to start or who to contact to proceed with the sanctuary project.

Cognizant of the ongoing struggle to make ends meet in the operation of the parish and school, I had never asked for financial assistance from the parish or the parishioners for the Sanctuary of The Divine Mercy. Even so, for the first time, out of desperation, I asked the parish accountant, Ed Schenk, if we could somehow squeeze $40,000 from our reserves to provide seed money to re-engage the sanctuary project. He told me what I already knew: there simply were no such funds available. Privately, I began to pray unceasingly for $40,000.

Two weeks later, the day after Thanksgiving, we celebrated a Mass of thanksgiving for the Statue of The Divine Mercy as we bid farewell to this symbol, that had helped open our eyes to the vision of the sanctuary. Within three days, the statue would go to the Shrine of Our Lady of Kibeho in Rwanda, on the continent of Africa. I was feeling melancholy. The money was gone, and the statue was going. Both were symbols of the Blessed Virgin Mary's request that there be a Sanctuary of The Divine Mercy on this property. My sadness was tempered by faith and trust in the miraculous manner in which the story had unfolded to this point.

GIFTS THROUGH PRAYER AND DEVOTION

A day later, I had returned from another funeral and was preparing for a wedding. A Mexican-American woman from the far south side of Chicago, who had no idea of the recent events surrounding the sanctuary project, came into the sacristy. We greeted each other, and she wasted no time in telling me that she had been praying in the church and felt the need to make a $40,000 donation to the Sanctuary of The Divine Mercy. Stunned for a brief second, I asked her to repeat what she had just said. Again she said, "I was praying and would like to donate $40,000 towards the Sanctuary of The Divine Mercy."

Two days later, only moments after the Statue of The Divine Mercy had left the grounds of St. Stanislaus Kostka, the woman, who chooses to remain anonymous, arrived and handed me a check for $40,000 — money designated solely for the Sanctuary of The Divine Mercy.

As I took the money, I felt it was Our Lady herself who placed the gift into my hands. The peace, the strength, and the humility of her presence filled my soul. My thoughts were suddenly turned to the parish school, as if Our Lady wanted me to know and understand that she had her plan for this holy ground well under control.

I was reminded in that moment that the generosity of the Big Shoulders Fund, under the direction of its Chairman, Jim O'Connor, was also a response to the hidden workings of her mysterious presence. Just months before, Big Shoulders had donated $4.4 million for renovation of the parish school, which was in dire need of repair. The exterior wall of the school had literally become a safety issue, and without a complete facelift, the school would risk closure.

The parish's commitment to Catholic education is evident in the nearly $100,000 it contributes annually to subsidize the cost of the school's operation, but financing the needed school renovation was far beyond the capacity of the parish. There are few words that adequately express the gratitude felt for Jim O'Connor and the many contributors to the Big Shoulders Fund. Suffice it to say, they, too, have been lured into Our Lady's story and will reap the rewards of their generosity.

A few days later, the parish received another gift. Having bid farewell to the Statue of The Divine Mercy, we received from Fr. Seraphim Michalenko, MIC, a replica of the original painting of The Divine Mercy. The nine-foot image is stunning in its beauty, emanating what has the appearance of intense light, as if from a flame perpetually burning in the Heart of Jesus. While I had seen other copies of the original, I had never seen one so striking as the image we received. The very sight of the image brings to life the experience of St. Maria Faustina, who writes in her own words:

> In the evening, when I was in my cell, I saw the Lord Jesus clothed in a white garment. One hand was raised in the gesture of blessing; the other was touching the garment at the breast. From beneath the garment, slightly drawn aside at the breast there were emanating two large rays, one red; the other pale. In silence I kept my gaze fixed on the Lord, my soul was struck with awe, but also with great joy. After a while, Jesus said to me, *Paint an image according to the pattern you see, with the signature: Jesus, I trust in You. I desire that this image be venerated, first in your chapel, and then throughout the world.*
>
> *I promise that the soul that will venerate this image will not perish. I also promise victory over its enemies already here on earth, especially at the hour of death. I Myself will defend it as My own glory.*

When I told this to my confessor, I received this for a reply: "That refers to your soul." He told me, "Certainly, paint God's image in your soul." When I came out of the confessional, I again heard words such as these: My image already is in your soul. *I desire that there be a Feast of Mercy. I want this image, which you will paint with a brush, to be solemnly blessed on the first Sunday after Easter; that Sunday is to be the Feast of Mercy.*

I desire that priests proclaim this great mercy of Mine towards souls of sinners. Let the sinner not be afraid to approach Me. The flames of mercy are burning Me — clamoring to be spent; I want to pour them out upon these souls (Diary, 47-50).

On December 12, 2003, the Feast of Our Lady of Guadalupe, we enthroned and blessed the newly received image of The Divine Mercy in a solemn rite. After the evening Mass, a young woman of Irish descent joyfully handed me a check for $50,000 and asked that the money be used exclusively for the building of the sanctuary and the printing of *A Mother's Plea*. As with the previous donor, she, too, requested anonymity.

In the moment, something hadn't quite registered, but the following morning it occurred to me. Two years ago, during the Novena to Our Lady of Guadalupe, I had specifically asked the Blessed Virgin for $50,000 in order to secure the architectural drawings for the sanctuary. As I wrote in previous reflections, heaven put it in my heart to be so bold in my request for the money. This was the burden I carried into the Hour of Great Mercy on her feast day two years ago. On that day at 4:00 in the afternoon, in the very moment I ended the hour of prayer, I received a call from "Big Shoulders" that a $75,000 donation had been offered for the parish school.

Even though the gift was designated for the school as opposed to the sanctuary, I gladly accepted the generous donation as a sign of Our Lady's answer to my prayers. Considering all that has transpired over the course of these two years, she seemed content with joy to placate me for the time being, knowing I was premature in my desire for the architectural drawings. She seemed to be waiting for the seed to sprout shoots in directions known only to her before finally granting my request for $50,000.

The Blessed Virgin Mary is, indeed, at the helm. Like a hurricane, her movements have been unpredictable, but, from that place of stillness in the eye of the storm, she has been consistent and constant in bringing her request for the Sanctuary of The Divine Mercy to fruition. She will bring us into safe harbor. For our part, we must be steadfast and persevering as the seed germinates, eventually to bear fruit in due season and in due time.

Faith is confident assurance
concerning what we hope for,
and conviction about things we do not see ...
By faith Abraham obeyed when he was called,
and went forth to the place he was to receive as a heritage;
he went forth, moreover, not knowing where he was going.
By faith he sojourned in the promised land
as in a foreign country,
dwelling in tents with Isaac and Jacob,
heirs of the same promise;
for he was looking forward to the city with foundations,
whose designer and maker is God.
By faith Sarah received power to conceive
though she was past the age,
for she thought that the one who made the promise
was worthy of trust.
As a result of this faith,
there came from one man,
who was himself as good as dead,
descendents as numerous as the stars in the sky
and the sand of the seashore.

Hebrews 11:1, 8-12

26

THE CALL TO ARMS: DEFINING THE PRIESTHOOD

April 8, 2004

The superficial and shallow trappings of the modern world create the illusion that all is well with humanity and that there is no need of God — certainly not a suffering God. Perhaps God may be accepted at best if He is kept at the level of the superficial and shallow. This is why the Eucharistic Jesus is so little appreciated today. He is too deep. He is too intense.

Even priests who put their hands to the Sacred Host may no longer feel its fire because too often they resist the descent into their own nothingness, to feel their own pain and behold Him who is their deliverer. Satan forbids the descent into the inner sanctum because it brings defeat to his reign. The enemy offers the superficial and the shallow to keep the priest at least lukewarm, or at best, cold and indifferent to the sacrificial and sacred character of his priestly consecration. The warrior shepherd, then, sleeps within him because he has relegated the Supreme Shepherd to the Garden of Paradise. Meanwhile, the sheep are alone in the Garden of Gethsemane, awaiting the kiss of death (Excerpt from Chapter 10: *Our Lady's Intervention*).

It is clear to me that on the day I consecrated my life to the Blessed Virgin Mary, she anointed me with the sword that pierced her heart and sent me into battle. She calls me to sacrifice my life in the holy work of redemption for the salvation and sanctification of souls.

My priesthood was transformed on the day I made the consecration and has since undergone a perpetuating purification. It is as if I was an entirely different person prior to September 14, 1999. On that day, the Feast of the Triumph of the Cross, something died in me. I became, as it were, a foreigner in a strange land. I recall walking several blocks to St. Peter's in Chicago for confession and feeling a light trying to break through the world's darkness. The world seemed sadly oblivious to the illuminating power of the Woman who seemed painfully desirous to bring the world to gaze on The Divine Mercy. The eyes of the Christ are the window to His soul, and His Heart is the door through which Our Lady guides us to drink at the fountain of mercy. To this end, she has requested of me a sanctuary. The Holy Spirit has infused me with a keen sense of the urgency of God's will to bring her call to fruition.

Symbols of Consecration

As known through history, the unfolding drama of God's self-revelation depends on the cooperation of persons who, in humility, respond perseveringly, prayerfully, and patiently to the promptings of the Holy Spirit. Herein lies the excruciatingly painful struggle of the soul to remain steadfast down the narrow road that leads to the fulfillment of heaven's plan. Knowing the natural inclinations and frailness of my manhood, along with the blatant contradictions I perceive within myself, I beg God's grace for perseverance. I ask Him to keep aflame the inner desire of my soul to remain an active and faithful participant in His story.

The consecration of my life to the Holy Mother of God seemingly brought a definitive demise to the already fragile sense of belonging I had to this world. At the same time, it brought to life an intense desire for sacrificial union with the Christ and the longing to become what I consume in the celebration of the Sacred Liturgy. This allurement to Jesus compelled me to consciously step away from anyone and anything that would impede my response to His call. This stepping away was an internal reality that demanded external expression. And so, along with the Rosary and the sword, I took a skull cap and a crucifix as symbols of my consecration.

The skull cap expresses total submission to the Christ in freely chosen slavery to the Blessed Virgin Mary. It keeps me fully conscious of my belonging to Jesus and thus serves me well in responding to the daily dying to self that is absolutely necessary for the fulfillment of God's will. Because it is a distinct and visible sign, it serves to safeguard the boundaries that define the priestly and religious character of my consecration.

The crucifix worn over and above the heart is the sword that pierced the heart of the Blessed Virgin Mary and the symbol of victory in suffering and death. The empathy of God is expressed in the image of the crucified Jesus who, in atonement for sin and in loving obedience to the Father, gave His life to the last drop of Blood. Jesus' victory in death gives me courage to cleave to Him, in loving obedience to our Father, that I faithfully suffer the sacrifice to which He calls me for the salvation and sanctification of souls.

Since the day I began the 33-day preparation for consecration of my life to the Mother of God, I have worn the rosary around my neck. The Rosary is the chain that binds me in slavery to the Blessed Virgin, that I may secure genuine freedom in Jesus.

Finally, the sword that adorns my bed reminds me that she calls me to live deeply the sacrificial nature of my priesthood. Indeed, on the day of my consecration, Our Lady turned her eyes away from me to embrace the rest of her children. The Holy Mother bid me farewell, as from afar Jesus beckoned me to Himself. She prodded me forward to fight for her children — for their salvation — for their sanctification.

Formed in Our Lady's Spirituality

The consecration of my life to the Blessed Virgin Mary and the subsequent transformation of my priesthood into sacrificial union with the Christ are woven into Our Lady's specific call that a sanctuary be built on the property adjacent to the Kennedy Expressway under the backdrop of the Chicago skyline.

Our Lady exercises her prophetic office in her request for a sanctuary on these grounds. She echoes the words of the prophet Hosea as she calls us into the desert in order to speak to our hearts. She asks that we come as in the days of our youth, when innocence made the heart receptive to the breath of God's Spirit. She wishes to espouse us forever in right and justice, in love and mercy. She will also espouse us in fidelity, so that we come to know, love, and serve God.

It is precisely in fidelity to her call that I recognize the need to be formed in her spirituality. For this reason, I consciously step away from the myriad of opinions being voiced to reshape the Church according to the standard of personal or political agendas as opposed to the standard of truth — a truth experienced in relation to the Incarnate God and communicated through the mysticism of Catholic spirituality — a Eucharistic and Marian spirituality. For too long, the Church's spirituality has suffered the assault of secularization, thus diminishing her sacrificial and sacred character, hurting her mission, and robbing innocence from the lives of the faithful.

Satan Befriends the Priest

I am not surprised that rather suddenly, after my consecration, I found myself in battle, asking Jesus to show me how to wield the sword. My soul deeply perceives the evil that seductively lurks to steal innocence from the beauty and good in God's creation. Evil has so manifested itself that since the time of my consecration, I have suffered severe attacks to my priesthood. I have felt myself spiritually raped, leaving me for a time seriously confused as to the genuine workings of the Holy Spirit and intrigued by the interplay of light and darkness — of good and evil.

As I continue to grow in Our Lady's spirituality, I am more keenly conscious that the sole purpose of the priesthood is to live in Jesus, with Jesus, for Jesus, and through Jesus. Every deep and good thing comes from this relationship which, by its very nature, is sacrificial and sacred. Jesus alone has the power to form the man that I am into the priest He calls me to be, thereby rekindling hope in the midst of the ever present forces of evil.

I believe the crisis being felt in priestly identity is rooted in the failure to seriously nurture the sacrificial and sacred character of the priesthood. If a man comes to the priesthood for comfort, prestige, or power, he is already guilty of the sin of Pharisaism, armed with the hammer in his right hand and the nails in his left. If he comes primarily in need of community, he has already made a dangerous contribution to the collective complacency that stifles the prophetic stirrings of God's Spirit. If a man comes to the priesthood for the sole purpose of serving others in friendship, he is doomed to suffer the devastating pain of rejection and betrayal by his closest confreres and those who build him up only to tear him down.

Like the Christ, the priesthood is not about good men doing good things. Priests are not professional good men. Priests have made a public profession of consecration to be configured to the Christ. If the sacrificial and sacred power of the Christ to conquer the demonic and lift humanity into another reality is dismissed as a fiction of the past, then priests will wallow in the sickness of their own self-absorbed disease. The sacrificial and sacred character of the priesthood will then be viewed as another aberration in the harlotry of the Roman Catholic Church. The unjust accusation that the Church is the beast or the Antichrist of the Apocalypse is, then, sinfully fed, and her sacrificial and sacred character is further desecrated.

A healthy and holy Church depends on the sanctity of those who set the standard. Priests have publicly surrendered themselves to Christ in a posture of self-giving sacrifice. In the footsteps of Jesus, they must step to the beat of a different drummer and make the lonely walk, leading others to sanctuary — to the solitude of the Christ, who brings rest to the soul.

They make the lonely walk donned in the flesh of their own humanity, with needs and inclinations no different from those of other men. Satan, who in unquestionable fidelity befriends the priest, remains the faithful foe whose slithering seductions militate against the sacrificial and sacred character of the priestly consecration. The priest knows that left to himself his spirit is willing, but his flesh is weak. If not centered in the Christ, Satan so easily lures him away from sacrifice and into selfishness — away from the sacred and into the secular.

The Master means to mince no words in the reminder that the devil deems to sift us all like wheat. As Jesus fore-warned, Satan, indeed, comes in the guise of light to strike the shepherd so that the sheep scatter. In fidelity to the Supreme Shepherd and in solidarity with many others who profess a deep and enduring love for the Christ, we suffer the assault. We do not succumb to defeat, but instead await the good that comes to those who love God. Having engaged the priest in battle, the enemy's demise is known only to the extent that the priest cleaves to the sacrificial and sacred character of the Christ. Configured to the Living Lamb who was slain, the priest is free to effectively lead others to proclaim victory in battle. In this right motivation to the priesthood, truth is uncompromised, and the call to sanctuary becomes essential to the identity of the priest.

THE SACRIFICIAL AND SACRED CHARACTER OF THE PRIESTHOOD

Living in a world that so easily succumbs to Satan's seductions, the lonely walk of a priest becomes all the more forsaken and all the more dangerous. This is especially true when, within the hallowed halls of the holy Church, her priests are themselves seduced, giving compromise with col-lective consent to the superficial and shallow agenda of those whose egos choose to secularize rather than surrender to the sacrificial and sacred character of the Church's mission. The veneer of religious verbiage may resound in profound words spoken, written, and worn, but the iconic identity of the Church's holy mystery is eclipsed.

The priest, then, bears within himself the responsibility for the reform. Deep-felt remorse leads to genuine repentance and recompense that the Christ be brought forth to rescue humanity from the depths of its own imperceptible darkness. Configured to the Christ, the priest lays his life on the altar of sacrifice in atonement for sin. In the sacrificial and sacred character of his priesthood, secure and strong in the solitude of sanctuary, the priest wields the sword that severs the head of the serpent to save and sanctify in the name and in the person of the Christ.

The Mother of God has made me understand that neither the Sanctuary of The Divine Mercy nor the parish will deeply reflect the sacrificial and sacred character of the Church unless I succumb to the sword that pierced her heart, so that *the secret thoughts of many be laid bare* before the altar of sacrifice and in the Sacrament of Reconciliation. In this, I feel my soul is infused with the soul of the Virgin of Nazareth as I am perpetually purified and perfected into the likeness of her Son.

I understand more than ever that the purpose of my priesthood is to participate with the Blessed Virgin Mary in the holy work of redemption. She makes it increasingly clear to me that as a priest I, more than anyone, must lay my life on the altar. I must remain there, perpetuating the atoning and healing grace of the solitary sacrifice of Golgotha. There my purifying wounds and the wounds of the world are seasoned in the slow suffering of sanctification. The goodness of God is manifested as I joyfully join my voice in concert with our ancestors, the saints, and the prophets. In communion with the pilgrim people of God, I give thanks in the celebration of the Sacred Liturgy, as flowing from the pierced Heart of the Christ, the Blood and Water washes us clean.

So strongly do I feel the truth of these words that they inspire my daily struggle to resist the inclination of the flesh towards the ideologies of the world. I choose instead refuge in sanctuary, where my priestly identity is lived, nurtured, and sustained. It is in sanctuary that I truly become a spiritual father. At a time when the people of the world turn a deaf ear to the voice of God and a hedonistic and narcissistic rebellion reigns, I await the return of the prodigal son. Our Lady implores me to cleave to Jesus in sanctuary, so that when the prodigal son comes, he finds me waiting. Through her, I become, as it were, a living sacrament that brings forth the salvific and sanctifying grace and the mercy of the crucified and risen Jesus.

To this end, my priesthood demands from me a life of asceticism that is absolutely essential for the opening of my soul to the transforming power of God's grace. Failure to respond to the grace conferred in my priesthood would conceal rather than reveal the sacred presence that permeates sanctuary. I would be, as it were, a veil that clouds the otherwise perceptible mystery of the Sacred Liturgy and the other Sacraments that flow from this fount of The Divine Mercy. I was ordained a priest not merely to perform a function, but, indeed, to become an icon of the very Christ who calls me. My response to His call to live in me and through me lifts this veil. Thus, the *Holy of Holies* becomes all the more accessible to those who seek to rediscover their innocence and make their hearts receptive again to the breath of God's Spirit.

THE LIFE-GIVING GIFT OF CELIBACY

If priests resist responding to the call of Jesus, it would be a travesty to the identity of the priesthood and treacherous to the mission of the Church. Having been chosen to live in the intimate company of the Christ, the call, woven through the pages of Sacred Scripture, demands that the priest befriend Jesus in the renunciation of much in the world that is good — not to mention the renunciation of all that is evil.

From the moment I heard His call, I have longed for this communion with Jesus and have prayed that He would weave my manhood into my priesthood that my spirituality might beget life. It seems to me that Jesus graced me with this longing in order to draw me into constant and unceasing prayer, nurtured and sustained in the willful renunciation of the world. In attending to this desire of my soul, I discover the joyful gift of celibacy and thus the potency of my manhood to beget and defend life.

That celibacy is truly a gift from God and not the trick of the institutional Church comes at great cost to the priest. He is called to offer his life in sacrifice and suffer the painful purgation that brings forth not his life, but the life of the Christ. Jesus, who calls the priest, indeed, makes Himself accessible but only after making Himself imperceptible to the senses. He does this to bring the priest to penetrate deeply the recesses of his own soul and there find Jesus in the joyful realization that apart from the Christ, the priest is nothing, has nothing, and can do nothing. The priest's life is no longer a mere meditation on the events that took place 2,000 years ago in and around the holy city of Jerusalem. His life becomes a contemplation of the unfolding drama of the Christ who teaches the priest to wield the sword of righteousness.

With the same zeal that provoked righteous anger in Jesus, I feel a fire burning in my soul as the ancient serpent, who smoothly seduces the world into submission, slithers his way into the hallowed halls of the holy Church. His venom brings the Woman to wail aloud in pain as her children are being ripped from her womb. She sends us into battle to fight for her children, anointing us with the sword that pierced her heart. The battle waged is against the powers and principalities of a world that is passing away. With zeal for love of the Father and configured to the Christ, the priest kisses the cross and lays his life on the altar of sacrifice. For this, he was ordained and in this, he begets and defends life.

The identity of the priest is so woven to the Sacred Mysteries that even if all the faithful turn away from the salvific and sanctifying grace of Calvary, the priest finds solace in the configuration of his life to the Christ in the solitary sacrifice that by its nature begets life and defends life. The sole purpose, then, for the sacrificial and sacred character of the priesthood is to perpetuate and proclaim the Paschal Mystery that life be propagated. In this, He is an expression of the Father's love for the world in sending the Son to atone for sins and the Son's loving obedience to the Father to bring it to completion. In the person of the Christ, at the altar of sacrifice, the priest is the instrument that graces the world with the means to be donned anew in the innocence of youth.

That the priesthood is an expression of God's love for the world brings me to reflect seriously on my identity as a priest in relation to the Father and in relation to Our Lady's request for a Sanctuary of The Divine Mercy. As I do so, I ponder the greatest challenge I face — the transformation of the rectory itself into sanctuary. Enveloped in the silence of the Blessed Virgin's prayer, the atmosphere of the rectory should not be unlike the sacred space where the Holy Sacrifice of the Mass is celebrated or the Sacred Species adored. The home of the priest becomes, as it were, the sacred space where, apart from everyone, in union with the Christ, the priest communes with the Father.

As Jesus so often went to an out-of-the-way place or sought the solitude of the desert, so, too, the priest safeguards his own space as sacred. There, in the paradoxical intimacy of the ever-hidden presence of the Christ, the priest, in the world but detached from the spirit of the world, wrestles with his own demons and dies the death that deepens his life in God. In this daily dying, the priest understands his celibacy in relation to the Christ and begins to accept and live the gift of celibacy out of love for the Father. Lived authentically, the experience of celibacy for the sole sake of the kingdom is a service rendered to the Church and an expression of indispensable support to the entire presbyterate in the nurturing and cultivation of its sacrificial and sacred character.

With deep-felt desire for authenticity, I battle against a multiplicity of opinions about what is acceptable in the lifestyles of priests — opinions that go so contrary to my perception of the call. Jesus calls the priest to walk down the lonely road bearing the cross, joyfully empowered and impassioned by His life. The call is nurtured and sustained by an asceticism that keeps the soul open to the transforming power of God's grace. Unfortunately, lifestyles that conflict with the radical call of Jesus are justified and defended in the name of plurality and pluriformity, while asceticism and prayer are sadly dismissed as practices relegated primarily to the lives of monks and hermits. If priests do not take seriously the call to holiness of life, then neither will the Church's sacred authority be given its due respect by virtue of God's command.

If a healthy and holy Church depends upon the sanctity of those who set the standard, then, in the footsteps of Jesus, priests must lead others in the walk to sanctuary. And so, the Sanctuary of The Divine Mercy requested by Our Lady, and the parish that receives the Sanctuary, will deeply reflect the sacrificial and sacred character of the Church to the extent that I succumb to the sword that pierced the heart of the Virgin Mother. As Jesus freely chose to undergo His passion and death, I freely choose to respond to His call to lose myself that He be found, to decrease that He increase, to die to myself that He live. Celibacy becomes, then, the gift I give to the Father that He freely use me for the sole purpose of His plan in the work of redemption.

THE MISSION

In her request for a sanctuary, the Holy Mother of God has defied the popular tendency in the Church to eradicate the sacrificial and sacred character of its mission as absolutely primary to its identity. In doing so, the Blessed Virgin has so affirmed the necessity of the priesthood to the nurturing and cultivation of Eucharistic and Marian spirituality that the priestly and ecclesial identity becomes one and the same thing. They express the mystery of covenant that safeguards and invites the faithful into loving relationship with the living God of history, who transcends both time and space.

In sanctuary, Our Lady offers holy ground for vigilant and persevering prayer, while keeping the hope expressed in the Sacred Liturgy ever present to perpetually satisfy the deep hunger of the soul's search for rest. As an extension of the Sacred Liturgy, sanctuary is an encounter with the Incarnate God who, without beginning and without end and by virtue of Baptism, has grafted us into His Body. Contemplation in the sacred silence of sanctuary has the potential to eradicate falsehood from the life of the adorer and reveal the truth that lies in the deep recesses of the soul — that is, the human person is loved into life and created in the very image and likeness of God.

As something died in me on the day I consecrated my life to the Holy Mother of God, something deeply beautiful came to life. The Mother of the Christ anointed me with the sword that pierced her heart and sent me into battle. My priesthood was redefined in the call to arms. I heard and understood the Mother's plea that a sanctuary of The Divine Mercy be built on these grounds. She made me understand that there can be no priest without sanctuary — to find one is to find the other. Without the sacrificial and sacred nurturing of sanctuary, my priesthood would be a farce. Simply speaking, I would be a fraud, at least to myself, if not to others.

Faithful to the sacrificial and sacred character of his consecration, the priest awakens the hope of the Church. His life, so woven to the spirituality of the Holy Mother of God and configured to the Christ, finds its deepest expression in sanctuary where eager anticipation of Jesus' return will bring rest to those who labor enveloped by the pain and persecutions and the trials and tribulations this side of death. In the meantime, the Church prods faithfully forward, armored in the Blood-stained victory of the cross. She awaits the sweet sound of the triumphal trumpeter, who brings an ever-enduring end to the wail of the Woman as her children, finally safe in sanctuary, savor salvation born from the sacrificial and sacred character of the supreme high and holy priest — the Christ.

Because we possess this ministry through God's mercy,
we do not give in to discouragement.
Rather we repudiate shameful, underhanded practices.
We do not resort to trickery or falsify the word of God.
We proclaim the truth openly and commend ourselves
to every man's conscience before God.
It is not ourselves we preach
but Christ Jesus as Lord,
and ourselves as your servants for Jesus' sake.
For God, who said, "Let light shine out of darkness,"
has shone in our hearts,
that we in turn might make known
the glory of God shining on the face of Christ.
This treasure we possess in earthen vessels,
to make it clear that its surpassing power
comes from God and not from us.

2 Corinthians 4:1-2; 5-7

27

LET THE CHILDREN COME UNTO ME

May 25, 2004

Some time ago, I had a dream that remains as vivid in my mind as the night it occurred. In the dream, I was just a boy, unsuccessfully trying to care for my brothers and sisters. I am the oldest son and the second of eight siblings — all of us born within a span of ten years. In the dream, the more I tried to keep order in the family, the more chaotic things seemed to become. The house was a wreck, and I was besieged by the biting and hitting and yelling, making me painfully aware that I had lost complete control of the situation. I frantically felt that I had failed my charge to the family.

I heard the doors of a car shut and saw through the window my father and mother walking toward the house. As soon as they walked through the door, a calm came over the whole household. I anxiously ran to my father who strongly stood, poised and polished in his military fatigues. Sobbing, I cried, "They don't obey. No one listens to me." Following alongside my father as he slowly and reflectively walked down the corridor, I continued crying and rambling about my deeply-felt failure.

All the while my father smiled. His countenance reflected serene strength as with utmost sensitivity and sincerity, he turned to me. His eyes betrayed a need to confide in me as he gently said, "You know, the general is on his way, and I'm very nervous." In that moment, I felt my father's love as I had never known it before. He was the calm in the chaos. His strength was enhanced in the truthful sharing of his own vulnerability. I wanted my father to continue to talk. I was so eager to listen. I felt strangely affirmed in that moment, as for the first time ever my father became my friend. Then suddenly, as I stood there listening to him, I saw myself become a man looking to him as if in a mirror.

Instantly, I was jolted from my sleep with a flashback flooding forward from the treasury of memories that have molded me and made me the man that I am. For several moments upon waking, I relived the day my father left for Vietnam, entrusting me with the charge to be man of the house. I was only ten years old.

Now, as a priest, that reality is ever so old, yet ever so new because at times I feel that I fail as the weight of the world bears down on my shoulders. Conditioned from the days of my youth to shoulder responsibility, I so often shun the whimpering child within me, who whines unceasingly for my attention. The little boy seems only to get in the way of my being a man.

Not so long ago, overwhelmed by the burden of my responsibilities, I went to pray. The crying child would not go away. He was just there in my face — a barrier that kept me from the consolation I sought in Jesus. With disdain and dislike for this child, I demanded that he depart from me and never return. He turned away, still sobbing. Suddenly with the eyes of my soul, I saw Jesus look at him and look at me. Jesus, pained at what I had done, spoke tenderly to the child, calling the boy to Him. My heart began to heal as Jesus lovingly embraced the child, doing for the child what I could not do and being for him what I had not been. Watching this, I felt a void well up inside me, and I boldly begged Jesus to bring him back. I wanted no longer to battle but to befriend the boy who was me.

That we should be attentive to the child within us is attested to in the Gospels. Sacred Scripture speaks of people bringing children to Jesus so that he would touch them, but the disciples kept them away. Jesus gently rebuked the disciples saying, "Let the children come to Me for to them belongs the kingdom of God" (Mk 10:14). He calls to Himself the child in all of us. Too often, though, we are reluctant to release the child to the loving arms of Jesus. Their sins, their tears, their wounds, their insecurities, their frailties, and their needs bring us shame. Their visions, their hopes, and their dreams embarrass us. We suppress their spontaneity before the throne of the Triune God, but they keep crying and He keeps calling.

How intriguing that the Risen Lord would call the apostles "children," even though they were grown men. In reading the Gospel of John, we learn that, unknown to the apostles, Jesus sat on the shore of the lake while they were out fishing. He called to them, "Children, have you caught anything to eat?" They hadn't, so He told them to cast the net over the right side of the boat. Obedient to the command, they cast the net and the catch was such that they could hardly pull the net in. At this, they realized it was the Lord, and coming to shore they found Jesus preparing a charcoal fire with fish on it and some bread. He invited them to eat.

Peter was still suffering as he sat there in the presence of the Risen Christ, whom he loved undyingly. Milling through his mind was the deed not done. Rather than defend Jesus, he had denied Him. In fear, he had failed Jesus. So, in his weakness, he wept bitterly.

It was a moving moment when after breakfast Jesus, knowing the stirrings of the soul, took Peter aside and purposefully questioned him. Three times Jesus asked, "Do you love me?" Then He commanded that Peter shepherd the flock. Simon Peter was validated and affirmed as the Master foretold the maturing of Peter into manhood — a maturing that would transform the weakness of flesh into the strength of spirit, giving Peter the courage to do what his soul had sought and to be what the desire of his dreams had demanded.

The child within Peter, exposed before the mercy of the Master, would one day look to Jesus as if in a mirror. The transforming power of God's grace would bring Peter to imitate the Incarnate Word. Configured to the Christ and in likeness to His life, St. Peter would testify with sacred power and authority to the sole Deity, resulting in the same descent into a similar death. With unwavering love for Jesus and true to the desire of his youth, in defense of the Christ, Peter would die in crucifixion, only to rejoice and revel in the resurrection.

PRIESTLY FORMATION

Twenty years ago today, the visions, the dreams, and the hopes that I guarded from the earliest days of my childhood became a reality when, on a rain-drenched evening, I was ordained a priest. Born on Holy Saturday, straddling the dark of Good Friday and the light of Easter morning, I have seen my priesthood as synonymous with my birth. Though my hair is thinning at an accelerated rate and beginning to show gray, I feel like a boy of twelve still asking God to make me a priest. It seems He keeps me forever young in order to mentor me into maturity, infused with His Spirit, but ever dependent upon Him. I am still the student and He the Master.

At times, I may wonder if I can truly endure the lifelong commitment to the priesthood without the shared intimacy of a partner in marriage. Occasionally, I may fantasize about children born from my own flesh and blood, but the wonder and the fantasy always yield to reality. Jesus has called me to Himself. That He has been my sole companion goes without question. The boy within me finds himself validated and affirmed as before Jesus I see myself become a man looking to Him as if in a mirror. This is the mysterious grace of the priesthood. To lose the gift would indeed bring unbearable sorrow to my soul.

If not for the sacred silence of sanctuary I would not, I could not, nor should I be a priest. Admittedly, on especially tense and stressful days, there are moments when I want to walk away, but every day I choose to stay. I never would have survived my own religious and priestly formation had I not discovered the sacred silence of sanctuary, where Jesus revealed Himself and opened my soul to the secrets of heaven. No professor of theology or psychology, nor any director of spirituality, nor the Pope himself could have done for me what Jesus did.

Instruments though they were to guide me on the way, it was the mysterious, incomprehensible, and enduring presence of the Christ in the Holy Eucharist that lifted me from the chaos, confusion, and cacophony of spirits competing for control of my soul. Jesus was the Master and I, so insecure and so inclined to the things of the world and the allure of the flesh, was his student. Through nine years of seminary, the adoration of the Blessed Sacrament in the sacred space of sanctuary kept me grounded as with unbridled zeal, religious and moral traditions of the faith were being subtly, seductively, and systematically dismantled under the guise of *Aggiornamiento* — the Renewal. The sacrificial and sacred were usurped by the sensual and the secular.

In the silence of sanctuary, Jesus opened my mind to rise above the rude noise of the world and to read history through the eyes of the saints and prophets. I saw how their childlike simplicity and humility kept them disposed to do great things for God with the mature passion of an adult, rather than the infantile ranting of an adolescent. Jesus' voice was in deep contrast to the eloquent voices with which the learned and clever sought to seduce me away from the suffering spirituality inherent in the faith of the Church and fully characteristic of the prayer life of the priest.

The Christ made this suffering spirituality clear to me on the occasion of my ordination to the priesthood. From across the country, my family gathered for the sacred event. I was ordained on a Friday evening and celebrated my first Mass the following day. Relieved of the tension, the solemn liturgies over, I was more than eager to relax and fully enter into the joy of a family reunion. In the basement of my Uncle's home, the violins and concertinas were being tuned and prepared to serenade the festive gathering. The aroma of my Aunt's home-cooked Polish cuisine billowed through the crowd, and everyone chatted and laughed as if in competition with the music. The whole scene added to the hustle of last-minute preparations for the banquet.

We could not have been happier when, with the suddenness of pain overtaking a woman in labor, the lighthearted joy turned to panic followed by a wave of frightening darkness. There, in the midst of celebration, my Uncle Ted, who had been key to the preparation of the ordination and the family reunion, suffered a massive heart attack. In moments that seemed like hours, the ambulance finally arrived to take my uncle to a nearby hospital where, like a thief in the night, death enveloped him and he was officially pronounced dead.

As the shock set in, I stood there with the profound realization that within the course of a day, my life had changed forever. As grieving eyes turned to me for consolation in the ritual mourning of the funeral liturgies of the Church, I became acutely aware that I was now forever a priest, according to the order of Melchizedek. Wearing the Roman collar hidden beneath the vestments of the Sacred Liturgy, my second Mass was offered in the company of grief-stricken relatives gathered around the coffin of our dearly beloved uncle. The marriage of my life to the Church was sealed in joy and consummated in sorrow as the oils of ordination were pressed into the palms of my hands and my heart wrenched in the sadness of the suffering faith of my grief-stricken family.

Now having served 14 years in the parish of St. Stanislaus Kostka, first as an associate pastor and now eight years as pastor, the joy that sustains me in sorrow is born from confident trust that victory will be fully realized just beyond the door of death. In the interim, the courage to sacrifice in the full commitment of my life to the Church is nurtured by a thirst that fuels the passion to mercifully labor for souls — souls that suffer the desecration of their true identities as created in the image and likeness of God.

THE DEVIL'S ILLUSORY LOVE

With sorrow, I have watched innocence drained from the eyes of countless young people, too many of whose bodies lie buried beneath the manicured lawns of numerous cemeteries around the Chicago area. The young and confused are led astray by the adolescent behavior of an adult world. They seek validation and affirmation in the wrong places, with the wrong people, and in doing the wrong things. Watching generations careening off the road of righteousness and falling fast into falsehood keeps me crying before the throne of the Triune God that "no one obeys — no one is listening." To a God whose unheard and unseen presence brings me peace, I am a priest, at times painfully, but always persevering in prayer.

In the silence of sanctuary, God puts into perspective the battle waging in the world, making me understand how hard it is to counteract the allure of Lucifer's lies when the principles of faith and morality are, at best, loosely defined or, at worst, completely obliterated. The devil's illusory love for the creature promises easy ways to power, prestige, self-adulation, and acceptance. His cost is the paid price of the soul's slavery to the superficial and shallow urges of the flesh, urges which in truth call us to the deeper realities of the Spirit. Satan's evil, masqueraded in light, knows only disdain for the suffering joy that is the fruit of self-surrender in submission to the Spirit of God. Those caught in the snare of his seduction share his disdain for the discipline of God and readily repudiate the faith of the Church. The child is most always the innocent victim of the lie.

It is in the nature of the world to wound the child, and, sadly, too often unknown to the child, God is its deepest desire and its laborious longing in the lonely sojourn. Through the valley of tears, into the dry of the desert, and through the dreadful night of darkness, the child's tears go undried if God is not known. The Blessed Virgin's request for the Sanctuary of The Divine Mercy is an expression of the holy will of God that tears of joy wipe dry the tears of sadness as the child is rescued from the fog fomented by the fury of the foe. God means to save those enslaved by the serpent's sly seductions that Christ be found and the soul set free from falsehood.

The Blessed Virgin's request keeps me humble as, perplexed by my powerlessness to fully comprehend her plan, my soul endures its own purification. Her call, nonetheless, is continually confirmed by the epiphanies sprinkled amid the aridity of my spiritual journey, keeping me steadfast on this narrow road. In powerlessness and nothingness, the consecration of my life to the Blessed Virgin Mary brings me to entrust all to the mysterious drama and design of God's action in a world that is passing away. In spite of my frustration and inability to completely grasp the mystery of God, with the trust of a child, I put faith in His incomprehensible presence. I am confident He will bring to fruition His specific will, vaguely understood, but burning nonetheless in the deep recesses of my soul.

In the meantime, the entrustment of my life to the Holy Mother of God brings me face to face with Jesus, looking to Him as if in a mirror. He makes me understand that I should do what only a priest can do, namely, open the doors so that access can be given to His Divine Mercy at the altar of sacrifice and in the safe-haven of the confessional. There, the secret thoughts of many are laid bare. There, I have seen innocence returned to the eyes of the child — the child so often hidden and buried in the depths of the soul. There, I have watched the transforming power of God's grace rekindle hope where hope had been lost.

THE HEROISM OF HOLINESS

How easy it is to be swallowed into the sea of self-pity until we see how the heroism of holiness brings heaven's healing power to shed light where darkness had prevailed. I have seen victory over the violence of vice in deliverance from the disease of drug addiction, salvation from the slavery to sex, purification from the propensity to pornography, faith restored in fidelity to family, and genuine humility nurtured where persistent perseverance bears the pain of the *thorn piercing the side*. The problem is that so few respond to the outpouring of God's grace or, perhaps unknown to many, the treasure remains untapped behind the locked doors of sanctuary.

With the natural instinct of a mother, the Blessed Virgin Mary hears the cry of her children. With the same suffering love that Jesus endured for ancient Jerusalem, she pleads for our attention, as in luminous transparency she shows anew the sorrow of Jesus weeping over the Holy City, "How often have I wanted to gather your children together as a mother bird collects her young under her wings and you refused Me" (Luke 13:34). Our reluctance to respond to Our Lady's plea would bring us to identify with the breed of unbelievers who Jesus calls wayward children. Squatting in the town square, the children called to their playmates: "We piped you a tune, but you did not dance! We sang you a dirge, but you did not wail!" (Mt 11:17). The parable chides the unbelievers for being like children who want to play a game other than the one suggested by their playmates. Neither the harsh utterances of John the Baptist nor the tender mercy of Jesus could bring a wayward people to repentance and conversion of life.

When overwhelmed by a world shamelessly unraveling into self-indulgent behavior, and when inundated by problems beyond my means to control or solve, at times I begin the spiral descent into the devil's darkness. Then I recall the joy in tragedy of the Vargas family, whose father and brother were murdered in Mexico. After the killings, their mother, accompanied by her eldest son, courageously made her way to Chicago to prepare a new home and a new life for her children. After the son was seriously injured in an automobile accident and left paralyzed for life, Maria de Jesus managed to bring her remaining nine children to Chicago. Once secure in their new home, the children, ranging in age from 6 to 18, were again shattered by the untimely death of their mother.

For six years, I have witnessed the simplicity and innocence of their young lives sustained in their shared faith that God had not, nor would He ever, abandon them. Together, they shoulder each other's burdens and bind themselves together in prayer and service rendered to God. They do it in a multiplicity of ways, giving consistent and joyful testimony to the light that pierces the darkness of tragedy.

Countless other examples abound to keep us joyful in the hope that the life flowing from the fountain of The Divine Mercy promises the only genuine means out of darkness and into light. The Divine Mercy takes us from a culture of death and into the culture of life. It frees us from the grip of the devil, so that we may savor God's abiding goodness. A litany of testimony, however, would confound the wise of the world, whose arrogance keeps them puffed-up by pride or forever chiding the child within — a child chastened by chains that bind it to a hedonistic preoccupation with the self — its cry for God crushed by the clamor of the world's rebellion.

The Virgin Mary's request for the Sanctuary of The Divine Mercy comes as a cry of remorse to rescue those robbed of innocence and return to them their inherent responsibility as disciples and members of the mystical body of the Christ. She calls us to conversion of life and patient and persevering prayer that the purification of the senses open the child within us to trust in the transforming power of the Triune God to bring the child to mature faith in the mission of mercy. We must express gratitude for this time of grace — this moment of mercy. Both victims and perpetrators in life that we are, the Blessed Virgin awakens us to defend truth or in death to travail. The choice is ours.

The religious and cultural crisis of our time is deeply rooted in the perversion of life lived apart from God — the disdain for the discipline of the Lord and the repudiation of responsibility for the cross we individually and collectively bear for the well-being of the whole. Centered on ourselves, we have become a people stuck in adolescent thinking and behavior, wreaking havoc on the innocence of youth and building barriers to the receptivity of their souls to the breath of God's Spirit. Because of a shameless persistence in personal sin, we are collectively guilty of robbing innocence from the child resulting in dire consequences for the well-being of society. Victims and perpetrators that we are in life, through the eyes of the child within us and in view of the children around us, the Holy Mother of God brings us to read history through the heroism and holiness of the saints and prophets. In faith and trust, they labored for love of a life that transcends the limits of time. She cautions us that to break the bonds that bind us to the faith of the ancients of old is to be tossed about by the whims and fancies of the present age and subsequently a condemnation of the future.

From the very lips of the Lord, echoed in the call of the Blessed Virgin, we learn that it is in the will of the Father to reveal the secret things of heaven. What is hidden from the learned and the clever is written in the heart of the child. This is the child in every man and woman who seeks salvation from seduction into slavery to the senses. The serpent's seducing of the soul into slavery keeps hidden the grace flowing from the dry of the desert and obscures the illumination of wisdom piercing the dark of night.

The Sanctuary of The Divine Mercy brings the promise of illumination, satisfying the soul's thirst and hunger for God — a thirst and hunger perhaps unknown to the pilgrim who, in silence, steps into the sacred space of sanctuary. There, the unheard call, having been suppressed by the cacophony of the world, awakens the soul to the child within and opens its ears to the whisper of God's voice, that to the child belongs the kingdom of God.

Unencumbered by the rude noise of the world and free from false teachers and false prophets who zealously labor to undo millennia of living tradition, the Sanctuary of The Divine Mercy promises the redefinition and the re-identification of a covenant people. As in the days of youth when innocence made the heart receptive to the breath of God's Spirit, the sanctuary opens the soul to the secret things of heaven. The Blessed Virgin Mary wishes to speak to our hearts, so that the sacred mysteries of the holy faith may be seen anew through the eyes of the child.

In a time when a covenant people are dangerously and despairingly disconnected, in her request for the sanctuary, the voice of the Holy Mother of God incarnates the words of the apostle Paul:

> We are strangers and aliens no longer. No, we are fellow citizens of the saints and members of the household of God.

We form a building which rises on the foundation of the apostles and prophets, with Christ Jesus Himself as the capstone. Through Him the whole structure is fitted together and takes shape as a holy temple in the Lord, in Him we are being built into this temple, to become a dwelling place for God in the Spirit (Eph 2:19-22).

THE CHORUS OF FIATS

The Church, conceived in the *fiat* of Abraham's response to God's self-revelation and gestating through the ages in the sojourn of Abraham's descendants, is visibly born in the Paschal Mystery of Jesus, the Christ. The suffering, death, and resurrection of the Blessed Virgin's Son is the birth whose pain of labor began in the silence of the Annunciation when Mary of Nazareth echoed the *yes* of Abraham's faith, bringing his descendants into one nation that knows no bounds — holy, truly catholic, and apostolic.

The Virgin of Nazareth, the bridge linking the Old and New Covenant, was not alone when she spoke her *yes* in the name of all humanity. There were others, too, who awaited the fulfillment of the promise made to Abraham. While Satan slept and the world wallowed indifferent to the things of God, a people kept faith — attentive to the prophets and vigilant to the signs of the times. Holy Scripture calls these faithful people the *Anawim* — the poor of Yahweh, the holy remnant — the Daughter Zion. There were Elizabeth and Zechariah, Simeon and Anna, and Joseph, the husband of Mary, to name a few.

The Blessed Virgin Mary, in a singular, unique, and most perfect way represents all the believing people — those who preceded her and those who come after her. It was through their vigilant faith that Jesus came in humility, a Babe born in Bethlehem. As it was, so it will be. The Blessed Virgin preceded

His first coming and is the advent announcing His Second Coming. The victorious Lamb once slain will come in the power of a King wielding the sword of justice — wielding but not wounding. This sword brings the reward that will be given to each man as his conduct deserves, separating the good from the evil, the wheat from the chaff, the flower from the weeds.

With the same vigilant faith, and in trustful abandonment to Divine Providence, the child within the man and woman, who by virtue of Baptism bears the name Jesus, shares in the same salvific and sanctifying mission of the saints and prophets of old. Our ancestors gave constant testimony to the power released by the humble submission of the soul to the supreme and sacrosanct authority of God. That the child within is known, loved, and served by God brings strength where once there was weakness, confidence where once there was insecurity, humility where once there was pride, and selflessness where once there was self-centeredness. The wounds of life, if not completely healed, are at least made sacred and become the source by which others are served and God is glorified.

In childlike humility and empowered by the Spirit, the ancients of old placed total trust in God. With mature faith they bore responsibility for the perpetuation and propagation of truths that ensured interior peace for their children. Rather than succumb to the venom of the slithering seductions of the ancient serpent of Genesis, the souls that suffer for the faith, imitating the saints and prophets of old, are set free from falsehood. They sing their *yes* in concert with the chorus of fiats that through the ages have borne abundant fruit in the regeneration of the faith.

We are the descendents of those whose faith has stood the test of time. Now, this is our time — the only time we have. We bear the same responsibility for the same faith that made our ancestors willing martyrs in the cultivation of the sacrificial and sacred character of their lives, lived configured to the Christ. Ours may be a bloodless martyrdom as we suffer the faith in the face of the world's repudiation of the Christ. This repudiation, often expressed in the world's indifference to truth, relegates Jesus to the myth of gods, prophets, or teachers whose relevancy makes for mere speculation.

THE POWER OF HUMILITY

Difficult as it is, the hostile disregard for the faith of the Church should come as no surprise. We were told it would be so. Before suffering His redemptive death, Jesus alluded to the sad reality that when the Son of Man comes, He would find the faith repudiated and the hearts of many gone cold, but He assured His disciples that He would always guard for Himself an *Anawim* — a little flock clothed in the Beatitudes and joyfully suffering in patient and persevering prayer. Disciples of The Divine Mercy, their childlike faith and trust in God and their openness to the secrets of heaven, are cause for hope in a world that is spinning out of control and drowning itself in a sea of egos. It would be naïve to deny that the world is moving dangerously down the wrong road. Hostility towards the Christian faith, with its life giving religious and moral principles, is overtly being fomented both from without as well as from within.

In spite of innumerable signs of God's ever constant presence in our midst, the rejection of the faith of the Roman Catholic Church by so many is symptomatic of a failure to respond to the perennial call of the Christ to "let the child come unto me." The refusal to be childlike results in the perpetuation of childishness characterized by the egocentricity of adolescent behavior that extends well beyond its years and too often remains the sole companion carried through life and into death.

No matter how beautiful her temples are or how faithful she may be to the rituals of her worship, if the Church resists the long-suffering faith and spirituality of her ancestors, devotion to the Christ in the cradle of the Catholic community reneges in its commission to be custodian and protector of the sacred truths and mysteries of the Christian faith. Built on the foundation of the Apostles — with Peter as its head and Christ Jesus its capstone and supreme authority — this commission, as with the grace conferred in Baptism, is permanent. The Christian faithful, then, have the responsibility to humbly submit in trust and obedience, in patient and persevering prayer, to the sacrosanct authority of the living God. This is the God who is ever active in and through the sacred Magisterium of the Church.

Her doctrine is pure but poorly propagated when her prayer suffers the pollution of the world's excesses. Infected by the spirits of a new age or espousing the corporate identity of a high-tech world, the Church's mysticism is diminished in the faithful's reluctance to bear responsibility for the unique mission entrusted to the Church by the Christ. Her sole mission is to nurture the child in the long suffering of a spirituality that brings a mature and responsible response to God's call to be disciples of the Christ in the daily dying to the self. When the Church, in her institutions, ministers, and members succumbs to the spirit of the world, the end result is sinful contribution to the evil breeding of social, psychological, and spiritual sickness. This evil breeding makes the soil fertile for the flowering of cults and cultic behavior that only desecrates the true nature of the Christ.

If the Church too often seems ineffective in this time, it is because the faithful give the appearance they have rejected, or at least do not understand, the sacrificial and sacred character of the Church as espoused to the Triune God and to Him alone. It is scandalous when, born of the waters of Baptism, the faithful have been formed in the spirit of the world. They are at a loss when they look to the Church's ministers and do not find confident strength in the power of humility. The truth, then, that the Church is the Mystical Body of Christ is too often concealed. The profound depth and perfection of her holiness is too often hidden in the life of her spouse, the Christ.

So, here in the heart of Chicago, as in innumerable places throughout the world, heaven is reaching out to humanity in a gesture of mercy to kindle within the soul a desire for God. The Holy Mother of God — the tabernacle that so long ago concealed the *Holy of Holies* — continues her apostolic mission to make Jesus known, loved, and served. She gently and tenderly, gracefully and mercifully, reminds a wayward, wandering, and wondering people that they, too, are known, loved, and served by God.

The same Virgin Mary, who after the Ascension of Jesus into heaven, kept vigil with the children of Abraham in the novena of prayer, remains steadfast and solicitous in her role as Mother of their descendants, the disciples of her Son. With this in her heart and ever united to the prayer of the Church, she has requested the Sanctuary of The Divine Mercy.

Nearly 2,000 years ago, as the children of Abraham were validated, affirmed, and empowered on the feast of Pentecost, the Blessed Virgin's call to sanctuary is reminiscent of the summons made to the apostles. They were called to return to the upper room of the Last Supper in anticipation of the promised outpouring of the Holy Spirit.

Our response to her call to step into the sacred silence of sanctuary brings the soul to drink at the fountain of The Divine Mercy. The soul's gaze on Jesus in the Blessed Sacrament, enveloped by the image of the Blessed Virgin Mary, prompts the child in every man and woman to look as if in a mirror upon the grandeur of its own identity. The child's soul is infused and animated with the mystery of incarnational spirituality. The soul discovers that it has a share in the very life of the Redeemer who is not frozen in the pages of Sacred Scripture, but is, indeed, alive and active in its deepest recesses.

Whether by the hidden virtue of grace already received in the holy Sacraments of the Church or perhaps through the stirrings of a newfound desire for life in God, the Iconic Monstrance of Our Lady of the Sign, holding within itself the Blessed Sacrament, awakens the soul to recognize that created in the image and likeness of God and loved into life, there is a child within who wants to be set free. That child's freedom is wrought through the healing, purifying, transforming, and sanctifying power of God's grace emanating from the Most Holy Eucharist. This is, indeed, the soul's personal encounter with the crucified and risen Jesus.

The Sanctuary of The Divine Mercy requested by Our Lady is an invitation to step into sacred space and, there, return to the days of youth, when innocence made the heart receptive to the breath of God's Spirit. Unencumbered by the distractions of the world's cacophony and the Church's own succumbing to the seduction of such chaos, the silence of sanctuary strips the masks that make the Master imperceptible to the senses. Soaring in the Spirit, the child called forth freely from within graciously gives gratitude to God on the holy ground that brings growth through grace. The sacred space of sanctuary brings the child in the man and woman to mature in wonder at the mystery of God who is ever present and ever active in creation.

See what love the Father has bestowed on us
in letting us be called children of God!
Yet that is what we are.
The reason the world does not recognize us
is that it never recognized the Son.

Dearly beloved, we are God's children now;
what we shall later be
has not yet come to light.
We know that when it comes to light
we shall be like Him,
for we shall see Him as He is.

1 John 3:1-2

Enediate dó   uerbum eius ad audiendi
nunum oŝ   uorem sermonum eius pŝ.
angeli eius   Benedic aiama mea dó
poientes uirtute qui faciis   mino et omnia que intra

28

An Apocalyptic Awakening

March 2007

The dragon sits by the side of the road, watching those who pass. Beware lest he devour you. We go to the Father of Souls, but it is necessary to pass by the dragon.

(St. Cyril of Jerusalem)

On the island of Patmos, in the Aegean Sea, I bled profusely — a wound to the head. There, on the island where the beloved John wrote the Book of Revelation, closing Sacred Scripture and defining the end of time, I had an unexpected brush with death. Now, with a scar forever on my forehead, I am visibly reminded that I am a marked man — a servant of the Living God.

The blessed wound I received on the little island of Patmos confirms my deep-felt conviction that ours is a suffering faith — sacred and sacrificial. That we try to see God in all things, even in the adversity of life, is a testimony to the truth that for those who love God, all things work for the good. And so it is that I interpret the affliction that enveloped what would otherwise have been a rather pleasant visit to the "island of the apocalypse."

PILGRIMAGE PRAYERS

This chapter began when I left Chicago on October 23, 2006, to lead 45 pilgrims through ancient shrines and sanctuaries in Italy. After eight days of travel, our intense and tightly packed pilgrimage ended in Rome with the celebration of the Papal Mass in the Basilica of St. Peter.

Following tradition, the pilgrimage had been permeated with prayers of gratitude for God's graciousness and with petitions both public and private. We prayed for world peace and for the mission of the Church. We prayed for our families and friends. We prayed for the sick and the dying. We also added special prayers for the sanctuary project at St. Stanislaus Kostka Parish.

This is the seventh year since we began laboring toward the fulfillment of the Blessed Virgin Mary's call to build a Sanctuary of The Divine Mercy on the grounds of St. Stanislaus Kostka Parish. Providentially, at the same time that I was leading the pilgrimage through Italy, Cardinal Francis George was in Chicago approving the revised design for the sanctuary.

In addition to both the public and personal petitions voiced by the pilgrims gathered in prayer, I am certain each pilgrim kept secret other supplications buried deep in the recesses of their own soul — petitions for deliverance from one or another affliction which can bind a person in a slavery of sorts. Or perhaps they prayed for liberation from a distress that keeps one walking that fine line, which when crossed brings a person to break from reality, even if only for a brief span of time.

A privilege of the priesthood is hearing sacramental Confessions, listening to people's stories, and trying to discern the state of their souls. I say privilege because hearing countless hours of Confessions has given me a deep appreciation for the sufferings of others and the absolute need we have of God's mercy and His desire to give it. The distresses we suffer in this world are woven into the larger story of man's good beginning and ultimate good end, and the battle that wages in between. Though we are redeemed by the Blood of the Cross, on this side of death, we are in exile. To the extent that we are estranged from God, we are distressed. We are in battle. We suffer a certain separation from our true selves — the self created in God's image and likeness. We long, therefore, to be whole.

Priest though I am, my consecration to God does not lift me from the realm of reality that keeps me in the battle between the forces of light and those of the dark. Perhaps my commitment to bring others into the light makes my battle all the more intense. In any case, I began the pilgrimage to Italy with an unspoken but specific request to be delivered from a torment I have suffered to varying degrees most of my life.

My personal affliction comes as an assault to my sense of well-being with God, with others, and with myself. Through the years, mirrors and cameras have become an increasing source of torment to me. At times, when I see a reflection of myself, I seem disfigured. My face especially may look distorted, and my thoughts become harsh and condemning. The mere sight of a camera pointed in my direction is enough to elicit an upsurge of those negative voices that tempt me into emotional paralysis. They shout into silence any good I perceive within me. They seem to sour any good fruit God produces in me. When this happens, I fall under the weight of those thoughts and distortions, and struggle to rise above the suffering they cause.

I have so often asked God to set me free from these torments. In fact, since the consecration of my life to the Blessed Virgin Mary and my response to her call to build the Sanctuary of The Divine Mercy, my personal afflictions have become more intense. Over the years, I had tried to accept what seemed perhaps the will of God. Yet, I found the interior battle would bring me at times to the brink of a cliff I feared could plunge me into an abyss of darkness from which there would be no return.

The pilgrimage to Italy was no respite from this battle. As soon as the trip began, the distortions — to my face and in my thoughts — returned with a vengeance. Joy and peace were being drained from my life. I fought to rise above the debilitating depression that ensued. My cry for deliverance was deep-felt. I begged God to finally set me free from this harassment to my soul. This became my personal, private, and unceasing petition.

On the Island of Patmos

After ending the pilgrimage, I arranged to meet Oscar Delgado in Rome. Oscar has been working with us on the sanctuary project since its conception. We had decided to make a retreat on the Greek island of Patmos, where John the Apostle wrote what became the last book of the Bible. The beloved disciple received a revelation — an apocalyptic vision — in a little cave while exiled to this tiny island. Since the iconography of the Sanctuary of The Divine Mercy will personify images from the Book of Revelation, Oscar and I thought it worthwhile to prayerfully visit the island.

We flew from Italy to Athens then transferred to a small propeller plane for the short flight to the island of Samos. After an overnight stay in Samos, we took a cab to a barren dock, where we waited all day for the arrival of a ferryboat. The tourist season had ended a few weeks earlier. Due to heavy winds and a rough sea, the boat didn't arrive until 8:00 p.m.

The boat ride seemed exceptionally slow. We docked at several other islands to unload freight, alight passengers, and pick up new ones. At one point, as the ferryboat was in sail, I went to the deck atop the ferry and walked in the open air. Although it was November, the weather seemed unusually harsh. My body shook from the wet, blustery wind that penetrated every pore of my skin. Looking out into the distance, I remember thinking how lonely it would be to die in the cold waters of a turbulent sea in the dark of night.

After what seemed like an all-night trip, we finally arrived on the small island of Patmos. It was nearly 11:30 p.m. We were met by Peter, whose family owned the apartments we stayed in that night. I was so tired. Not only was the trip from Samos to Patmos long and slow, I was worn out from the intense and varied travels of the pilgrimage. All I wanted to do was to go to bed. I longed for a night of deep and peaceful sleep.

Oscar suggested that we both read the Book of Revelation before going to sleep. He thought it would be a nice way to prepare for the next day's visit to the "cave of the apocalypse." I agreed, but my hope that night was to dream rather than to read the book. Oscar's apartment was on the floor above mine and Peter's was directly below. We wished each other a good night and God's blessing and parted our ways. We planned to meet for breakfast at 8:00 in the morning before going to the cave.

I entered my apartment. I locked the door, leaving the key in the lock. I brushed my teeth and washed my face. The last memory I have before going to bed was of looking at myself reflected in the mirror. I was more than pleased by what I saw. Not only did I look normal, but I looked virile and handsome. My face radiated a light I had never before perceived. I was certain in that moment God had answered my prayer for deliverance from my personal torment. That was the last thought I remembered that night. I must have fallen sound asleep the moment my head hit the pillow.

Meanwhile, Oscar was on the terrace outside his apartment, reading the Book of Revelation. As I slept soundly, his thoughts were fixed on John's vision of the cosmic upheaval brewing there on the horizon of history — the final battle between good and evil, the shedding of blood, the seal of the living God branded into the foreheads of God's servants, and the mark of the beast on those who reject God. Soon Oscar would go to bed, and only a few hours later I would awake in the dark of my apartment, a dark so black that I could not see my hands before my eyes.

It must have been about 4:00 in the morning when I got out of bed, disoriented and wondering where I was. Immediately I sought the light, but to no avail. My arms and hands reached out into the space before me, searching for walls, light switches, lamps — anything to dispel the darkness enveloping me.

Still half asleep, I gave up trying to find the light and went back to bed. Morning would come soon enough. Bending over, I reached for the bed, but couldn't find it. "Where is the bed?" was the last coherent thought I had before I plunged headfirst with loud force into something that sent a wave of shock through my entire head and neck. For a second, I was stunned into oblivion. In the next second, fear forced my hand to my head, from where I felt a sudden, dull sting. In the black darkness of this lonely and unfamiliar place, my forehead felt foreign to my touch, and in the silence of that solitary space I shivered and gasped. In a whisper, I groaned, "Oh, my God." Somehow, even as panic surged through me, I was certain God was there.

I don't know how I got there, but the next thing I remember was standing before the mirror — the same mirror that left me exceptionally proud only hours earlier. This time I was terrified at what I saw: my blood-covered hand pressed against my forehead, my face and t-shirt drenched in blood. I lifted my hand away from my head, and to my horror my forehead opened and blood spilled with the rapidity of a faucet turned wide-open.

The instinct to survive kicked in. Within seconds, I was upstairs banging on Oscar's door, shouting his name as loud as I could. Just as Oscar opened the door, Peter yelled from the banister below, "What happened?" and ran up the stairwell. I quickly turned in his direction, and as I looked down toward him, my blood cascaded, splashing on the steps below.

With Oscar to my right and Peter to my left, I felt a momentary relief, knowing I was no longer alone. As we hurried into my apartment, still bleeding profusely, I began apologizing at the sight of blood splattered across the floor — on the door, in the bathroom, and in the bedroom. The whole apartment looked like the aftermath of a slaughter. Alongside the bed, I saw for the first time the sturdy wood table that had been the *cause* of my fall. A thick glass top, now broken, was the *weapon* that ripped open my head.

I remember pressing a large towel to my head, and then my memory lapsed. I have no recollection of dressing myself, but I was fully dressed. The next thing I recall was walking toward a car for the short ride to a nearby clinic. There were no hospitals on the island. We waited in the car outside a small clinic while the island police located the only available medic. Peter and Oscar kept reassuring me, "You'll go to the cave. Don't worry. You'll go to the cave."

When the medic arrived, he opened the clinic. Still holding the blood-soaked towel to my head, I was quickly ushered into a small room. Even though my eyes were drenched in blood, I could see the room was colorless and barren. The only exception was a cabinet against the wall and a lone metal table in the center of the room. I would lie on that table for the next four hours. As I lay down, I knew I no longer had control. By God's grace, I was able to let go of all fear. I simply placed myself in the hands of God.

At one point, I heard Oscar say, "Father, the icon of Jesus hangs on the wall behind you. He's looking down at you." My blood-soaked eyes opened wide. I wanted to turn around to see the icon, but I couldn't. Suddenly, the medic looked down into my eyes, his face only inches from mine, and asked, "Anthony, are you okay?" His words were sincere and spoken with compassion. For the first time, I saw his face. He was so young. His eyes were dark and caring. Consoled by the sight, I simply answered. "Yes, I'm okay." He tried to stop the bleeding as he wiped the blood from my eyes and face. Sometime later, the medic's face again hovered over me. Looking into my eyes, he said with great empathy, "Anthony, this is going to hurt." I quietly answered, "Yeah, I know."

The sting of cold alcohol washed into the wound, and the sharp pain of the needle challenged my senses. The constant flow of blood was a block to any anesthetic. The medic knew the pain would be excruciating, and it was. His empathy gave me the courage to endure whatever would come. I knew I wasn't alone in my suffering. I couldn't see the icon of Jesus behind me, but it didn't matter. The medic had become for me a living icon of the Christ. My life was in his hands.

My hands tightly gripped my belt and my legs wrenched with spasms as each stitch was sewn. The persistent bleeding gave a welcome respite from the pain of the needle-drawn thread. At one point, I became colder than ice and my body shook uncontrollably. My teeth began to chatter so hard I thought they would break from the pressure. A little relief came after blankets were thrown over my body.

Three hours since lying down on that table, the suturing now done and my head bandaged, I was told to sit up slowly. I was so weak and so cold. My only desire was to stay where I was, but with the help of the medic, I complied. I was no sooner upright than blood began to trickle from beneath the bandage into my eyes and down my face.

Once again on my back, the bandage now removed, Oscar told the young medic I needed more stitches. After that, I remember little else. At some point, both Oscar and Peter had left. I was aware others had entered the small room, but I was oblivious to what was being said. That well-known phrase "it's all Greek to me" suddenly became literal. I sensed all eyes were on me. At this point, I didn't care what was being said or what was being done. I was just tired and dazed.

Oscar and Peter returned with clean clothes. I was unaware my clothes were soaked in blood. My hair felt wet with what I thought was sweat. I brushed my hand against the back of my head to dry the sweat. As if to recall an earlier image, I brought back my hand, now covered in blood. I was amazed that I had lost so much blood and yet was still alive.

I was taken to another room, where I was given a bed. Preparations were being made for an immediate trip back to the island of Samos, where I was to check into the hospital. I stepped from the door of the clinic, and for the first time since arriving on the island, I saw the light of the sun.

Before leaving Patmos, the promise was kept. Oscar and I paid a brief visit to the cave of the beloved John, only yards from the clinic. Within minutes, we were at the cave. My legs felt like rubber. I was dizzy and my head throbbed with pain. With little strength to support my body, I managed to descend down the stairs and into the cave. There, I dodged the low ceiling and protruding rock wall. I was extremely sensitive to anything in close proximity to my head.

I sat on a bench for a brief five minutes. It was all so surreal. The thought of John's apocalyptic vision and the writing that ensued would not register with me. Near the stroke of midnight, I had arrived on the island of Patmos. Now, less than twelve hours later, I could not remove myself from the drama of my own apocalyptic reality. My blood had been shed and my forehead marked forever.

A PERPETUAL IMPRINT

After leaving Greece, I returned to Rome. Doctors' orders would not allow me to make the international flight to the States for a full eight days, so I used my recuperation in Rome as a time for retreat. During this time of prayer and reflection, I was haunted by two conflicting images looking back at me from the same mirror. One image seemed to cancel the other. The virility reflected in the mirror at midnight on Patmos was shattered by the image of my open forehead and a blood drenched face reflected from the same mirror only hours later. The radical shift from total control to utter vulnerability had opened my soul, in an instant, to complete dependence on God.

Rather than take away the debilitating distortions I perceived in my face, it seemed God had given them a perpetual imprint. Rather than remove the "thorn in my side," He had pushed it in all the more deeply. Indeed, God reproves and chastens those whom He loves. The trauma I suffered on the "apocalyptic island" was a loud awakening to the sound of God's voice — a strong voice that admonished me and the enemy within me. He permitted a hard blow to be dealt. I felt not only the pain of my forehead ripped open, but also the suffering of my soul exposed to God's scrutiny. I became aware that it is not by appearances that a man is judged, but by the state of his soul.

Indeed my soul was being scrutinized and found lacking.

And the judgment, in a word, was mistrust. I had not fully trusted the affirming voice of God that named me and blessed me as a beloved son. Instead I cleaved to those voices of condemnation that come from the battleground of the mind. In so many ways and through so many years, God had tried unceasingly to set me free from the torment, but all the while I had yielded to the lies. So many years of my life had been lived in the service of God, and yet I had kept so many things for myself. I had attempted to maintain control of my life and had not relinquished everything to the healing and transforming power of God's Spirit.

Now, I was not only weak from a large loss of blood, but I was faint with fatigue from the awareness of this sin and other sins weighing down on my conscience.

As a confessor, I am keenly aware of God's infinite mercy for His children. Now as penitent, I, too, must humble myself, examine my conscience, and with a contrite heart ask God's forgiveness. At the Basilica of St. John Lateran, I made the most complete and comprehensive Confession of my life. If on the "apocalyptic island" I had been purged of impurities and depleted of energy in the shedding of my own blood, I was now being washed anew and replenished in the Blood of the Lamb.

After Confession, I attended Mass, knowing that the Holy Eucharist is the fount from which His Blood brings the bath that bathes and the food that feeds our souls. I was there in the silent embrace of God's infinite mercy. During the silence, I vividly recalled a dream I had shared with my parishioners just before leaving on pilgrimage.

In my dream I was walking to Mass through a hilly, rugged, and weedy terrain. It was night, and I could see a small chapel off in a distance, looking a little shabby and lonely as it stood there alone on one of the hills. There was no evidence that anyone was in the chapel. No lights were burning. The little chapel looked as though it had been abandoned for years.

As I walked, I became keenly aware of the presence of evil. My reflective walk quickened to a pace that was propelled by the adrenaline beginning to rush through my veins. I turned around, and four thugs were running rapidly toward me. Looking forward, I felt fear begin to surge as I now stepped into a gallop that would never be. I was pounced on, and with force I was thrown to the ground — the four thugs on top of me. In an instant, I felt the pressure lift. As quickly as the four thugs came, with the

*same swiftness, they left. The foreboding evil that
had enveloped the scene seemed to evaporate immediately.*

*Surprisingly, my body felt no pain. Lying there, face down
as though dead, I drew my hands under my chest and
pressed them to the ground as leverage. Then I pushed my
torso up and raised my head slightly. As I looked forward,
the rugged and weedy terrain appeared to have been
transformed into a beautiful landscape of hills of various
sizes and shapes, sprinkled with an assortment of trees in
every shade of green. It was still night, but the night's
darkness was bathed in a radiant light. Small houses were
scattered throughout that looked like cottages painted into
the pages of a child's book of fairytales. The peace I had
was quite a contrast to the previously felt evil. Children
were at play, and as I looked to my right, I saw young men
playing touch football.*

*I turned my gaze toward the night sky only to behold the
heavens opened. The Blessed Virgin Mary appeared surrounded by the brightness of a dazzling light that made it
almost impossible to see her. She descended suddenly and
swiftly — her whole presence embracing the landscape.
Instantly, though, I sensed the return of evil's fury. My
eyes were again drawn upward to the place from where
Our Lady had come. A dragon lunged forward from
nowhere, but was detained by a net of some sort, making
it impossible to disturb or disrupt the beauty and peace
that lay before me.*

As I woke from the dream, I remembered feeling a great
confidence that indeed the Blessed Virgin Mary was bringing
her plan for the parish to fulfillment. It was as if she suddenly

descended anew to embrace the parish of St. Stanislaus Kostka and make it holy ground.

The previous seven years since the consecration of my life and that of the parish to the Mother of God has been a walk unlike any I had ever imagined. Now in Rome, sitting in the Basilica of St. John Lateran, the events on the Island of Patmos and this dream were beginning to coalesce. Both summoned me to the daily dying to self necessary for the fulfillment of God's plan in my life. Only in dying to self will I behold victory in the battle, the battle to build the sanctuary and the fight to be free from forces that try to bind me in falsehood.

THE WOUNDS OF HER SON

In Patmos, God had challenged me to see Christ by looking beyond those two conflicting images reflected back at me from the same mirror. Both images, the one of virility and the other of vulnerability, are true to who I am. But, seen apart from Christ, they enslave me in the drudgery of a battle that cannot be won. I should instead behold the icon of the Christ in the young medic who, as he wiped the blood from my eyes and face, gently called my name. With empathy, he warned me that it would hurt. I was reminded that in my response to God's call I had chosen the narrow road, and there, to cleave to Christ and carry the Cross. In His vulnerability, Jesus shows His virility. From His sacred Wounds, He heals humanity. In the shedding of His blood, He gives life. The fulfillment of God's will in my life demands that I look away from myself and turn towards Him.

Now it seemed God had set me back on track. And, true to His promise, He protects His own. Everywhere I had gone, at the clinic in Patmos, the hospital in Samos, in Rome and Chicago, the same scenarios were spoken as a reminder of the blessed wound I now bore on my forehead. I was told, "If you had been knocked unconscious, you would have bled to death. If the impact had been only an inch lower, you could have died in an instant. You could have lost an eye. Your face could have been grossly disfigured."

None of these tragedies would necessarily have destroyed me nor would they have caused my defeat. People suffer far worse everyday and give noble testimony to the good that can come from the traumas of life. Even death is not cause for despair for those who die in God's grace.

But for me, the shedding of blood and the marked forehead awakened me to the state of my soul and to whose voice I should listen, to whose power I should yield, and to whose reign I should serve. The wound I suffered on the island of Patmos reminded me that I had long ago been *knighted* into the service of Our Lady. As priest, I stand in solidarity with her people, but before them I must be both shield and sword in the protection and defense of their lives.

After eight days of recuperation, I left Rome, looking like a soldier returning from battle. When my parishioners learned of the freak accident I suffered in Patmos, and when they saw the wound so freshly branded into my swollen forehead, and my eyes enveloped by black and blue bruises, they assured me they shared the pain.

They reminded me that the bloody awakening on the island of Patmos was only one in a series of struggles to bring the Blessed Virgin's call to fruition. Our response to her call exposes us to those forces that wish only the death of the soul. Our faith and trust must be rooted in the truth that God is always faithful to His promises. In the battle we may be wounded, but our lives in God will not be destroyed.

We would be wise to trust in the apocalyptic vision of the beloved John. The little cave became, as it were, a window by which John would peer through history. There he saw an angel sent by God to mark the forehead of God's servants. The seal to the forehead would protect the servants of God from the four evil winds whose fury would destroy the world. Knowing the battle that envelops the world, Christ gave the Sacraments to the Church as seals that bind us to God and safeguard us in times of trial and tribulation.

Rather than listen to the voices of condemnation that come from the battleground of the mind, rather than yield to the powers and principalities of this world, rather than serve the seductive and illusory reign of Satan, God has inspired us once again to turn our attention to the *Woman Clothed with the Sun*. Not only should we imitate the journey of faith she trod, when as a pilgrim like ourselves, she pondered the mysteries of God unfolding in her life, but we should trust that from Heaven she continues to care.

A growing flock believes that the Woman of the Apocalypse has placed in our hearts and our souls her wish that a Sanctuary of The Divine Mercy be built on the grounds of St. Stanislaus Kostka Parish. In her Sanctuary, Our Lady promises shelter from the storms of life — a respite from the battle. From the fount of God's mercy, that is, from the Wounds of her Son, she will give drink to God's people. In Sanctuary, the Blood and Water flowing perpetually from the Wounds of Jesus will bring refreshment, renewal, and rejuvenation to a wayward, wondering, and wandering people.

Preparation for Victory

I believe more than anything else the story woven through the pages of *A Mother's Plea* is about perseverance in the struggle — to listen and respond with faith and trust to the mysterious movement of God's Spirit. This story is about persistence as we make the walk through the perilous journey into the light.

In January 2007, the Archbishop of Chicago, Francis Cardinal George, granted permission for St. Stanislaus Kostka to be named the Sanctuary of The Divine Mercy for the Archdiocese of Chicago. We received this as official confirmation that our walk in faith to build Our Lady's sanctuary has not been in vain. What began as a flicker of faith seven years ago is now a blazing fire.

The call to build sanctuary is not unique to St. Stanislaus Kostka Parish. In many places near and far, the same scenario has been played out. As far away as Africa, the Blessed Virgin Mary called for the world's return to God. The refusal to respond to her call brought dire consequences as seen in the massacre of untold thousands. In November 2004, I was in Rwanda and saw firsthand the sad aftermath of the genocide that took the lives of a million people.

Immaculée Ilibagiza, a survivor of the 1994 genocide and the author of the international best-selling book *Left to Tell*, came to St. Stanislaus Kostka Parish on February 12, 2007. She came to thank the parish for the gift of the 18-foot statue of The Divine Mercy that links our sanctuary to theirs. The statue was erected on the age-old *Hill of God*, overlooking the Shrine of Our Lady of Kibeho. Our Lady had said in Kibeho that God alone can bring genuine and enduring peace. Immaculée closes her book with words of gratitude to Our Lady of Kibeho, but then sighs, "If only we had listened."

Yes, if only we'd listen.

The Blessed Virgin Mary has requested a Sanctuary of The Divine Mercy on the grounds of St. Stanislaus Kostka Parish, and she is showing herself throughout the world with a frequency never before known. We would be foolish not to listen to this woman who bore the Prince of Peace. She reigns for the sole purpose of establishing in the hearts of her people the Kingdom of her Son. She prepares the way by which the King will come to separate, in a definitive way, the forces of light from those of darkness. Every Mass celebrated, every Creed recited, and every Our Father prayed, is an anticipation of the glorious reign of Christ.

The cosmic upheaval so mystically imaged in the Book of Revelation is, in a word, about victory. The Sanctuary of The Divine Mercy is a preparation for the full realization of this victory. It is a means by which God wishes to bring healing and transformation to a people who know too well the battle that wages within them and around them. In a world where light and darkness are so intricately woven together that sometimes hope is overridden by despair, the Mediatrix of Mercy brings the Christ whose reign has already begun. Yes, the Lamb of God, slain and yet standing in the heavenly courts, reigns upon the throne with the Ancient of Days. He is victorious.

Millennia ago, from the little cave on the tiny island in the Aegean Sea, the heavens opened and a vision was revealed. Since then, the world has been fascinated by the cosmic upheaval brewing on the horizon of history. The upheaval is upon us. It is within us. To some degree it has always been, but there has been a sudden and violent change in the affairs of the world. Heaven will not be silent.

In her request for the Sanctuary, the *Woman Clothed with the Sun*, stands at the door and knocks. Do we dare open the door?

I have opened the door. The veil has been lifted to the plea of a Mother. It takes courage to respond to her call. I say courage because no one who answers the call will go forward unscathed. But the sweet taste of victory brings joy enveloped in the mystery of God, who is ever present in the inner sanctuary that lies within all of us.

Borrowing the words of the beloved John, *A Mother's Plea* is pure and simple, a testimony to *the distress, the kingdom, and the endurance we share in Jesus.* May the Blessed Virgin Mary inspire courage and strength for the mission entrusted to all who are willing to make the sacrifices needed to bring hope to a world still so new to the third millennium.

EPILOGUE

Then afterward I will pour out My Spirit upon all mankind.
Your sons and daughters shall prophesy,
your old men shall dream dreams,
your young men shall see visions;
even upon the servants and the handmaids,
in those days, I will pour out My Spirit.
and I will work wonders
in the heavens and on the earth,
blood, fire, and columns of smoke;
the sun will be turned to darkness,
and the moon to blood,
at the coming of the day of the LORD,
the great and terrible day.
Then everyone shall be rescued
who calls on the name of the LORD;
for on Mount Zion there shall be a remnant,
as the LORD has said,
and in Jerusalem survivors whom the LORD shall call.
(Old Testament, Book of Joel 3)

A Mother's Plea is a testimony to God's persistence in pursuing a wandering people. Heaven is reaching out to humanity in a plea to drink at the Fountain of The Divine Mercy. This is a story about Our Lady's intervention. She asked for the parish, and I gave it to her. Indeed, she is here.

I am responding to Our Lady's call from the depths of my nothingness and from the fiscal poverty of this parish. In the process, I am learning that heaven brings people into the path of its unfolding plan for humanity's salvation and sanctification.

Some people are consistent and persevering in their response to God's will. Others may respond for a time and then move on when the burden of God's demands makes life uneasy. Still others simply choose not to respond. No one is forced to respond to the will of God, and in fact, such a response is not easily discernable. Then, of course, there are those who fall into Satan's trap and succumb to his deceptions, lusting after illusions or finding themselves caught in his seductions.

Whatever the case may be, Jesus never stops loving. He longs to allure us into His Heart through the penetrating gaze of His Divine Mercy. His eyes are the window to His soul. His Heart is the door through which Our Lady guides us to drink at the Fountain of The Divine Mercy. To this end, she has requested a sanctuary.

The need for the sanctuary is at the heart of this story, which continues to unfold through the purgative and trans-forming power of the Holy Spirit. The story is about the living and the dead and includes both the sacred and the secular. In the midst of spiritual warfare, the mysticism of the Church weaves itself through the lives of the faithful who respond to a call heard from that sacred place in the depths of the soul.

This story is unfolding and will not end until Jesus comes in glory as the just judge. In the meantime, we are living in a time of grace. This is the only time we have. Our indifference to the call would be chilling. Our silence would be condemning. We must build the sanctuary.

Fr. Anthony Buś, on a balcony at St. Stanislaus Kostka school looking out over the Kennedy Expressway in the shadow of the proposed Divine Mercy Sanctuary. Chicago Sun-Times, Inc.

A Father's Plea

It costs only our lives to open the interior
sanctuary of our souls to the indwelling presence
of God. We die that He live, we decrease that
He increase, we lose ourselves that He be found.
Indeed, only then do we come into our true
identity as a people created in His image and
likeness. Only then does the purpose and meaning
of life transcend the limits imposed
by time and space.

That we are destined to share in God's eternity
compels our commitment to life in a world
that is passing away.

Your assistance in the building and
nurturing of the sanctuary is a commitment to
life and the means to genuine *metanoia*, that is,
the transformation from darkness to light, from
evil to good, from death to life.

Fr. Anthony Buś, CR
Pastor
St. Stanislaus Kostka Parish
1351 West Evergreen
Chicago, Illinois 60622-2362
www.amothersplea.org
www.SanctuaryofTheDivineMercy.org

The Proposed Sanctuary of The Divine Mercy

Sanctuary Mission and Vision

The Sanctuary of The Divine Mercy is quiet refuge from the labor of life's journey where the soul is opened to the transforming power of God's ever-abiding presence.

Through adoration of the Blessed Sacrament, which is enveloped by the Iconic Monstrance of Our Lady of the Sign, humanity will be restored to its rightful identity, as conceived and created in the image and likeness of God — an identity clothed in dignity, nobility, and grace. The grace of the Blessed Sacrament will assist a covenant people in its return to childlike trust in Jesus and inspire enthusiasm for the work of life.

Core Values

* The need for sacred silence that God's voice be heard.
* The Holy Eucharist as God's unique and perfect presence among us.
* The Blessed Virgin Mary's solicitous care and concern for her children.
* The sacrificial and sacred character of the Church's mission and that of her members.
* Connection to the Jewish roots of our faith and the religious and spiritual traditions of the Catholic faith as exemplified in the lives of the Saints.
* Humility, modesty, and hospitality to safeguard the sacred in the space of sanctuary.
* Detachment from many good things in life in order to be single-minded in our devotion to Christ.
* The fulfillment of the spiritual and corporal works of mercy.
* Humble recognition that we are sinners and always in need of conversion.
* Joy in the incomprehensible desire of God to transform us through His Mercy.
* Vigilance and persevering prayer in preparation for the Second Coming of Christ.

I want to live
in the temple of the Great God,
where everything is to be found.
In this sanctuary, I find all
that I loved most rapturously,
all that I thought most truly,
all of those most beautiful things
I wished to accomplish.

Bogdan Janski
Founder of the Resurrectionists
November 15, 1830

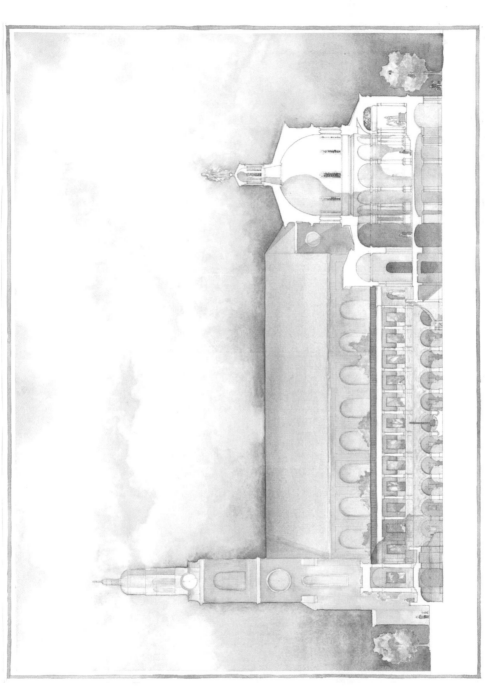

Cross section of the Sanctuary of The Divine Mercy schematic design next to Saint Stanislaus Kostka Parish facing North.

Front view of the Sanctuary of The Divine Mercy schematic design next to Saint Stanislaus Kostka Parish facing East.

THE THEOLOGY OF THE SANCTUARY
OF THE DIVINE MERCY

The Sanctuary of The Divine Mercy starts with the premise that liturgical art and architecture are sacramental and therefore reveal to our senses the otherwise invisible realities of heaven through sign and symbol (*Sacrosanctum Concilium*, 122). As such, every architectural choice is a theological choice. The architecture of the Sanctuary is more than an architectural tent to keep out rain and wind. It is a three-dimensional building which makes present the very reality of The Divine Mercy in the same way that an icon is a two dimensional vehicle for making present the presence of a heavenly being. The primary theological motif of the Sanctuary of The Divine Mercy is the history of salvation as evidenced in the Garden of Eden, the Temple of Solomon, the Church, and the heavenly Jerusalem. Pilgrims to the Sanctuary will be welcomed into an oasis of prayer in the city, but also encounter in microcosmic form the great deeds of God in salvation history as well as an anticipated eschatology of their heavenly future. All the while, the greatness of God's mercy is shown as the means for returning to the embrace of the Father.

The large narrative of salvation history follows a fairly simple timeline: God was complete and perfect in Himself; He chose to create the world and human beings, who were happy with him in the Garden of Eden; humanity chose to reject God at the Fall and was ejected from the Garden; at the Fall, chaos and disorder entered the world; man's relationship with God, with other human beings, and with nature was no longer in harmony and balance. God's merciful plan of salvation, then, centers on drawing humanity back by reordering it towards right relationship with him. In the Old Testament, this included the Ten Commandments as a merciful revelation of how God wanted his creatures to return to him. It also included the commands of ritual worship and the building of the Solomon's Temple. The Sanctuary of Divine Mercy will be informed by this history in order to represent an "undoing" of the Fall in art and architecture.

TEMPLE TYPOLOGY AND THE SANCTUARY OF THE DIVINE MERCY

According to Scripture and contemporary documentary evidence, the Temple of Solomon was not simply a large building for ritual activities. It was understood to be an evocation and making present of the reunification of God and humanity. It was composed of three portions: a porch, a large inner room, and a smaller cubic room at the rear.

The porch was framed by two large bronze columns and served as a transitional space from the earthly world into a realm of sacramental presentation of the restored Eden and heaven beyond. The large inner room, known as the *hekal*, is described in scripture as being covered in sculpted leaves, flowers, gourds, palm trees and cherubim, evoking the Garden of Eden and the harmonious state of humanity, angels and God as it was in the beginning. The Jewish high priest passed through the "garden" and the veil to enter the Holy of Holies, the place of God's presence. The Holy of Holies held the Ark of the Covenant which contained the tablets of the Ten Commandments as well as manna and the rod of Aaron. The space above the ark was called the Mercy Seat and is where the presence of God rested. The high priest brought the petitions of the Twelve Tribes to the presence of God in the Holy of Holies, sprinkling animal blood, and then came forth to share the blessings of God with the people. This same high priest wore a breastplate studded with twelve gems, each representing the Twelve Tribes of Israel, and by extension all of humanity. He therefore brought all of humanity to God.

The design of the Sanctuary of The Divine Mercy begins with this three-fold temple typology. Between the sidewalk and the garden courtyard will be be a transitional porch, perhaps using columns of brown stone to suggest the great bronze columns of the temple porch. Passing through the porch, the visitor will enter an enclosed courtyard garden, intended to be an oasis of order, peace, and beauty in the noise and chaos of the city. This garden corresponds to the *hekal* of the temple. With its ordered plantings, fragrant flowers, and fountain at the center which signifies the rivers of paradise, this garden will begin to "undo" the Fall in that it replaces city noise with peace, chaos with order, and engine fumes with sweet fragrance. As the iconographic plan continues, we hope to include imagery that helps the visitor understand this garden as something more than a botanic experience. It will include imagery in the iron gates which suggest the reentry into Eden and inscriptions in the architecture itself.

The architectural and theological destination of the Sanctuary, however, is the large adoration chapel at the east end, which corresponds to the Holy of Holies in the Temple. As in the Temple of Solomon, the chapel will be an evocation of heaven. Whereas the Holy of Holies in the temple contained the ark of the Old Covenant of the Law, the Sanctuary will show this reality fulfilled. A rectangular pedestal recalling the Ark of the Covenant will become a setting for the "Iconic Monstrance," an image of the Virgin Mary which contains within it the Eucharist for adoration. Here, Christ, who is the New Covenant, is set within the womb of His Mother who is the new Ark. Therefore, representationally, the New Covenant literally stands on the Old Covenant, not abolishing it but fulfilling it.

The adoration chapel of the Sanctuary of The Divine Mercy will also take many allusions from the Book of Revelation and its descriptions of heaven. Since this room is meant, like the Holy of Holies, to sacramentally present the "signs and symbols of heavenly realities" (*SC*, 122), the heavenly realities described in scripture are given pride of place. In the Book of Revelation, John sees a throne with one seated on the throne, surrounded by an emerald rainbow. The throne of this chapel, of course, will be the Iconic Monstrance, and the setting on the wall behind it will be developed in glass mosaic as an emerald "rainbow" in the manner often represented in traditional eastern icons. Around the throne in scripture are described twenty-four white robed elders, and the architecture of the room contains twenty-four columns in twelve pairs, building on the biblical comparison between Christians as "pillars of the Church" (Galatians 2:9) and the twelve foundations of the Heavenly Jerusalem as the twelve apostles.

Additionally, the Heavenly Jerusalem is described as being jewel-like, radiant with light, crystalline, and golden. The walls of the city are described as being composed of the same twelve gems originally placed on the high priest's breastplate, meaning that God's presence is now in his creation who form "God's building," but one glorified and perfected in heaven at the Banquet of the Lamb. The architecture and iconography of the Sanctuary will sacramentally present this glorified, divinized heavenly reality in conventionalized form.

Therefore, the building will partake of colored marbles, gold mosaic, and gem-like colors. The dome mosaic over the room will be composed of a night-blue sky with golden stars, arranged in geometric patterns to suggest the new heavens over the new earth.

Many smaller iconographic details are yet to be finalized, but the large theological picture is clearly sketched out. The Sanctuary of The Divine Mercy will come as close as possible to being a coherent whole, organized around the centrality of The Divine Mercy as evidenced in the Sacrament of Mercy, the Eucharist. It will nonetheless recall the story of salvation history in poetic architectural, iconographic and textual terms. The rich layering of meaning will not be mere lavish display, but will adequately and gloriously make knowable to the senses a foretaste of the heavenly liturgy while keeping primary things primary, secondary things secondary and peripheral things on the periphery. The goal of this building is to draw people to The Divine Mercy. The beauty of the building and its art will not become an aesthetic end in itself, but be transparent to the formative and transformative presence of Christ. The hope is that people will be attracted by its beauty, engaged in the truth of its content, and transformed by the goodness they find in Christ. They will then go forth to transform the world, making disciples of all nations as they preach the revelation of The Divine Mercy.

Dr. Denis McNamara, Assistant Director
The Liturgical Institute, University of Saint Mary of the Lake, Mundelein Seminary
Author, Heavenly City

THE SPIRIT OF OUR EFFORTS
THE CHURCH'S CALL — OUR RESPONSE

BACKGROUND

In 1870, the Congregation of the Resurrection began working at St. Stanislaus Kostka Parish. By 1897, St. Stanislaus Kostka was one of the largest parishes in America, with 40,000 parishioners, and at the end of the century the parish had given birth to 20 new parishes throughout Chicago — an unparalleled legacy of spiritual multiplication in the city. With the construction of the Kennedy Expressway in the 1950s, and with it, changing patterns of immigration, gentrification, and the arrival of new forces of social disruption, the parish began a slow decline. By the end of the century, the parish had dwindled to less than 500 families.

The material and spiritual poverty brought by these changes prepared the people of St. Stanislaus Kostka to receive a call at the dawn of the New Millennium — a call rooted in the renewal and resurrection of society. The Sanctuary of The Divine Mercy is a call to a new ministry and a wider mission. Since August 1999, the people of St. Stanislaus Kostka have walked in faith, discerning the Spirit of God under the guidance of the Blessed Virgin Mary. That initial call has developed, not without trials, into the clearer vision that it has become today.

Every day over 300,000 people travel along the Kennedy Expressway. This main artery feeding the engine of the American economy is symbolic of the frenetic nonstop life of certain aspects of the American culture that leave little room for contemplation and even less room for God's mercy to touch the deep recesses of the soul. The Sanctuary of The Divine Mercy will stand as an oasis on this crossroad of America, where the weary traveler can be enveloped in the mercy of God in a place of sacred silence. The Sanctuary will be a sign of contradiction, and the healing silence it offers will be a powerful antidote to a culture that tries to silence God's voice.

Since August 1999, this new mission has been discerned and has slowly and painfully matured. A steady and growing number of souls already recognize and experience the Sanctuary of The Divine Mercy on the grounds of St. Stanislaus Kostka Parish. The charism to renew and resurrect society animates the mission of the Sanctuary of The Divine Mercy and seeks to serve this people in union with the Church and in response to the particular needs of our place in history. In January 2007, the Cardinal Archbishop of Chicago, Francis George, officially designated St. Stanislaus Kostka Parish as the Sanctuary of The Divine Mercy for the Archdiocese of Chicago.

This new mission and ministry of St. Stanislaus Kostka Parish should be viewed as a response to the Church's call, her pastoral plan and priorities for the Third Millennium. Pope John Paul II believed that his particular mission was to lead the Church into the New Millennium with a superabundant outpouring of grace and mercy. At that great moment in history, the turn of the century, he articulated a vision and issued a call to the Church, guiding her into the future. Three encyclicals form a unified pastoral plan for the Church of the New Millennium — *Novo Millennio Ineunte, Rosarium Virginis Mariae,* and *Ecclesia de Eucharistia.* Along with Pope Benedict XVI's *Deus Caritas Est* and *Sacramentum Caritatis,* a clear path has been laid as we are confronted with the unique challenges and opportunities of our time in history.

At the same time, on the threshold of the New Millennium, the call to build the Sanctuary of The Divine Mercy was heard and began to be discerned. What follows is the fruit of that discernment — an understanding of the new mission and ministry at St. Stanislaus Kostka within the framework of the Church's pastoral plan and her priorities for the New Millennium.

THE CHURCH'S CALL:
DUC IN ALTUM (PUT OUT INTO THE DEEP)!

At the beginning of the new millennium, and at the close of the Great Jubilee during which we celebrated the two thousandth anniversary of the birth of Jesus and a new stage of the Church's journey begins, our hearts ring out with the words of Jesus when one day, after speaking to the crowds from Simon's boat, he invited the Apostle to "put out into the deep" for a catch: "Duc in altum" (Lk 5:4). Peter and his first companions trusted Christ's words, and cast the nets. "When they had done this, they caught a great number of fish" (Lk 5:6).

Duc in altum! These words ring out for us today, and they invite us to remember the past with gratitude, to live the present with enthusiasm and to look forward to the future with confidence: "Jesus Christ is the same yesterday and today and for ever" (Heb 13:8).

John Paul II, *Novo Millennio Ineunte*

Our Response:

The rallying cry issued by John Paul II carries the spirit of trusting, surrender, courage, and boldness to "put out into the deep." From the initial call for the Sanctuary of The Divine Mercy, the character of this new mission and ministry has embodied the same spirit of surrender, courage, and boldness as it is an ambitious mission in the midst of significant challenges. Symbolically, the Sanctuary of The Divine Mercy is a kind of net that seeks to catch souls being carried along the current of the Kennedy Expressway. In both the spirit and in the imagery of the Holy Father's thematic rallying cry, the Sanctuary of The Divine Mercy at St. Stanislaus Kostka Parish gives a positive response.

The Church's Call:
Be Profoundly Rooted
in Contemplation and Prayer

It is important however that what we propose, with the help of God, should be profoundly rooted in contemplation and prayer. Ours is a time of continual movement which often leads to restlessness, with the risk of "doing for the sake of doing." We must resist this temptation by trying "to be" before trying "to do." In this regard we should recall how Jesus reproved Martha: "You are anxious and troubled about many things; one thing is needful" (Lk 10:41-42).

John Paul II, *Novo Millennio Ineunte*

OUR RESPONSE:

The Kennedy Expressway aptly symbolizes our "time of continual movement" and a culture that finds little value in the quest for "being" and the spiritual fruits born from contemplating the mystery of Christ. The Sanctuary of The Divine Mercy answers the deep-seated thirst for stillness in our time. Our noisy world longs for silence and contemplation. The Sanctuary offers an oasis where this need is met. Wrapped in the beauty that speaks of these mysteries and before the living King and the fountain of Mercy Himself, the traveler finds more than rest, he or she finds Life. When the road weary person finds a place of quiet to discover the sanctuary within his or her soul, God's voice can be heard. It is there that the renewal and resurrection of society begins to take root, within the spiritual shelter of Sanctuary.

Here in the heart of Chicago, as in innumerable places throughout the world, heaven is reaching out to humanity in a gesture of mercy to kindle within the soul a desire for God. The Holy Mother of God — the tabernacle that so long ago concealed the Holy of Holies — continues her apostolic mission to make Jesus known, loved, and served. She gently and tenderly, gracefully and mercifully, reminds a wayward, wandering, and wondering people that they, too, are known, loved, and served by God.

Our Lady's request for a Sanctuary of The Divine Mercy is a mother's plea to her children to seek refuge in God. To this end, she prepares holy ground where sacred silence gives way to the sound of God's voice. She will not permit the cacophony of the world to interrupt or distort the voice of the living God. She will provide the means to draw the pilgrims to the Sanctuary of The Divine Mercy and into the silence of the adoration chapel where Jesus will give to drink from the fountain of mercy.

The Sanctuary of The Divine Mercy will be an encounter with the living God in the silence of sacred space. There, away from the noise of the world, the soul will "contemplate the face of Christ in the school of Mary."

A Mother's Plea, Chapter 10

THE CHURCH'S CALL:
CONTEMPLATE THE FACE OF CHRIST
IN THE SCHOOL OF MARY

To Contemplate the face of Christ, and to contemplate it with Mary, is the "programme" which I have set before the Church at the dawn of the third millennium, summoning her to put out into the deep on the sea of history with the enthusiasm of the new evangelization. To contemplate Christ involves being able to recognize him wherever he manifests himself, in his many forms of presence, but above all in the living sacrament of his body and blood. The Church draws her life from Christ in the Eucharist; by him she is fed and by him she is enlightened. The Eucharist is both a mystery of faith and a "mystery of light."

John Paul II, *Ecclesia de Eucharistia*

May Mary Most Holy, the Immaculate Virgin, ark of the new and eternal covenant, accompany us on our way to meet the Lord who comes. In her we find realized most perfectly the essence of the Church. The Church sees in Mary — "Woman of the Eucharist," as she was called by the Servant of God John Paul II — her finest icon, and she contemplates Mary as a singular

340

model of the Eucharistic life. For this reason, as the priest prepares to receive on the altar the verum Corpus natum de Maria Virgine, speaking on behalf of the liturgical assembly, he says in the words of the canon: "We honor Mary, the ever virgin mother of Jesus Christ our Lord and God." The faithful, for their part, "commend to Mary, Mother of the Church, their lives and the work of their hands. Striving to have the same sentiments as Mary, they help the whole community to become a living offering pleasing to the Father." She is the tota pulchra, the all beautiful, for in her the radiance of God's glory shines forth. The beauty of the heavenly liturgy, which must be reflected in our own assemblies, is faithfully mirrored in her. From Mary we must learn to become men and women of the Eucharist and of the Church, and thus to present ourselves, in the words of Saint Paul, "holy and blameless" before the Lord, even as he wished us to be from the beginning (Col 1:22; Eph 1:4)

Benedict XVI, *Sacramentum Caritatis*

OUR RESPONSE:

Enthroned at the heart of The Sanctuary of The Divine Mercy will be the Iconic Monstrance of Our Lady of the Sign. Already approved by Francis Cardinal George, the nine-foot monstrance is being sculpted by Stefan Neodorozo. This original iconography reflects John Paul II's program for the third millennium "to contemplate the face of Christ in union with, and at the school of, his Most Holy Mother."

The iconic monstrance is a symbol of the union of Jesus with his bride, the Church. It expresses the immutable bond between the Mother and Child. It shows the complementary union between the Man and the Woman and the sacred power of God's reign in the mutually shared authority of the King and the Queen. Subject to the Christ, the Virgin Mary is exalted and thus the whole of humanity is donned in dignity, nobility, and grace.

A Mother's Plea, Chapter 24

The design and plans for the Iconic Monstrance of Our Lady of the Sign were well established when the words of John Paul II and Benedict XVI were written. Their words serve to confirm the inspiration for the Iconic Monstrance of Our Lady of the Sign. The theological inspiration for the Iconic Monstrance of Our Lady of the Sign is the following:

Then God's temple in heaven was opened, and the ark of his covenant could be seen in the temple. There were flashes of lightning, rumblings, and peals of thunder, an earthquake, and a violent hailstorm. A great sign appeared in the sky, a woman clothed with the sun, with the moon under her feet, and on her head a crown of twelve stars. She was with child and wailed aloud in pain as she labored to give birth.

Revelation 11:19-12:1-2

As long as the sacrifice of the Cross is perpetuated in the celebration of the Holy Eucharist, the Blessed Virgin Mary is in the pain of labor, and with her, the whole Mystical Body of Christ. As with the ancient Ark of the Covenant, like Mary, the Church holds within herself the Holy of Holies and is commissioned to safeguard and show forth the jewel of her faith. Appropriately, the Blessed Sacrament, that is, the Sacred Host, enveloped by one of the most ancient icons of the Blessed Virgin Mary will be at the heart of the Sanctuary of The Divine Mercy. The icon, which dates back to the earliest centuries of the Church and is commonly called Our Lady of the Sign, evokes the prophesy of Isaiah and the apocalyptic vision of St. John the Apostle. Their prophecies recall the onset of man's salvation in the sign of the woman bringing forth the Child. The monstrance bearing the image of Our Lady of the Sign safeguards and shows forth the jewel of Catholic spirituality which is the Body, Blood, Soul and Divinity of Jesus Christ present in the consecrated Host. Both the image of Our Lady and the Blessed Sacrament are symbols of victory in battle and together define the Sanctuary of The Divine Mercy.

A Mother's Plea, Chapter 24

THE CHURCH'S CALL:
ADORATION OF THE MYSTERY OF MERCY

When the Church celebrates the Eucharist, the memorial of her Lord's death and resurrection, this central event of salvation becomes really present and "the work of our redemption is carried out." This sacrifice is so decisive for the salvation of the human race that Jesus Christ offered it and returned to the Father only after he had left us a means of sharing in it as if we had been present there. Each member of the faithful can thus take part in it as if we had been present there. Each member of the faithful can thus take part in it and inexhaustibly gain its fruits. This is the faith from which generations of Christians down the ages have lived. The Church's Magisterium has constantly reaffirmed this faith with joyful gratitude for its inestimable gift. I wish once more to recall this truth and to join you, my dear brothers and sisters, in adoration before this mystery: a great mystery, a mystery of mercy. What more could Jesus have done for us? Truly, in the Eucharist, he shows us a love which goes "to the end", a love which knows no measure.

John Paul II, *Ecclesia de Eucharistia*

Mary is the one who has the deepest knowledge of the mystery of God's mercy. She knows its price, she knows how great it is. In this sense, we call her the Mother of mercy: our Lady of mercy, or Mother of divine mercy; in each one of these titles there is a deep theological meaning, for they express the special preparation of her soul, of her whole personality, so that she was able to perceive, through the complex events, first of Israel, then of every individual and of the whole of humanity, that mercy of which "from generation to generation" people become sharers according to the eternal design of the most Holy Trinity.

John Paul II, *Dives in Misericordia*

OUR RESPONSE

More than a private devotion, the mystery of mercy holds the key to salvation history and the heavenly storehouse of grace. John Paul II, through his life and papacy, called the Church into the mystery of mercy unlike any pontiff in history. Before becoming pope, he was instrumental in advancing the message of The Divine Mercy and the cause of St. Maria Faustina Kowalska. As pope, his most personal encyclical, *Dives in Misericordia*, contemplated the theme of God's mercy and perhaps most defined his papacy. He instituted the Feast of The Divine Mercy to end the Easter Octave, or perhaps, to more completely insure the celebration of the great Feast of the Resurrection from the Easter Vigil to the Eighth Day. Saint Maria Faustina Kowalska was canonized the "Apostle of The Divine Mercy" — the first saint canonized in the new millennium. Providentially, John Paul II died moments after the vigil mass was celebrated, marking the Feast of The Divine Mercy in 2005.

John Paul II has rightfully been called the pilgrim pope whose message of Christ's mercy went to all four corners of the earth at a great pace and with great urgency. He is the spark prophesied in the writings of St. Maria Faustina that would set the fire of The Divine Mercy ablaze across the world. That fire is kindled in sanctuary.

At the heart of the Sanctuary of The Divine Mercy will be the Mediatrix of Mercy Adoration Chapel — a powerful visual statement of the role of Mary as Mother of Mercy. It is in her heart that The Divine Mercy is known so deeply. She will come to the aid of the frightened, the disheartened, and the wounded. She will help them say with confidence, "Jesus, I trust in you." Each, in his or her way, will be equipped with the gifts needed to "put out into the deep" — to be clothed in the beatitudes and to live with authenticity the spiritual and corporal works of mercy.

The new mission and ministry of St. Stanislaus Kostka, the Sanctuary of The Divine Mercy, is born from a call to respond to the particular needs of the *Anawim* of the third millennium. Its aim is to draw them out of the restless culture symbolized by the Kennedy Expressway, east of the church. The call is heard in Jesus' cry from the cross — *I thirst*. His thirst is for souls. It is heard in the cry of the commuter. Symbolically, the mission of St. Stanislaus Kostka turns to the East — the direction of the rising sun, the hope of a new day, the expectation of Christ's return, and the fulfillment of the promise to his people.

The Sanctuary of The Divine Mercy at St. Stanislaus Kostka Parish seeks to respond to the complex needs of the people of today with a multifaceted mission and ministry. The Sanctuary is rooted in the call to renew and resurrect society, according to the plan and program of the Church so recently embarked upon the third millennium. At its core, the mission and ministry is a call to sanctuary where a Marian and Eucharistic spirituality can profoundly transform the soul. All the various initiatives and plans of the Sanctuary seek to support the soul's encounter with God, assisting the growth of this relationship into maturity and active witness in the world.

THE CHURCH'S CALL:
THE PASTORAL PRIORITIES FOR THE THIRD MILLENNIUM

We must gain new impetus in Christian living, making it the force which inspires our journey of faith. Conscious of the Risen Lord's presence among us, we ask ourselves today the same question put to Peter in Jerusalem immediately after his Pentecost speech: "What must we do?" (Acts 2:37).

With its universal and indispensable provisions, the pro-gramme of the Gospel must continue to take root, as it has always done, in the life of the Church everywhere. It is in the local churches that the specific features of a detailed pastoral plan can be identified — goals and methods, formation and enrichment of the people involved, the search for the necessary resources — which will enable the proclamation of Christ to reach people, mold communities, and have a deep and incisive influence in bringing Gospel values to bear in society and culture.

What awaits us therefore is an exciting work of pastoral revitalization — a work involving all of us. As guidance and encouragement to everyone, I wish to indicate certain pastoral priorities which the experience of the Great Jubilee has, in my view, brought to light:

> *Training in Holiness*
> *Training in Prayer*
> *The Sunday Eucharist*
> *The Sacrament of Reconciliation*
> *Primacy of Grace*
> *Listening to the Word*
> *Proclaiming the Word*

John Paul II, *Novo Millennio Ineunte*

OUR RESPONSE

The gap in catechesis and religious education of more than two generations has created a great thirst for the Church's riches to be known and lived. Following John Paul II's pastoral priorities for the New Millennium, the vision for the Sanctuary of The Divine Mercy, as a center for the New Evangelization, foresees robust on-going programming and initiatives that will open the storehouse of the Church's patrimony for generations to come. The providential location on Chicago's Kennedy Expressway (I90/94) permits the Sanctuary to offer these programs to the commuter and the whole Archdiocese due to this easily accessible location. In addition to presenting practical training in holiness, prayer, Sabbath rest, Eucharistic and Marian spirituality, the sacraments, discernment, scripture study, evangelization, catechesis and apologetics, the Sanctuary will have a particular focus on forming Catholic culture and worldview. The Sanctuary will be supported in its evangelization efforts with a media center that will use new and traditional media to reach out with the message of the Gospel and The Divine Mercy.

Special Perpetual Novena Prayer to Our Lady of Good Remedy

O QUEEN OF HEAVEN AND EARTH, Most Holy Virgin, we venerate thee. Thou art the beloved Daughter of the Most High God, the chosen Mother of the Incarnate Word, the Immaculate Spouse of the Holy Spirit, the Sacred Vessel of the Most Holy Trinity.

O Mother of the Divine Redeemer, who under the title of Our Lady of Good Remedy comes to the aid of all who call upon thee, extend thy maternal protection to us. We depend on thee, Dear Mother, as helpless and needy children depend on a tender and caring mother.
Hail, Mary....

O LADY OF GOOD REMEDY, source of unfailing help, grant that we may draw from thy treasury of graces in our time of need. Touch the hearts of sinners, that they may seek reconciliation and forgiveness. Bring comfort to the afflicted and the lonely; help the poor and the hopeless; aid the sick and the suffering. May they be healed in body and strengthened in spirit to endure their sufferings with patient resignation and Christian fortitude.

Hail, Mary....

DEAR LADY OF GOOD REMEDY, source of unfailing help, thy compassionate heart knows a remedy for every affliction and misery we encounter in life. Help me with thy prayers and intercession to find a remedy for my problems and needs, especially for... *The spiritual and material resources needed to build the Sanctuary of The Divine Mercy in the heart of Chicago on the grounds of St. Stanislaus Kostka Parish.*

On my part, O loving Mother, I pledge myself to a more intensely Christian lifestyle, to a more careful observance of the laws of God, to be more conscientious in fulfilling the obligations of my state in life, and to strive to be a source of healing in this broken world of ours.

Dear Lady of Good Remedy, be ever present to me, and through thy intercession, may I enjoy health of body and peace of mind, and grow stronger in the faith and in the love of thy Son, Jesus.

Hail, Mary....

V. Pray for us, O Holy Mother of Good Remedy,
R. That we may deepen our dedication to thy Son, and make the world alive with His Spirit.

AFTERWORD

FR. S. SERAPHIM MICHALENKO, MIC

For over 20 years, I had the privilege of being the vice-postulator for the canonization cause of the first saint of the Great Jubilee Year 2000, St. Maria Faustina Kowalska. In light of my familiarity with the urgent message of The Divine Mercy that God entrusted to this saint, Father Anthony Buś, CR, the author of *A Mother's Plea*, requested that I serve as a theological advisor in his mission to respond to what he perceives to be Our Lady's call to build the Sanctuary of The Divine Mercy at St. Stanislaus Kostka Parish in Chicago.

In an effort to evaluate the authenticity of this mission, I read *A Mother's Plea* and discovered fascinating parallels between the story that has been unfolding in this inner-city parish and St. Faustina's perseverance in receiving and spreading the message of The Divine Mercy throughout the world. I believe that these parallels or connections are signs of God's providence that can encourage each of us — even as we experience difficulties — to see Jesus, The Divine Mercy, and His mother, the Blessed Virgin Mary, very much alive in our lives and our world. Readers of these reflections should be prepared for a life-changing encounter with the living God.

THIS IS GOD'S WORK, NOT OURS

After the sacred image of Jesus, The Divine Mercy — revealed in a vision to St. Maria Faustina Kowalska on February 22, 1931, in the city of Plock, Poland — was finally painted by June of 1934, it was hidden in the corner of a dim cloister corridor. Yet the Lord repeatedly insisted to Sr. Faustina, the "Secretary of My Divine Mercy," that it be blessed and solemnly exposed for public veneration.

It was nine months before that request was fulfilled during a three-day celebration of the Jubilee Year of the Redemption in 1935. The image of The Divine Mercy was unveiled, blessed, and exposed for public veneration at the celebration of the Mass concluding the Octave of Easter in this Jubilee Year at the famous Shrine of The Mother of Mercy of the Dawn Gate in Vilnius (then in Poland and now the capital of Lithuania). Sadly, however, after the celebration, the sacred image was returned to the cloister corridor — and hung up, face to the wall!

During one of the sermons preached on that occasion by her spiritual director, Sr. Faustina was greatly overcome by the many sinners who were sincerely repenting, placing their trust in God's mercy, and confessing their sins at the sight of the image. Further, she saw how many demons were fleeing from their hearts and souls.

While St. Faustina was hurrying back to the convent after the celebration, the demons, in the form of evil people, attacked her, threw her into the gutter, and beat her up. They angrily reproached her for ruining, in one night, their labor of many years. On seeing her returning in such a horrible condition, the Sisters at the convent pleaded for an explanation. Her response was: "The Lord God is being so greatly offended, and people couldn't care less about His mercy, and so deserve punishment. I am greatly suffering on account of this, and I deeply sympathize with those chosen by God who receive revelations."

As I immerse myself in these reflections of an inner-city parish priest, of whom our Blessed Mother is demanding a very similar commitment — and as I follow, and take part in, his efforts to realize her will — I, too, greatly sympathize with him. The vicissitudes undergone during the unfolding of God's projects are often challenging. Were we to ask Our Lord and Our Lady (as Sr. Faustina did) why one must go through so many obstacles and put up with so many and such great difficulties in the fulfillment of their requests for the good of souls, most likely we would receive the answer they gave her: That it be evident this is God's work, not ours.

FIDELITY TO GOD'S GRACE

The second parallel between these two stories became obvious to me as I recalled an important lesson St. Faustina learned well and recorded in her spiritual *Diary* in this illuminating entry from October, 1936:

> The Lord said to me today: Go to the Superior and tell her that I want all the Sisters and wards [the women and girls the Sisters ministered to] to say the chaplet, which I have taught you. They are to say it for nine days in the chapel in order to appease My Father and to entreat God's mercy for Poland.
>
> I answered the Lord that I would tell her, but that I must first speak about this with [the] Father [confessor], and I resolved that as soon as the Father comes I will speak to him at once about this matter. When Father arrived, the circumstances were such that they prevented me from seeing him, but I should not have paid any attention to the circumstances and should have gone and settled the matter. I thought to myself, "Well, I'll do it when he comes again."
>
> Oh, how much that displeased God! In one moment, the presence of God left me, that great presence of God, which is continuously within me in a distinctly felt way. At that moment, however, it completely left me. Darkness dominated my soul to such an extent that I did not know whether I was

in the state of grace or not. Therefore, I did not receive Holy Communion for four days, after which I saw [the] Father [confessor] and told him everything. He comforted me, saying, "You have not lost the grace of God, but, all the same, be true to him."

The moment I left the confessional, God's presence enveloped me as before. I understood that God's grace must be received just as God sends it, in the way He wants, and one must receive it in that form under which God sends it to us.

O my Jesus, I am making at this very moment a firm and eternal resolution, by virtue of Your grace and mercy, of fidelity to the tiniest grace of yours *(Diary of St. Faustina, 714-716)*.

I don't know whether Fr. Anthony is aware of these passages from St. Maria Faustina's *Diary*, but I know that he is not swerving from fidelity to what seems to be *A Mother's Plea*.

THE LIGHT OF FAITH

Another palpable connection between these stories was the prophetic tone found in both Sr. Faustina's writings and Father Anthony's reflections. Both of these writings advise the reader to be attentive to "the signs of the times." In Matthew's gospel, Our Lord complains that "You know how to read the face of the sky, but you cannot read the signs of the times" (Mt 16:3). Prompted by this complaint, Our Lord wept over the Great King's City with this lament:

Jerusalem! Jerusalem! Killer of the prophets! Stoner of those who were sent to you! How often I wanted to gather together your children as a hen gathers her brood under her wings — and you would not! (Lk 13:34).

The role of prophecy in the Church was clearly explained by Joseph Cardinal Ratzinger on the occasion of the presentation to the world of The Third Secret of Fatima:

The Apostle [Paul] says: "Do not quench the Spirit, do not despise prophesying, but test everything, holding fast to what is good" (1 Thes 5:19-21). In every age the Church has received the charism of prophecy, which must be scrutinized but not scorned. On this point, it should be kept in mind that prophecy in the biblical sense does not mean to predict the future but to explain the will of God for the present, and therefore show the right path to take for the future.

The prophetic word is a warning or a consolation, or both together. In this sense there is a link between the charism of prophecy and the category of "the signs of the times," which Vatican II brought to light anew: "You know how to interpret the appearance of earth and sky; why, then, do you not know how to interpret the present time?" (Lk 12:56). In this saying of Jesus, the "signs of the times" must be understood as Jesus Himself. To interpret the signs of the times in the light of faith means to recognize the presence of Christ in every age. In the private revelations approved by the Church ... this is the point: they help us to understand the signs of the times and to respond to them rightly in faith (*The Message of Fatima, Theological Commentary, Public Revelation and Private Revelations — Their Theological Status*, Vatican City, Libreria Editrice Vaticana, © 2000, p. 36).

A Mother's Plea, as with St. Maria Faustina Kowalska's revelations of The Divine Mercy, must also be understood as "the signs of the times" for this Third Millennium. In his homily on the occasion of St. Faustina's canonization the Holy Father, John Paul II, declared:

Sister Faustina's canonization has a particular eloquence: By this act I intend today to pass this message on to the new millennium. I pass it on to all people, so that they will learn to know ever better the true face of God and the true face of their brethren.

Saint Faustina's private revelations about Jesus, The Divine Mercy, are, therefore, a prophetic message to the Church and the world for our times. The canonization of the bearer of that message is the Church's stamp of approval as to their divinely supernatural origin and authenticity. The Pope's following declaration on that occasion, I believe, is its highest endorsement:

> Today my joy is truly great in presenting the life and witness of *Sr. Faustina Kowalska* to the whole Church as a gift of God for our time. By Divine Providence, the life of this humble daughter of Poland was completely linked with the history of the 20th century, the century we have just left behind. In fact, it was between the First and Second World Wars that Christ entrusted His message of mercy to her. Those who remember, who were witnesses and participants in the events of those years and the horrible sufferings they caused for millions of people, know well how necessary was the message of mercy.
>
> Jesus told Sr. Faustina: *"Humanity will not find peace until it turns trustfully to Divine Mercy"* (*Diary*, 300). Through the work of the Polish religious, this message has become linked forever to the 20th century, the last of the second millennium and the bridge to the third. It is not a new message but can be considered a gift of special enlightenment that helps us to relive the Gospel of Easter more intensely, to offer it as a ray of light to the men and women of our time.
>
> What will the years ahead bring us? What will man's future on earth be like? We are not given to know. However, it is certain that in addition to new progress there will unfortunately be no lack of painful experiences. But the light of Divine Mercy, which the Lord in a way wished to return to the world through Sr. Faustina's charism, will illumine the way for the men and women of the third millennium.

THE SPARK OF THE DIVINE MERCY

Through the life of St. Faustina, the light of Divine Mercy has been slowly spreading throughout the world to give hope to humanity in our time. At the consecration of The Divine Mercy Basilica near the resting place of St. Faustina's mortal remains in

Poland, the Holy Father, referring to a statement made by Our Lord as recorded in St. Faustina's *Diary*, boldly asserted:

> Today, therefore, in this Shrine, I wish *solemnly to entrust the world to Divine Mercy.* I do so with the burning desire that the message of God's merciful love, proclaimed here through Saint Faustina, *may be made known to all the peoples of the earth* and fill their hearts with hope. May this message radiate from this place to our beloved homeland and throughout the world. May the ***binding*** promise of the Lord Jesus be fulfilled: From here there must go forth "the spark which will prepare the world for His final coming" (cf. *Diary,*1732).
>
> This spark needs to be lighted by the grace of God. This fire of mercy needs to be passed on to the world. *In the mercy of God the world will find peace and mankind will find happiness!* I entrust this task to you, dear Brothers and Sisters, to the Church in Kraków and Poland, and to all the votaries of Divine Mercy who will come here from Poland and from throughout the world. *May you be witnesses to mercy!*
> (*Homily* of Pope John Paul II at the Dedication of The Divine Mercy Shrine in Kraków-Lagiewniki, Poland, August 17, 2002; published in the August 21 issue of *L'Osservatore Romano*).

"What," the benevolent reader might ask at this point, "has all this to do with these reflections of *A Mother's Plea* and its author?" Let me tell you what happened to St. Faustina before she entered the religious life, when she was only nineteen. As she made her way home from a dance during which Jesus upbraided her for putting him off, she dropped into the city's cathedral. There, the Lord gave her instructions concerning her calling as the "Secretary" and "Apostle" of His mercy. The cathedral's patronal title is: *Of Saint Stanislaus Kostka.*

The connection continues in the New World. The first church in the Western Hemisphere where the image of The Divine Mercy was publicly venerated is that of a Polish community in Adams, Massachusetts. Built in 1904, it, too, bears as its patronal title: *Of Saint Stanislaus Kostka.*

Is it any wonder, then, that "the spark" of The Divine Mercy, of which Our Lord and the Holy Father speak, has now alighted on the first church built in Chicago over a hundred years ago for the benefit of the overwhelming number of Polish immigrants to that city — a parish that now serves a rather diverse people of distinct ethnicities? Is it any wonder that we discover in *A Mother's Plea* that Our Lady is now requesting of this church's pastor, the author, that a sanctuary or shrine be built there in honor of Her Son — The Divine Mercy Incarnate?

Further, is it any wonder that this church's heavenly patron is Stanislaus Kostka, whose obedience to his heavenly Mother's instructions to follow the vocation to the consecrated life was all that mattered in spite of his father's worldly plans for him? Still further, is it any wonder that the same thing happened with St. Faustina as her parents opposed her vocation to the religious life?

For these two saints, God's will was sovereign. Utmost faithfulness to His will and to the inspirations that flowed from it was imperative — such obedience was absolutely necessary and urgent!

May all who immerse themselves in the timely reflections of *A Mother's Plea* respond aright to "the sign of the times" — God's call to trust in His mercy while there is yet the time for mercy: JESUS, I TRUST IN YOU! The Sanctuary of The Divine Mercy at St. Stanislaus Kostka Church is to be that urgent sign beckoning Chicagoans and all visitors to that city to find secure refuge under the tender mercy of the Savior of the world and of His Immaculate Mother Mary!

Fr. S. Seraphim Michalenko, MIC

✝ Vice Postulator emeritus for North America in
St. Faustina's Canonization Cause

✝ Co-founder and Director Emeritus of the
John Paul II Institute of Divine Mercy

✝ Rector Emeritus of the National Shrine of The Divine Mercy

✝ Present Director of the Association of Marian Helpers—
the first proclaimers on a worldwide scale since 1944
of The Divine Mercy Message and devotions granted
to the Church through St. Maria Faustina Kowalska,
5 August 2004

✝ Written on the Memorial of Our Lady of Mercy, Patroness
of the Congregation of Sisters of Our Lady of Mercy, of
which St. M. Faustina was declared Honorary Co-Foundress

Prayers and Devotions
Referenced in A Mother's Plea

Message of The Divine Mercy

JESUS I TRUST IN YOU

The Humble Instrument

On October 5, 1938, a young religious by the name of
Sister Faustina (Helen Kowalska) died in a convent of the
Congregation of Sisters of Our Lady of Mercy in Cracow,
Poland. She came from a very poor family that had struggled
hard on their little farm during the terrible years of World War I.
Sister had had only three years of very simple education. Hers
were the humblest tasks in the convent, usually in the kitchen or
the vegetable garden or as porter.

The Image

On February 22, 1931, Our Lord and Savior Jesus Christ appeared to this simple nun, bringing with Him a wonderful message of Mercy for all mankind. Sister Faustina tells us in her diary under this date: "In the evening, when I was in my cell, I became aware of the Lord Jesus clothed in a white garment. One hand was raised in blessing, the other was touching the garment at the breast. From the opening in the garment at the breast there came forth two large rays, one red, and the other pale. In silence I gazed intently at the Lord; my soul was overwhelmed with fear, but also with great joy. After a while Jesus said to me: 'Paint an image according to the pattern you see, with the inscription: Jesus, I trust in You!'"

Some time later, Our Lord again spoke to her: "The pale ray stands for the Water which makes souls righteous; the red ray stands for the Blood which is the life of souls. These two rays issued forth from the depths of My most tender Mercy at that time when My agonizing Heart was opened by a lance on the Cross ... . Fortunate is the one who will dwell in their shelter, for the just hand of God shall not lay hold on him."

Divine Mercy Sunday

As a further sign of His forgiving love, Jesus called for a Feast of The Divine Mercy to be celebrated in the whole Church. The Second Sunday of Easter is now celebrated as Divine Mercy Sunday throughout the Church. He said to Sister Faustina: "I want this image to be solemnly blessed on the first Sunday after Easter; that Sunday is to be the Feast of Mercy. On that day, the depths of My Mercy will be open to all. Whoever will go to confession and Holy Communion on that day will receive complete forgiveness of sin and punishment. Mankind will not enjoy peace until it turns with confidence to My Mercy."

THE NOVENA

Jesus further asked that Divine Mercy Sunday be preceded by a Novena to The Divine Mercy, which would begin on Good Friday. He gave her an intention to pray for on each day of the Novena, saving for the last day the most difficult intention of all, the lukewarm and indifferent of whom He said: "These souls cause Me more suffering than any others; it was from such souls that My soul felt the most revulsion in the Garden of Olives. It was on their account that I said: 'My Father, if it is possible, let this cup pass Me by.' The last hope of salvation for them is to flee to My Mercy."

THE CHAPLET

In 1933, God gave Sister Faustina a striking vision of His Mercy. Sister tells us: "I saw a great light, with God the Father in the midst of it. Between this light and the earth I saw Jesus nailed to the Cross and in such a way that God, wanting to look upon the earth, had to look through Our Lord's wounds. And I understood that God blessed the earth for the sake of Jesus." Of another vision on September 13, 1935, she writes: "I saw an Angel, the executor of God's wrath ... about to strike the earth. ... I began to beg God earnestly for the world with words which I heard interiorly. As I prayed in this way, I saw the Angel's helplessness, and he could not carry out the just punishment. ..."

The following day an inner voice taught her to say this prayer on ordinary rosary beads:

"First say one 'Our Father,' 'Hail Mary,' and 'I believe.'

Then on the large beads say the following words:

'Eternal Father, I offer You the Body and Blood, Soul and Divinity of Your dearly beloved Son, Our Lord Jesus Christ, in atonement for our sins and those of the whole world.'

On the smaller beads you are to say the following words:

'For the sake of His sorrowful Passion have mercy on us and on the whole world.'

In conclusion you are to say these words three times:

'Holy God, Holy Mighty One, Holy Immortal One, have mercy on us and on the whole world.' "

Jesus said later to Sister Faustina: "Say unceasingly this chaplet that I have taught you. Anyone who says it will receive great Mercy at the hour of death. Priests will recommend it to sinners as the last hope. Even the most hardened sinner, if he recites this chaplet even once, will receive grace from My infinite Mercy. I want the whole world to know My infinite Mercy. I want to give unimaginable graces to those who trust in My Mercy."

SUBSEQUENT HISTORY

One day in the same year, 1935, Sister Faustina wrote for her spiritual director: "The time will come when this work, which God so commends, [will be] as though in complete ruin, and suddenly the action of God will come upon the scene with great power which will bear witness to the truth. It will be as a new splendor for the church, though it has been dormant in it from long ago." This indeed came to pass. On the 6th of March, 1959, the Holy See, acting on information that was inaccurately presented, prohibited "the spreading of images and writings advocating devotion to The Divine Mercy in the form proposed by Sister Faustina." As a result, there followed almost twenty years of total silence. Then, on the 15th of April, 1978. the Holy See, after a thorough examination of original documents previously unavailable to it, completely reversed its decision and again permitted the devotion. The one man primarily responsible for this reversal of decision was Karol Cardinal Wojtyla, the Archbishop of Cracow. On October 16, 1978, he was elevated to the See of Peter as Pope John Paul II. On March 7, 1992, Sr. Faustina's virtues were declared heroic; on December 21, 1992, a healing through Sr. Faustina's intercession was declared a miracle; on April 18, 1993, Pope John Paul II had the honor to declare the Venerable Servant of God Sister Faustina Blessed; and on April 30, 2000, Pope John Paul II canonized Blessed Faustina and also called for the celebration of the Second Sunday of Easter as Divine Mercy Sunday throughout the Church.

A NOVENA TO OBTAIN GRACES THROUGH THE INTERCESSION OF SAINT MARIA FAUSTINA

O Jesus, who filled Your handmaid Saint Faustina with profound veneration for Your boundless Mercy, deign, if it be Your holy will, to grant me, through her intercession, the grace for which I fervently pray. My sins render me unworthy of Your Mercy, but be mindful of Saint Faustina's spirit of sacrifice and self-denial, and reward her virtue by granting the petition which, with childlike confidence, I present to You through her intercession.

Saint Faustina, pray for us.

THE CHAPLET OF DIVINE MERCY

The Chaplet of Mercy is recited using ordinary rosary beads
of five decades.

Our Father...Hail Mary...The Apostle's Creed.

ON THE OUR FATHER BEADS SAY THE FOLLOWING:

**Eternal Father, I offer You the Body and Blood, Soul and
Divinity of Your dearly beloved Son, Our Lord Jesus Christ,
in atonement for our sins and those of the whole world.**

ON THE TEN SMALL BEADS OF EACH DECADE, SAY:

**For the sake of His sorrowful Passion, have mercy on us
and on the whole world.**

CONCLUDE WITH:

**Holy God, Holy Mighty One, Holy Immortal One,
Have mercy on us and on the whole world.**
(Repeat 3 times)

THE ANGELUS

In the name of the Father, and of the Son, and of the Holy Spirit. Amen.

V. The Angel of the Lord declared unto Mary.

R. And she conceived of the Holy Spirit.

Hail Mary, full of grace, the Lord is with thee. Blessed art thou among women and blessed is the fruit of thy womb, Jesus. Holy Mary, Mother of God, pray for us sinners, now and at the hour of our death. Amen.

V. Behold the handmaid of the Lord.

R. Be it done unto me according to thy Word.

Hail Mary, full of grace, the Lord is with thee. Blessed art thou among women and blessed is the fruit of thy womb, Jesus. Holy Mary, Mother of God, pray for us sinners, now and at the hour of our death. Amen.

V. And the word was made Flesh.

R. And dwelt among us.

Hail Mary, full of grace, the Lord is with thee. Blessed art thou among women and blessed is the fruit of thy womb, Jesus. Holy Mary, Mother of God, pray for us sinners, now and at the hour of our death. Amen.

V. Pray for us, O Holy Mother of God.

R. That we may be made worthy of the promises of Christ.

Let Us Pray. Pour forth, we beseech Thee, O Lord, Thy Grace into our hearts, that we, to whom the Incarnation of Christ Thy Son was made known by the message of an angel, may, by His Passion and Cross, be brought to the glory of His resurrection, through the same Christ Our Lord. Amen.

V. Glory be to the Father, and to the Son, and to the Holy Spirit. As it was in the beginning, is now, and ever shall be, world without end. Amen.

(Repeat three times)

The Act of Consecration
St. Louis Marie De Montfort

I, (Name), a faithless sinner, renew and ratify today in thy hands the vows of my Baptism; I renounce forever Satan, his pomps and works; and I give myself entirely to Jesus Christ, the Incarnate Wisdom, to carry my cross after Him all the days of my life, and to be more faithful to Him than I have ever been before.

In the presence of all the heavenly court I choose thee this day for my Mother and Mistress. I deliver and consecrate to thee, as thy slave, my body and soul, my goods, both interior and exterior, and even the value of all my good actions, past, present, and future; leaving to thee the entire and full right of disposing of me, and all that belongs to me, without exception, according to thy good pleasure, for the greater glory of God, in time and in eternity.

Prayer to St. Michael

St. Michael the Archangel,
defend us in the day of Battle;
be our safeguard
against the wickedness and snares of the devil.
May God rebuke him, we humbly pray,
and do thou, O prince of the Heavenly Host,
by the power of God,
cast into Hell, Satan and all the other evil spirits,
who prowl about the world,
seeking the ruin of souls.
Amen.

BOGDAN JANSKI
FOUNDER OF THE RESURRECTIONISTS

Why did I return to the holy Catholic faith…?
Because you, O merciful God
wished me to do so!
Your grace alone accomplished this,
and not any of my reasoning, or merits,
or works. I feel this deep within my soul,
and I thank you, O God, for deigning
to look upon my misery and my sufferings,
for hearing me as I groaned and sighed
for the true and universal good.
All-powerful God, help me!
Throughout the rest of my life
give me the strength to become
worthy of your goodness!

December 28, 1834

From Addiction to Conversion
The Story of Brother Bogdan Janski, Founder of the Resurrectionists

"This must be proclaimed to a sinful world, and it is something a person is unable to find out by himself: God loves you."

Brother Bogdan was born in Poland in 1807 and baptized as Theodore Ignatius Bogdan Janski. In the years before and during Theodore's childhood, his country was annexed, freed, and invaded again and, as is always the case, it was poor people like Theodore's family who bore the brunt of the collapse of nation and society. His family lost their land, and both food and clothes were hard to come by.

His father and mother separated when he was in elementary school, but Theodore grew up under the influence of religious teachers in his village who taught him to seek God and strive for holiness. His teachers recognized that he was smart and imaginative, and they made it possible for him to stay in school and even move on to further studies.

Before he left for the University of Warsaw, his mother wrote him a letter which he kept in his diary: *"Don't get into bad company; avoid those who would lead you into worldly and bad habits. Look for companions who have a good reputation . . . ."* She also reminded him that he was just turning sixteen and that he would have to take responsibility for his own life in Warsaw because there would be no father or mother to guide him.

At the university, Theodore got his first taste of the secular world and soon rejected Christianity for materialism.

Despite his mother's warning, Theodore made friends with a classmate who introduced him to drinking parties and brothels.

Theodore often met his friends for bouts of drinking and sex in the tombs beneath the floor level of the Carmelite Church in Warsaw. During one meeting, Theodore poured his drink into a human skull and served up a toast from it. Lifting his gruesome cup, he cursed death and laughed at the thought of eternal life. Life was to be lived now and, since the fullness of pleasure was life's purpose, he entered passionately into the thrills of sensuality.

Just before he left his hometown for an appointment to the Department of Economics and Law at the University of Paris, he impulsively married a pregnant girlfriend named Alexandra. The son born to Theodore and Alexandra was not Theodore's, but he had married Alexandra to save her from embarrassment. Later, he would spill out his regret in his diary: "*A woman has deprived me of my greatness.*" Much later he would admit that he had no one but himself to blame for his inability to reign in his emotions and impulses.

From time to time, he thought of Alexandra. He wrote her letters and, when he had it, sent her money, but the threat of war kept Alexandra and Bogdan apart. They would never see each other again, and he would never meet Alexandra's son.

In Paris, Theodore was attracted to student groups among the Polish refugees. Like him, these companions were poor, confused and unable to do anything positive about the political turmoil in their homeland. Now twenty, Theodore began to call himself "Bogdan," his less formal middle name.

With his new name, things began to change for Bogdan, but very slowly. He began to make a living by translating works from Polish to French, writing articles on economics, and tutoring high school students. He was becoming responsible.

THE DREAM TAKES SHAPE

"Help me to be able to help others on the road to salvation."

Poland's great Romantic poet, Adam Mickiewicz, was one of the political refugees in Paris. His home had become a gathering place for young men like Bogdan. The poet was a strong believer in the gospel of Jesus Christ and attended Mass regularly. Under Mickiewicz's influence, Bogdan began to wonder if he could find God's grace once again.

After many years of avoiding Mass, he found himself wandering into churches to pray, though still drinking and roaming the nighttime streets of Paris. He found it more and more difficult to get up in the morning. Consequently, his research and teaching position at the university was in jeopardy. His diary recounts a daily struggle between sin and God's grace:

> *"Merciful God, support me with your grace. Complete within me this work of salvation, of reconciliation with you.... In you, O God, is all my hope."*

Soon he joined a study group of like-minded individuals. They went to Mass each Friday and then gathered to study sacred scripture at the house of Mickiewicz. Eager to apply the biblical message of salvation to their circumstances, they asked: What would happen if they began living like true disciples of Jesus? Is a regeneration of society based on Christian principles even possible?

In Acts 4:32-33 they found hope: "*The whole body of believers was united in heart and soul....everything was held in common, while the apostles bore witness with great power to the Resurrection of Jesus Christ.*" A Christian social revolution might be possible, Bogdan thought. Society could be reborn, this time formed by the Gospel. The dream of Bogdan Janski began to take shape.

APOSTLE OF HOPE

He realized that to begin a new life he had to seek forgiveness and healing through the sacrament of Confession. His grand ideas were still locked behind his sinful habits. So he and several others began to prepare for their confession, the first since they were children. Bogdan prayed with all his heart that God would free him from his sins of sensuality.

It took him a year of soul searching but, with the help and direction of the prior of a local Benedictine abbey, he confessed his sins and experienced a powerful conversion of life.

He notes in his diary: "*Father Prior was dismayed and frightened by my confession. He called my conversion miraculous.... I received his blessing, my eyes filled with tears, and that is the way he left me. I fell on the ground in the form of a cross.*"

Like a child, this man of great intellect had to learn basic Catholic devotions. He joyfully tells us that after his conversion "*I learned to recite the Rosary.*" And, he kept in contact with the Benedictines who taught him how pray with greater trust. He brought all his hopes and dreams to prayer.

Once Bogdan found God through Jesus Christ in the sacrament of Confession, nothing could stop him from telling others about his new life and the hope that it brought him.

He began to speak to his companions about his dream for a new Christian society.

Peter Semenenko was the first to respond. A twenty-one year old from a militant group of exiles, Peter had left the Church and joined a failed uprising in 1831 in Poland. He then escaped to Paris disillusioned and in danger of going to prison if he were caught. Bogdan took him in and began counseling the young man to return to the Faith and to make something of his new life.

"A truly religious person does not have to regret his past because it was a condition for his call."

CONGREGATION OF THE RESURRECTION

"Why did I return to the Catholic faith? Because You, O God of mercy, wished me to do so. Your grace alone accomplished this, and not any of my reasoning, merits or works."

Bogdan led Peter to confession at the same monastery where he had been reconciled. Another young revolutionary, Jerome Kajsiewicz, also began to experience a new hope and he, too, joined Peter in receiving the sacrament of Confession. Now there were three converts, and a spiritual awakening began to occur among the exiles in Paris.

Bogdan's dream of a new life for himself and his friends became a reality when he rented a house in Paris and invited Peter and Jerome and several other men to live with him, just like the small group of early Christians mentioned in Acts.

On Ash Wednesday in 1836, four of these friends with Janski as "Elder Brother" formed a community of young men that became the inspiration for the Congregation of the Resurrection. Soon, two more men joined them. Brother Bogdan was twenty-nine years old when he formed his new community.

From the beginning the new community was apostolic. In his memoirs, Jerome wrote of those earliest days: "*We felt called by God to serve our brothers but (at first) only a few people believed in us.... (But) one cannot fall in love with the Lord, taste how sweet He is, and not at the same time, be inflamed with the holy desire to see others share this same happiness.... (And, so) we tried to help others to know and love Jesus....*"

Bogdan again took to the streets of Paris, but this time it was to seek out poor exiles and to offer them the gift of hope, the same hope that had saved his life. He fed the hungry and sheltered the homeless with money he begged from some of the well-off exiles in Paris. His new brothers eagerly followed his example.

Bogdan, now known as the "Elder Brother" of the community, became a public penitent and developed an amazing patience and calm. A friend writes of him in those days: "*How many hardships he had to endure....how many evil things he had to listen to before he was able to convince this or that friend of his errors....and take them to Mass and finally lead them to the confessional.*"

Jerome, Peter and the others watched and learned as Brother Bogdan showed the way: "*He sought out straying compatriots in all corners of the great city of Paris. For some he found food, and he assured the conversion of others by taking them into (our) house and going to great trouble to find money to feed a dozen or more people.*"

He was seen in the streets in tattered work clothes while dealing with the poor. Someone saw the miserable condition of his shoes and bought him a new pair. The next day, the donor saw him wearing old worn-out shoes. *"What happened to the shoes I bought you yesterday?"* *"Don't be angry,"* Bogdan answered, *"I met a very poor person and exchanged shoes with him."* For the poor immigrants of Paris, Bogdan Janski became an apostle of hope.

"May I spend my life laboring to erect a temple in which all of humanity will love and honor You. I want to live in the temple of the great God.

ENDLESS POSSIBILITIES

"I continue to hear the anguished cry of those who have been treated unjustly...oppressed by exploitation, extreme poverty and lack of education."

During the next few years, Bogdan intensified his mission to the poor of Paris. Soon the other brothers joined him in this work, and they divided up the poor sector of the city, each accepting responsibility to visit and assist the needy in his area.

Then Brother Bogdan began to cough. At first it was just annoying. With the cough came fatigue and weakness. When he began to cough up blood, he knew that he had little time left to do all the things he had hoped to do in his life. He had dreamed of little houses of brothers living together and forming a network of passionate Christians who would change the world. What would happen now?

He envisioned a transformation of society where the poor could find inns devoted to their care and hospitals that were not just places to go to die but to receive healing. His ideas and plans continued to develop: homes for invalids; Christian schools, even colleges and universities; print shops to produce Christian literature; lay societies to serve the poor as Jesus did. Under the inspiration of God's grace, Bogdan dreamt of a new world transformed by the Gospel. The possibilities were endless.

Meanwhile, Brother Bogdan continued to encourage his brothers, especially Jerome and Peter. When both of these young men felt a call to the priesthood, Brother Bogdan dissuaded them from leaving their group to join the Benedictines and, instead, introduced them to the idea of going to Rome to work and study. Soon, these two brothers left for the eternal city while Brother Bogdan continued to maintain the community in Paris.

Brother Bogdan's ministry was to seek out those who needed him in the streets of Paris but, by 1838, he was feeling weaker. *"Last Saturday....I went to confession after a few days of illness related to the lungs."* He rallied after that but by spring of 1839 he was clearly failing: *"(I am) poor in spirit, poor in health but with a never failing hope of improvement...and once again (I am) reconciled with the Lord."*

By late 1839, he was so sick that the brothers in Rome asked him to come there so they could take care of him. Brother Bogdan died in 1840 at Rome among his brothers when he was only thirty-three, too soon to see his community fulfill the dream of a new society formed and energized by the Gospel of Jesus Christ. But at his death, surrounded by Peter and Jerome and the other brothers, Brother Bogdan was assured that his vision would live on.

And, indeed, the dream did not end with the death of Brother Bogdan, Today, in sixteen countries, the Congregation of the Resurrection works to establish the kingdom of God and to live out Brother Bogdan's dream of transformation of the individual and society.

RISE FROM DARKNESS

The Fathers and Brothers of the Resurrection

You have read the story of our founder, Brother Bogdan Janski. We, the Congregation of the Resurrection, have dedicated our lives to his dream for the world.

Our message is simple and clear: we strive to help those who are struggling with sin and who feel powerless or dead inside. We tell them of God's love and grace freely available through belief and commitment to Jesus Christ. We help them rise up from the darkness of sin to live in the light of the Gospel.

Beyond bringing hope to the individual, we also have a unique way of looking at society. We know that the world can be a dark, sinful place and that there are many people who live in a culture of death. Wherever we Resurrectionists work, we endeavor to bring life. We offer a new way of living and promote a new society founded on the example of the Acts of the Apostles where the original community of Christians was united in heart and mind. Sharing the Eucharist binds us together and helps us form a new society in Jesus Christ. With all our hearts we strive for the resurrection of those dead in sin and despair.

We are faithful to the charism of our Elder Brother Bogdan, who illuminated his world with the light of Jesus

Christ. We, the members of his Congregation, carry that light wherever we go. Brother Bogdan's dream is our dream, too.

ALLELUIA

A Prayer to Follow the Example of Brother Bogdan

Lord Jesus Christ, in Your great love You called Brother Bogdan Janski to leave a life of sin and darkness and to found a community of men who would discover the hope of resurrection for themselves and the world.

You chose Brother Bogdan as a marvelous example of how true repentance leads to conversion and loving ministry to the poor. I want to follow his example and experience for myself Your healing grace. When I am down, lift me up Lord as You comforted and raised up Brother Bogdan.

Use me to help bring light to those in darkness and permit me to carry the message of life to those who live in the shadows of the culture of death. Through the intercession of Brother Bogdan assist with Your grace those addicted to alcohol and other drugs as well as those who sin against purity.

Grant also that one day we who embrace the spirit of Brother Bogdan, the Apostle of Hope, may celebrate his beatification for Your greater honor and glory. We ask all this through Christ Our Lord. Amen

The Congregation of the Resurrection is a religious community in the Catholic Church which continues the work of Brother Bogdan and his original community. We are priests and brothers ministering in parishes, schools, retreat centers and health facilities throughout the world. We keep Brother Bogdan's dream alive.

By Rev. Gerald Watt, CR

ST. STANISLAUS KOSTKA CATHOLIC CHURCH PARISH HISTORY

CULTURAL AND SOCIAL HISTORY

By 1850, the close proximity of Chicago's important waterways and numerous railroads helped transform a little settlement into an industrial and commercial city with job opportunities for crowds of courageous pioneers from around the entire world. After the Civil War ended in 1865, European immigration gathered momentum and poured new life and energy into a country bent on a rapid recovery from the ravages of a devastating conflict. Drawn by the powerful influence of the steadily increasing vitality of this city overflowing with energy, a Polish colony was formed in the northwestern part of the city where St. Stanislaus Kostka is located today.

In the early days, the St. Stanislaus district of today resembled a veritable and immense farm, where swamps and muddy plains stretched out at great length, so much so that some of the first settlers related that they hunted for wild ducks and set traps for rabbits in this region. In 1864, as the influx of Poles multiplied, the small colony grew stronger. A benevolent society eventually formed and organized itself more tenaciously day by day under the patronage of St. Stanislaus Kostka. The practice of the faith and the preservation of the customs of their homeland were the primary goals of this Polish community.

In 1871, the first St. Stanislaus Kostka church building was completed and became the physical manifestation of the strong faith of this newly formed society[1]. At the same time, a complete drought penetrated the city, followed shortly thereafter by the Great Chicago Fire and a terrible epidemic known as "Black Smallpox." The disease raged so tremendously that the number of victims equaled that of the Chicago Fire.

Following the devastation, conditions throughout Chicago began to improve in every respect, especially in manufacturing and trade, and the parish grew further as a feverish reconstruction of the city began. Since laborers were needed, a great many Poles immigrated to the area, making Chicago the seat of contemporary American Polonia and, in general, one of the greatest Polish cities.

In 1893, Chicago hosted the Columbian Exposition, establishing Chicago as a major city in the United States and demonstrating that urban harmony could be achieved through good planning and hard work[2]. As visitors from all over the world converged on Chicago to witness the latest in human achievement, tour groups made regular stops at St. Stanislaus Kostka Parish. By 1897, St. Stanislaus Kostka became the largest parish in the United States, if not the world, with a population of 40,000[3].

As the twentieth century progressed, the neighborhood surrounding the parish began to change. Up until the late 1930s, St. Stanislaus Kostka continued to be the center of religious and cultural life for Polish immigrants. By the end of the 1930s, however, parishioners began moving from the neighborhood in search of a better life in the suburbs. Migration to the suburbs continued to increase when, at the end of the 1950s, many parishioners had no choice but to move out of the neighborhood when the Kennedy Expressway was built. Original plans to build the expressway called for the demolition of St. Stanislaus Kostka Parish. Parishioners gathered in thousands to sign petitions in protest until the city finally agreed to divert the expressway and build it approximately one and one half feet from the rectory building[4]. By 1981, demographics had changed so drastically that parish membership consisted of only 850 families.

The apostolic mission of the parish has been renewed over the last several decades as immigrants from Latin American countries have arrived to make their home here. The majority of immigrants come from Mexico, and the large number of Mexicans and Mexican-American parishioners have brought a new dynamism and vitality to the parish[5].

The neighborhood today still retains a Polish population. Poles with roots at the church continue to return to the parish from all across the Chicago area for baptisms, weddings, and funerals. Now, an entirely new phase is under way as not only Poles, but Mexicans routinely visit the parish to return to their roots. The bilingual skills of the parish priests serve the diverse mix of parish membership, and Masses are offered in English, Spanish, and Polish[6].

In addition to Poles and Hispanics, the parish is comprised of Anglos, Asians, Africans, and African Americans. The diversity of the parish's membership is considered one of its greatest strengths today because it reflects the challenge to true catholicity – that God is, indeed, the God of all people.

St. Stanislaus Kostka Parish is also dedicated to serving the needs of the poor through its soup kitchen. Located in the lower church, the soup kitchen currently serves between 100 and 200 people a day and is efficiently managed by Sr. Anne Schaeffer. Sister Anne has raised funds to keep the soup kitchen open six days a week since its dedication by Joseph Cardinal Bernardin in 1986.

Those traveling the Kennedy expressway will be beckoned by the imposing presence of the Sanctuary of The Divine Mercy where perpetual adoration to the Eucharist under the loving gaze of Our Lady will provide a sanctuary in the city, where all are welcomed. Until that time, the parish continues to offer Sunday Masses in English, Polish, and Spanish. Daily services include confession, a morning and evening Mass, a holy hour at the Hour of Great Mercy, recitation of the Rosary, and Eucharistic Adoration. The Stations of the Cross are observed on Sunday afternoon.

ARCHITECTURAL HISTORY

In 1867, four lots were purchased for $1,700 at the corner of Noble and Bradley Streets with the expressed intention of building a Polish Catholic Church. A two-story wooden structure was built on the property that included classrooms on the ground floor and the church above. The original church was destroyed by fire in 1906[8].

In 1875, Patrick C. Keely, an award-winning architect from Brooklyn, designed the current old-world Renaissance church. Its Romanesque architecture with white brick and stone trimmings took 16 years to complete. Oak choir stalls flank the baroque altar in the upper church, which is filled with paintings and sculptures by well-known Polish artists of the time. Stained-glass windows from the Royal Bavarian Art Institute in Munich were installed in 1903. In 1964, one of its twin towers was destroyed when it was struck by lightning. The cost of replacing the tower was prohibitive, so it was never rebuilt.

The future site of the Sanctuary of The Divine Mercy is the property between the church and the school where the previous school building with its impressive auditorium once stood. The auditorium once hosted a Democratic rally where William Jennings Bryan addressed more than 10,000 Chicago Democrats. In 1917, Ignace Jan Paderewski addressed a group of clergymen at the auditorium. In his speech, Paderewski pinpointed the solution for the liberation of Poland. His message reached the President, convinced him that a free Poland was a necessary condition to save the world for democracy, and Poland was freed. From a spiritual viewpoint, this situation brought on a high motivation to prayer and numerous devotions at the parish as well as prayers and pleas for peace and freedom.

The school, which is run by the School Sisters of Notre Dame, recently celebrated its 130th Anniversary. The current structure, originally built for high school students and completed in 1959, was also badly in need of major capital improvements. At the beginning of 2004, Big Shoulders generously awarded a $4.4 million grant for these improvements, making St. Stanislaus Kostka a "flagship school" within the Archdiocese of Chicago. Because of its strategic location along the Kennedy Expressway, these improvements symbolize the strong commitment to quality Catholic education by the Big Shoulders Fund and the Archdiocese of Chicago.[9]

HISTORY OF RELIGIOUS LIFE

The Congregation of the Resurrectionists arrived in 1871 to administer the church. Motivated by overcrowded conditions that had resulted from a rapid increase in population, the pastor of St. Stanislaus Kostka Parish, Fr. Vincent Barzynski, CR, helped found five additional Polish parishes throughout the city. As the Polish community continued to grow throughout the 1890s, the pastor of St. Stanislaus

Kostka was instrumental in starting eight additional parishes in the Chicago area. Between 1871 and 1900, approximately 20 Polish parishes in all were founded in the Chicago area under the leadership of the Resurrectionists.

In 1874, the School Sisters of Notre Dame took over the management of the school. The Congregation of Notre Dame was founded in 1597 at Mattaincourt, in the French Province of Lorraine. In 1906, a devastating fire completely destroyed St. Stanislaus Kostka School, together with its equipment, the library, the furniture, and the Sisters' convent home, which was located on the fifth floor of the school building. By 1908, the school was rebuilt and St. Stanislaus Kostka had 4,500 children attending its parochial school.

In the 137 years of its life, St. Stanislaus Kostka Parish nurtured the vocation to the religious life of nearly 354 young women, with 197 becoming School Sisters of Notre Dame.

VENERABLE MARY THERESA DUDZIK

Among all the religious whose vocations were nurtured in the parish of St. Stanislaus Kostka, Josephine Dudzik's unique place in the history of Chicago deserves special recognition since she founded a religious congregation of sisters and is now a candidate for beatification.

In 1881, at the age of 21, Josephine left Poland and arrived in the United States where she took residence with her family in the neighborhood surrounding St. Stanislaus Kostka. Under the spiritual direction of the pastor, Fr. Vincent Barzynski, CR, she began the journey that would eventually lead to the founding of the Franciscan Sisters of Blessed Kunegunda, presently known as the Franciscan Sisters of Chicago.

Taking the religious name, Mary Theresa, Josephine Dudzik laid the foundation for her new community of religious sisters in the corporal and spiritual works of mercy whose apostolic mission extended throughout the Chicagoland area and continues to this day.

Venerable Theresa Dudzik's story and the history of her religious congregation are the subject of a book by Sr. Anne Marie Knawa, OSF called *As God Shall Ordain.*

[1] *St. Stanislaus Kostka 125th Anniversary Celebration,* Narod Polski May 21, 1992

[2] *City of Big Shoulders, A History of Chicago* (DeKalb: Northern Illinois University Press, 2000)

[3] Ibid

[4] *Since 1867, Immigrants Welcome at St. Stan's.* John Stebbins, ChicagoSun- Times May 30, 1987

[5] *Catholicism, Chicago Style,* Ellen Skerrett, et.al., (Chicago: Loyola University Press, 1993); *Chicago Churches and Synagogues,* George Lane and Algimantas Kezys, (Chicago: Loyola University Press, 1981)

[6] Ibid

[7] Ibid

[8] *Since 1867, Immigrants Welcome at St. Stan's.* John Stebbins, ChicagoSun- Times May 30, 1987

[9] *Vicariate III, New Facelift for an Old Friend,* Office of Catholic Schools, Archdiocese of Chicago Annual Report 2004 History of Religious Life

[10] *www.franciscanservices.com*

Tribute to Mary Stachowicz

City of Chicago Tribute
Presented by Alderman Colom
of the 35th Ward

Mrs. Mary Stachowicz
A Proposed Resolution Reading as Follows:

WHEREAS, Citizens in today's society seem to have become desensitized to random acts of violence aimed at innocent people; and

WHEREAS, While the print and broadcast media are full of reports of such incidents, one particularly heinous and outrageous murder galvanized the residents of the city of Chicago and prompted them to raise their collective voices in anger and sorrow; and

WHEREAS, The senseless murder of Mary Stachowicz touched many hearts in the community surrounding the St. Hyacinth parish where she worshiped and the Sikorski Funeral Home where she worked, soothing and interpreting for grieving families; and

WHEREAS, From all accounts, Mary Stachowicz was especially suited to perform the duties of this position because of her compassionate and caring nature and her ability to convey those feelings to people in mourning; and

WHEREAS, That same caring nature appears to have been the catalyst for her murder as she reached out to offer her help to the alleged perpetrator of this egregious act because she felt he was in need; and

WHEREAS Mary Stachowicz leaves behind a loving family, countless relatives, and devoted friends who will mourn her. However, a whole city grieves for her loss and struggles to come to grips with yet another random act of violence that deprives us of a citizen of Mary's caliber and any contributions she would have made for the benefit of Chicago society as a whole; now, therefore,

Be It Resolved, That we, Mayor Richard M. Daley and the members of the Chicago City Council gathered here this fourth day of December, 2002, do hereby offer our deepest sympathy to the family and friends of Mary Stachowicz and extend our most fervent wish that the coldness of their grief be soon replaced by the warmth of their memories of her; and

Be It Further Resolved, That a suitable copy of this resolution be prepared and presented to the family of Mary Stachowicz.

Alderman Colom moved to Suspend the Rules Temporarily to permit immediate consideration of and action upon the foregoing proposed resolution. The motion *Prevailed*.

On motion of Alderman Colom, the foregoing proposed resolution was Adopted by yeas and nays as follows:

Yeas—Aldermen Granato, Haithcock, Tillman, Preckwinkle, Hairston, Lyle, Beavers, Stroger, Beale, Pope, Balcer, Frias, Olivo, Burke, T. Thomas, Coleman, L. Thomas, Murphy, Rugai, Troutman, DeVille, Munoz, Zalewski, Chandler, Solis, Ocasio, Burnett, E. Smith, Carothers, Wojcik, Suarez, Matlak, Mell, Austin, Colom, Banks, Mitts, Allen, Laurino, O'Connor, Doherty, Natarus, Daley, Levar, Shiller, Schulter, M. Smith, Stone—48.

Nays—None.

SOURCES

Catholicism, Chicago Style (Chicago: Loyola University Press, 1993);
Ellen Skerrett, et.al.

Chicago Churches and Synagogues, Fr. George Lane and
Algimantas Kezys (Chicago: Loyola University Press, 1981)

(*Chicago Tribune*, June 27, 2000, Steve Kloehn) Fr. Richard Fragomeni

City of Big Shoulders, A History of Chicago, Robert G. Spinney
(DeKalb: Northern Illinois University Press, 2000)

Diary of St. Maria Faustina: Divine Mercy in My Soul, Marian Press,
Stockbridge, MA: 1987

Legionaries of Christ, Chapter 26 Photograph of St. Peter's Basilica
in Rome, Italy

Our Lady of Good Remedy image courtesy of Tan Books and Publishers, Inc.

Pietá, Giovanni Bellini, Chapter 14 Painting

Pope John Paul II, inside back cover image courtesy of ©Marians of the
Immaculate Conception, Stockbridge, MA 01263, used with permission

St. Michael defeating the dragon above Mont St. Michael (vellum);
Image in Chapter 28; Pol de Limbourg (d.c.1416); Musee Conde,
Chantilly/The Bridgeman Art Library

St. Stanislaus Kostka 125th Anniversary Celebration, Narod Polski
May 21, 1992

St. Stanislaus Kostka Centennial Yearbook 1867-1967

St. Stanislaus Kostka Diamond Jubilee Yearbook 1867-1942

Since 1867, Immigrants Welcome at St. Stan's, John Stebbins,
Chicago Sun-Times May 30, 1987

Thunder of Justice 1993 Ted Flynn (for quote from Pope Paul VI
Homily dated June 29, 1972)

The Eucharist and Its Relationship to the Church,
Pope John Paul II Encyclical

True Devotion to Mary, St. Louis Marie De Monfort. Translated
by Fr. Frederick William Faber, D.D. Tan Books and Publishers, Inc.
Rockford, IL: 1941

The Divine Mercy: Message and Devotion, Fr. Seraphim Michalenko,
MIC, with Vinny Flynn and Robert A. Stackpole. Marian Press,
Stockbridge, MA: revised 2001

The Most Holy Mother of God Empress of All, Artist Unknown,
Chapter 24 Icon

The Statue of The Divine Mercy in Kibeho, Chapter 23 photograph of the
Statue of The Divine Mercy in Kibeho. © Marians of the Immaculate
Conception, Stockbridge, MA 01263. Used with permission.

Vicariate III, New Facelift for an Old Friend, Office of Catholic Schools,
Archdiocese of Chicago Annual Report 2004

www.franciscanservices.com

Author's Biography

Father Anthony Buś, CR

Father Anthony Buś, CR, was ordained a Roman Catholic priest in 1984 and is a vowed religious of the Congregation of the Resurrection—a religious community of priests and brothers, founded in 1836 in Paris, France. Born in Cristobal, Panama, Father Anthony was raised in a military family. He is the second eldest of eight siblings. Father has a B.A. degree in sociology from St. Louis University, and a Masters of Divinity from Aquinas Institute in St. Louis, Missouri. Since 1996, he has been pastor of St. Stanislaus Kostka Parish in Chicago, Illinois.